CLEMENTINA BLACK was born in Brighton in 1853, the eldest daughter in a family of eight children. Her father was a solicitor and for many years Town Clerk of Brighton. When Clementina was twenty-two her mother died, and she was left in charge of her invalid father and the younger children in the family so it was several years before she came to London to study, teach and write. In the early 1880s she became involved in the problems of women's work and wages, and in 1886 she was made Secretary of the Women's Protective and Provident League, a position she held until 1889, when she resigned to found the Women's Trade Union Association (formed after the famous Bryant and Ma___ match girls' strike). By 1893, Clementina Black and s_____ her colleagues decided that another type of stru___ ___ ___s-sary if the social and economic conditions ___ were to be permanently improved, and ___ Industrial Council was formed, wit___ founder member and later as P___ President of the Anti-Sweat___ ___rous articles and books, as w___ before Parliamentary committees o___ ___er fight for a minimum wage was based on ___ ___belief that low pay was at the root of most of ___ ___rings of working women.

Her books include *Sweated Industry and the Minimum Wage* (1907), *Maker of Our Clothes: A Case for Trade Boards* (1909), *The Linleys of Bath* (1911) and *Married Women's Work* (1915).

She wrote novels and short stories, some of which were structured, according to her nephew David Garnett, 'on the traditional pattern of the tom-boy damsel in distress and travellers upon the Dover Road': they include *A Sussex Idyll* (1877), *Orlando* (1880), *Miss Falkland and Other Stories* (1892), *An Agitator* (1895), *The Princess Desirée* (1896), *The Pursuit of Camilla* (1899), *Caroline* (1908)

Clementina Black was an ardent suffragist, though never a militant one; she was an early member of the National Union of Women's Suffrage Society, acting editor for a time of the *Common Cause*, and inaugurator of the great suffrage petition of 1906. She died in 1922.

If you would like to know more about Virago books, write to us at 41 William IV Street, London WC2N 4DB for a full catalogue.

Please send a stamped addressed envelope

VIRAGO
Advisory Group

Book Tokens

Give them the pleasure of choosing
Book Tokens can be bought and exchanged at most bookshops.

MARRIED WOMEN'S WORK

BEING THE REPORT OF AN ENQUIRY
UNDERTAKEN BY THE
WOMEN'S INDUSTRIAL COUNCIL

EDITED BY
CLEMENTINA BLACK

NEW INTRODUCTION BY
ELLEN F MAPPEN

Virago

Published by Virago Press Limited 1983
41 William IV Street, London WC2N 4DB

This Virago edition is offset from the first edition of this book,
published in 1915 by G. Bell, London.

New Introduction © Ellen F Mappen 1983

British Library Cataloguing in Publication Data
Women's Industrial Council.
Married Women's work.
1. Wives—Employment—Great Britain—History
—20th century
I. Title   II. Black, Clementina
4.3′094   HD135
ISBN 0-86068-410-5

Printed in Great Britain by litho
at the Anchor Press, Tiptree, Essex.

The cover shows a photograph of Annie Birch, taken at The Albion
Towel Mill, Farnworth, Lancs. It is reproduced by kind permission
of her niece Mrs E. Thomas, who later worked at the same factory.

CONTENTS

NEW INTRODUCTION

Commenting on the report of the four Lady Assistant Commissioners to the Royal Commission on Labour in the January 1894 edition of *The Fortnightly Review*, Agnes Amy Bulley, a former Newnham undergraduate and writer on women's work, noted that 'the public mind had become agitated upon the subject of women's labour'. She concluded that

whatever direction social progress may take, the position
of women in the industrial world, bound up as it is with
the question of the home and the welfare of the coming
generations, must receive much closer attention in the future,
both from social reformers and from legislators.[1]

The Lady Assistant Commissioners' report, *The Employment of Women*, was just one fruit of the concern over women's life and labour which arose in the last decades of the nineteenth century and continued into the twentieth. Beginning with the investigations of Charles Booth, who sent Clara Collet into the East End so that she could observe the conditions of women's work firsthand, to Collet's appointment as the first woman Labour Correspondent of the Board of Trade in January 1893, collecting detailed information as the first step to social reform became increasingly popular. It was especially seized upon by feminists who sought to improve the position of women. In many cases, the employment of married women and the effect of such work on both women and their children was the subject of inquiry.

From the 1880s, women, mostly but not all middle-class,

formed political pressure groups to achieve social and economic rights for women. Sometimes, as in the case of the Women's Industrial Council, they welcomed men as members.[2] These women were social feminists because they connected social reform with obtaining women's rights. Some, but not all, were socialists. Many were also active in the suffrage movement but at the same time they did not allow other women's issues to be ignored by the general public or by government officials. The groups they formed, which included the Council, the Women's Co-operative Guild, the Women's Labour League, and the Fabian Women's Group, became an informal but wide-ranging network of women committed to ameliorating women's position in society. Most importantly, they maintained that women had a role in public life even if they did not have the parliamentary vote – that women could and should create and implement social policy, particularly as it affected other women and their families. The knowledge they gained as a result of investigative efforts became, in some measure, ammunition in their struggle.

The Women's Industrial Council was organised in 1894, partly to collect and publish 'trustworthy information about the condition of women's work'. But its efforts were much broader in scope. Briefly, the Council was an outgrowth of the Women's Trade Union Association which had been formed as a result of the women's trade union movement of the late 1880s. The Association had been created in October 1889 after the Bryant and May match girls' strike 'to establish self-managed and self-supporting Trade Unions' for women and girls. By 1893, however, its leaders, including Clementina Black and Amie Hicks, had decided that another type of structure was necessary if they were to improve 'permanently... the social conditions of working women'. Trade unions for women, they felt, were unstable and could not be relied upon to bring about social change.

As a result, the Council was formed to establish 'on a broader basis,...a body whose aim it should be to watch over women engaged in trades, and all industrial matters which concern women'. At its inaugural meeting, held in London in November of 1894, Clementina Black stated the aims of the Council. In addition to making 'special and systematic inquiry into the conditions of working women', it would also 'provide accurate information concerning these interests, and...promote such action as may seem conducive to their improvement'.[3]

Clementina Black's emphasis on action is important. Council members were social activists as well as social investigators. Over the next twenty-five years, members used the information they had gathered: they wrote numerous articles, published their own quarterly, the *Women's Industrial News*, organised and served on deputations to ministers, testified before Parliament, and held conferences and public meetings, at times in co-operation with other groups. In short, Council members were vigorous in their endeavour to carry out the Council's objectives.

Although the Council was not involved with organising women's trade unions, the members still maintained contact with working-class women and girls. One of the Council's aims was to educate, through the efforts of its Organisations Committee, chaired by Amie Hicks, these individuals 'in social questions, economics, and legislation affecting their trades'. Other members included the drill instructor Clara James, Lily Montagu, a leader in the girls' club movement, and Mary Neal. The committee was responsible for four activities: the Clubs' Industrial Association; the Girls' Club Library; the Physical Drill for Working Girls; and the Association of Trained Charwomen. The Clubs' Industrial Association arranged industrial lectures, social meetings and special citizenship classes for the girls' clubs. It eventually became the National Organisation of Girls' Clubs. The

Library lent books to the clubs. The girls in the Drill, under the supervision of Clara James, gave annual displays in Queen's Hall. The Association of Trained Charwomen was an attempt to train and find work for charwomen in London.

The Council's inquiry into the economic and hygienic effects of the industrial employment of married women and widows, resulting in the publication of *Married Women's Work* in 1915, should be viewed against the background of its commitment to investigation as a tool for understanding social problems and for achieving change. The events surrounding its compilation and eventual publication illustrate the methods employed by the Council and the connections between the different groups – connections which were, for various reasons, sometimes shattered. The fact that the Council leadership decided to undertake such a wide-ranging study on married women's work, and the emphasis placed upon infant mortality and child welfare, indicate the importance of these subjects to feminists and other reformers alike. Although 'nearly all the social questions of the day [were] affected by the fact of married women's labour', the Council thought that only fragmentary and often inexact information existed about it. Moreover, as stated in a letter to *The Times* requesting monetary support from the general public, the Council believed that[4]

the collection and publication of a large body of facts concerning the employment of married women will be of especial value to the various health authorities of the country; it will probably throw light upon infant mortality and physical deterioration, as well as upon many industrial and some social problems.

The book focuses on problems of women's work that Clementina Black and other social feminists were attempting to overcome through the various organisations in which they were active. Although on first reading the book may appear to be a collection of isolated facts, it actually presents 'the true conditions of some thousands – probably many thousands – of married women's lives in Great Britain in [the] earliest quarter of the twentieth century'– the type of work they did, the low wages they usually received, their health, their homes, their relationships with their husbands, and their children .

By 1908, when the Council began this inquiry, it had already investigated numerous trades in which women and girls were employed, including laundry work, jewellery and jewel-case making, millinery, artificial flower-making, embroidery, machining and tailoring. By 1914, the Council's secretary, Lucy Wyatt-Papworth, could report that the Council had investigated one hundred and seventeen trades. It had also undertaken extensive inquiries into home work. As a result of their efforts, Council members wrote to Herbert Gladstone in 1907 concerning the parliamentary inquiry into home work, that "our experience of years of study of the question of home work...convinces us that in order to understand the elements of the subject we must have first-hand knowledge of the work done and the surroundings in which it is done', thus again emphasising the Council's belief that 'without full investigation it [was] impossible either to legislate or to organise wisely'.[5]

The Investigation Committee actually formed 'the basis for all the rest' of its endeavours. Clementina Black was the committee chairman. Margaret MacDonald, B. L. Hutchins, Edith Macrosty, Horatio Player, and Minnie Nodin were also members. B. L. Hutchins, a school manager, lecturer and writer on factory and social questions, was an active Fabian and a member of the Fabian Women's Group. The other women were members of the Women's Labour League. Membership in more than one society enabled the women to co-operate on issues of mutual concern while still maintaining independent groups with slightly different approaches to achieving their social feminist goals.

The investigators for *Married Women's Work* were charged
with obtaining a substantial body of information about each
individual visited, using a standard format. In addition to
biographical information about the woman worker, her
occupation, and whether she had continued to work after
marriage, each investigator was to inquire about or make
comments on such questions as living conditions, rent,
number of rooms, number of living children and their 'state',
whether any of the children worked, their occupations and
wages, the number of children who had died and the cause
of death, whether the mother had been working when the
child died, arrangements for child care, the effect of work
on the woman's health, her earnings, whether they were
seasonal, the husband's occupation and earnings (if any),
the total family income and the weekly budget. Other
questions asked whether women workers were competing
with men, whether women were being replaced by machinery,
general characteristics of the trade, and whether legislation
on the subject of married women's work was desirable.

Investigators were given a booklet of suggestions, *Hints
to Investigators*, on how to proceed. They were told not to
write down their responses while interviewing but to make
rough notes immediately after leaving a dwelling. Other
instructions illustrate further what the Investigation Committee was looking for, and explain why the final report
was so full of detail. *Hints to Investigators* suggested that

reports should be as lifelike and complete as possible.
Details that seem, in the individual case, unimportant,
become significant when they recur again and again. Thus,
the appearance of good or bad health, cheerfulness or the
reverse, are points worth noting; and so are any little
details that may be given of family history in the previous
generation. Too much detail is far preferable to too little.

By 1910, at least 1506 cases, excluding those from Yorkshire,
had been received in the Council's office.

The committee members had decided that, for the results to be significant, the inquiry had to extend beyond London and into the large provincial towns. They realised that 'we should have to undertake a great deal of hard work and incur a large amount of expense'. A letter to *The Times* of 28 May 1909, estimated that at least £500 would be needed to pay for skilled investigators and related expenses. Appeals were made to other organisations for help in collecting the information. The interest aroused by the investigation was considerable. For instance, the Central London Branch of the Women's Labour League, at its meeting on 16 June 1908 agreed to co-operate with the Council. Clementina Black was asked to speak at a meeting of the branch either on married women's work or the state maintenance of mothers; she agreed to speak on the former.[6] The December 1908 issue of the *Women's Industrial News* also indicated that in several towns, local branches of the National Union of Women Workers wished to be involved. The extent of mutual co-operation is further illustrated by the Council's willingness to share its cases with the Fabian Women's Group when the latter began a study in 1913 on the proportion of women workers who partially or wholly supported others.[7]

The employment of Dorothy Lenn, who was also an organiser for the Women's Labour League, and the involvement of Margaret Bondfield in the investigation in Yorkshire are just two more examples of the benefits resulting from the co-operation within the Council and with other groups at the initial stages of the inquiry. Margaret MacDonald was influential in raising funds from individuals in Leicester so that the Council could send Lenn there; she even donated her own money to aid Lenn's work.

Margaret Bondfield, in addition to her connection with the Council, was also a Fabian and a member of the Women's Labour League. She spent, as the *News* reported in its July 1910 issue, some months of energetic and valuable work in Yorkshire. Her reports are extremely full, not only of plain facts about work and wages, but also of most interesting human details. She has stayed in the homes of the workers themselves during many of her journeyings and has succeeded in winning their confidence and friendship, which has enabled her to give us a picture of their lives from the inner side.

In July of 1909, Bondfield had lectured at a quarterly meeting of the Council on her experiences as an investigator and the importance of the work they had undertaken. A report on her speech noted that she

spoke of the difficulties of her subject, as nearly a million of the married women of this country were engaged in industrial work of varying kinds and conditions. . . she hoped they would have sufficient courage to face the facts which they had elicited. Social reformers wanted to know what effect married women's work had on home and children, and consequently on the health of the nation.

As a result of her lecture, a long discussion ensued. The report also noted that 'much diversity [existed] as to the right methods of dealing with an undoubted evil'.

A letter from Clementina Black to Margaret MacDonald in May of 1910 suggests that by then there was at least some internal diversity of opinion, not just, as the *News* had remarked, over a solution to a social problem, but over the handling of the book. At the same time, other issues surfaced which led to disagreement between these two leading members and conflict within the Council. Although the details are somewhat sketchy, it is apparent that some members were also upset over a proposed incorporation of the Council which would give the Executive Committee more power. In addition, there is some indication that there was dissension over the role of the secretary of the Council.[8] Surprisingly, the *News*, which usually gave concise summaries of meetings, is fairly cryptic in describing the 15 July 1910 meeting at which a crucial resolution was passed.

All this resulted in the resignation of Margaret Mac-Donald and her followers, including a number of women who belonged to the Women's Labour League. Amie Hicks also resigned as a vice president of the Council. Lily Montagu decided to sever the Clubs' Industrial Association's connection with the Council. Miss Potter, who ran the Association of Trained Charwomen, resigned. Gertrude Atkins (who had spent three months in the chief centres of the cotton industry for the inquiry in Lancashire), Margaret Bondfield, Sister Kerrison, Dorothy Lenn, Ramsay MacDonald, Mary Macpherson, Mary Middleton, Lily Montagu, Minnie Nodin, and Horatio Player all left the Council.

Clementina Black, B. L. Hutchins, Lucy Wyatt-Papworth, together with newly-recruited members and others who stayed, carried on with the book, with investigative work, and with the Council's role of watching over all industrial matters which affected women and girls. By 1912, the Annual Report noted that the report of the inquiry, which was being written by members of the Investigation Committee under Clementina Black's editorship, was nearing completion. The following year the committee discussed the report's conclusions which were considered to be 'of very great interest, raising many new points and throwing fresh light on a difficult problem'. The start of the war had some impact on further delaying publication but the book finally saw the light of day in 1915.

Clementina Black's introduction and the sections which follow are important not just for the information about the work and lives of working-class women and their families but also because the conclusions provide a summary of some of the major concerns of early twentieth-century social feminists, including the low level of remuneration of women workers and the overall issue of married women's work and its effect on infant mortality and child welfare.

Clementina Black concluded 'that what is wrong is not the work for wages of married women, but the under-payment, both of men and women'. She also believed that the lack of training for girls led to poor wages for women in later life. Over the years the Council had been prominent in attempts to improve trade training for girls, particularly in London. Some progress had been made, but obviously more was left to do. These facts are evident in reading through the cases in the book.

On the related questions of whether married women wanted to work or why they worked there was only slight diversity of opinion. Some indicated that women worked because of the independence it gave them and because it allowed them and their families to live above mere sub-sistence. B. L. Hutchins pointed out that there was some evidence 'of a growing sense in some women that work is a thing to take a pride and a pleasure in'. She also noted, as did others, that it was 'unreasonable that in one class women should be bitterly blamed for finding a substitute for nursery work while, in another, such action is regarded as quite normal'. Still, most remarked that the majority of married women worked because of economic necessity – because of poverty and of unemployment or under-employment and the low wages paid to men. Finally, the evidence on the heated question of infant mortality sup-ported, as one review in the *News* noted, the view that 'grinding poverty is worse for the infant even than only partial care from its mother'. Most realised that restriction of married women's work would only lead to more hardship of which there was already a considerable amount; choice was a necessity if not a right.

For the most part, the views expressed in the book are in the words of middle-class writers; of the women interviewed, the descriptions are, overall, sympathetic and understand-ing. The reader does get an idea, however, of the 'type' of working-class women that middle-class feminists admired and with whom they felt most comfortable. It was, according to Margaret Skinner, 'usually the intelligent woman earning a good wage who [was] the best manager and has most care of her family'. In her classification of married working-class women, Clementina Black clearly considered those women who needed to work but did not inferior to those who did work, whether they needed to or not. She admired most, though, the 'great body of intelligent, able, and efficient mothers, examples of whom may be seen at meetings, large or small, of the Women's Co-operative Guild'. They were the women who formed 'the very bulwark of national prosperity' and who supported women's suffrage and easier divorce. They were likely to be the same type of women described by Jill Liddington and Jill Norris in *One Hand Tied Behind Us* – that is, the 'radical suffragists' who joined with the middle-class women of the National Union of Women's Suffrage Societies in a common cause.

The editor of *Married Women's Work*, Clementina Black, was a pivotal figure in this struggle for a common cause. Although there is unfortunately a dearth of information about her personal life, a brief sketch reveals the scope of her activities, which included literary as well as social feminist endeavours.[9] Because of her knowledge of the conditions of women's work and her commitment to ameliorating its evils, she is central to any study of this earlier women's movement.

Clementina Black was born in Brighton at her parent's home on Ship Street on July 27 1853. She was the eldest girl in a family of eight children. Her mother, Clara, was the daughter of George Patten, a portrait painter: her father, David, was a solicitor and for many years the Town Clerk of Brighton, also serving as Brighton's coroner from 1856 to 1893. Her mother died when Clementina Black was in her early twenties. After that, she spent time caring for her family, and was able to do some teaching and writing as well. Her first short story, 'The Troubles of an Automaton', was printed in an issue of the *New Quarterly Magazine* in 1876 and her first novel, *A Sussex Idyll*, was published in London in 1877.

Shortly after this, she and her sisters moved to London where she continued to write. In 1880, she published a three-volume romance, *Orlando*. At this time, she was also secretary to a debating society. The mid-1880s appear to have brought changes to her life and to the life of at least one of her sisters. In 1885 and 1886, she was working at the British Museum where she was helped by Dr. Richard Garnett, Keeper of Printed Books at the Museum. She developed a friendship with him, visited him at his home, and on one occasion brought her sister Constance with her. The latter, who is well known for her work as a translator of Russian classics, met Edward Garnett. They subsequently married and in 1892, David Garnett, the writer was born.

Around the time that Constance Black met Edward Garnett, Clementina Black took steps which added a new dimension to her life. In late 1886 or early 1887, she became Secretary of the Women's Protective and Provident League, subsequently the Women's Trade Union League. She held that position until 1889, when she resigned and helped to found the Women's Trade Union Association which later evolved into the Council. In any evaluation of the Council's history she emerges as its main protagonist, generally recognised as the Council's 'chief inspirer and a devoted friend of the woman worker of all classes.'[10]

It was not only her involvement with the Council on the married women's work inquiry or its other investigations which led Clementina Black to her conclusion about the evils of low wages. Her belief that a minimum wage was necessary as a way of solving many industrial evils was an outgrowth of years of experience. Beginning in the mid-

1880s, when she served as an organiser, first with the League and then with the Association, she realised that low pay was 'at the root of most of the wrongs and sufferings of working women in this country'.[11] This belief shaped many of her actions as the years passed. Later on, she became active in the Anti-Sweating League and was a strong advocate of the establishment of trades boards to set minimum wages in selected trades. In fact, she even resigned temporarily the presidency of the Council in January of 1909 because she wanted to devote what time she had to 'the most vital of industrial reforms – a reform to which the Council has decided to remain inactive'. Because Council members had been divided about the usefulness of trades boards in sweated industries, they voted not to take an official stand on the issue.[12] The MacDonalds were among those on the Council opposed to trades boards. Clementina Black wrote that she was 'worried' about the split but felt that she could no longer represent the Council.[13] Her strong belief in the need for trades boards was summed up eloquently in an article she wrote for the *Daily Chronicle*. She noted[14]

only those who know the poorer working woman at firsthand can tell what it would mean if a hope of betterment could be held out to her. Until now none of us have been able honestly to tell her that there was a chance of things being appreciably better in her lifetime. Certain evils, indeed, breaches of the Factory Acts, for example, well-wishers can help to get set right, but the worst evils of all, the compulsory acceptance of 2d. or 1½d., or even 1d. for an hour's work, the cruelty of seeing rates of pay decreasing year by year, these there has been no means of alleviating, and until they are alleviated our civilisation remains but a mockery, and the absence of slavery in our country little more than a form of words.

Once the legislation passed through Parliament though, she did return to her leadership role on the Council.

Clementina Black's involvement with the Council and with the Anti-Sweating League were just two aspects of her social feminist work. While she was most active in trying to achieve economic rights for women through social reform, she did not forsake the suffrage arm of the women's movement. She was 'an ardent suffragist though never a militant one'.[15] She held office both in the London Society for Women's Suffrage and in the National Union of Women's Suffrage Societies. In 1906, she drew up a suffrage declaration which by June 1907, had been signed by 52,000 women.[16] This commitment to women's suffrage continued side by side with her social reform and literary endeavours until the vote was won. She was also, like many of the women involved in the struggle for women's rights in the late nineteenth and twentieth century, 'a Socialist at heart'.[17] In her case, she was, at least in the late 1880s, a member of the Fabian Society.[18]

Although over the years she wrote numerous didactic articles and books and gave testimony before Parliamentary committees on questions related to women's work, she also continued her literary efforts. For instance, she wrote more novels which her nephew David Garnett described as structured in 'the traditional pattern of the tom-boy damsel in distress and travellers upon the Dover Road'.[19] *The Princess Desirée* (1896), a romantic historical novel about a princess who had 'the stuff of a man in her', is a good example.

She wrote short stories, and in 1892 published a collection of these under the title, *Miss Falkland and other stories*. In addition, she translated several works; one, on Auguste Rodin by Camille Mauclair, was published in 1905. She was considered an expert on the eighteenth century. In 1885, for instance, she wrote an article for *The Gentleman's Magazine* on Sarah Fielding, the sister of Henry.

At times, she turned her hand to reviews and to poetry. She reviewed both Thomas Hardy's *Tess of the D'Urbervilles* and George Gissing's *The Odd Women* for the *Illustrated London News*, in 1892 and 1893. One of her poetic efforts tied her literary and social feminist activities together. In the late 1890s, she wrote 'The Rhyme of the Factory Acts' which was intended for distribution by the Council in working girls' clubs. It laid out the various regulations in poetic form and ended with lines that conveyed one of Clementina Black's passionate beliefs:

> So overwork and underpay
> Go gaily on from day to day
> And will, till those who work unite
> To see their own affairs kept right.

Clementina Black was much admired and loved by those who knew her well. Her letters indicate her great devotion to her niece, Speedwell, whom she raised. David Garnett wrote of her in warm terms: she was, according to him, charming, 'so wise', with a clear mind. She also knew 'more than most women what sort of thing is to be expected of the human race'.[20] In spite of her later disagreement with Margaret MacDonald, Clementina Black was once described by Lily Montagu as the person on the Council who was 'best for soothing'.[21] When she died in 1922, one of her obituaries was entitled 'Women's Friend'.

In January 1915, an article written for the *Women's Industrial News* could justly claim that 'modern industrial legislation owed much to women' since investigation and administration went together and women did both efficiently. The work of Clementina Black and her colleagues on the Council, of which the married women's work inquiry is just one example, is an important aspect of the larger effort of social feminists to attain equality for women in British society.

Ellen F Mappen,
1983
Highland Park, New Jersey

NOTES

I would like to thank the Rutgers University Research Council for a grant enabling me to look at the letters of and about Clementina Black in the Garnett Collection at the Humanities Research Center of the University of Texas at Austin. I would also like to thank the librarians at the Humanities Research Center, the Fawcett Library, the Trades Union Congress Library, the Labour Party Library, and the British Library of Political and Economic Science for allowing me access to their collections. Finally, I would like to thank Richard Garnett and Anne Lee Michell for permission to quote from material in the Garnett Collection of the University of Texas.

1 'The Employment of Women. The Lady Assistant Commissioners' Report', *The Fortnightly Review*, LV (January 1894), 39. The term 'Lady Assistant Commissioners' is used in the text since that was the title given to the women investigators.

2 For the most part, unless noted, the published records of the Women's Trade Union Association and the Women's Industrial Council provide the basis for information about the Council and the publication of *Married Women's Work*.

3 Black quoted in *The Times* (London), November 27, 1894, 12.

4 See typescript letter dated September 25, 1908 in Tuckwell Collection, Trades Union Congress Library. Tuckwell Collection 340. See also *The Times* (London), May 28, 1909, 11.

5 Letter to Gladstone quoted in *The Morning Post*, July 3, 1907. Clipping in Tuckwell Collection 202.

6 See Women's Labour League/169. Central London

Branch Minute Book and Women's Labour League/171 Central London Branch Executive Committee Minutes, Labour Party Library.

7   See *Fabian News*, XXIV (July 1913), 61.

8   MacDonald Collection, Collection J, Vol. 5, Item No. 36, Black to Mrs. McDonald, May 22, 1910, British Library of Political and Economic Science (BLPES) and also un-catalogued materials relating to incorporation of the Council in Box A, Women's Industrial Council, BLPES.

9   Some useful biographical information can be found in: Mary Cameron, 'Clementina Black: A Character Sketch', *The Young Woman*, I (June 1892), 315–316; Carolyn Heilbrun, *The Garnett Family* (London: George Allen and Unwin Ltd., 1961), esp. pp. 68–69, 178; and David Garnett's three-volume autobiography, *The Golden Echo*. The first volume entitled *The Golden Echo*, (N.Y.: Harcourt, Brace and Company, 1954) is the most helpful of the three.

10   Clipping from the *Westminster Gazette*, September 20, 1918 in Tuckwell Collection 340.

11   'The Organization of Working Women', *Fortnightly Review*, XLVI (November 1889), 699.

12   See letter to Gladstone. Tuckwell Collection 202.

13   Manuscript letter in Fawcett Autograph Collection, II, Pt. C., February 22, 1909, Clementina Black to Miss Strachey, Fawcett Library, City of London Polytechnic.

14   Clipping from the *Daily Chronicle*, April 19, 1909. Tuckwell Collection 2001.

15   Garnett Collection, notes by Anne Lee Michell to Olivia Rayne Garnett's 'A Bloomsbury Girlhood', un-published manuscript, 554, Humanities Research Center, the University of Texas at Austin.

16   *The Times* (London), December 20, 1922, 13 and *The Englishwoman's Yearbook and Directory*, ed. G. E. Mitton (London: Adam and Charles Black, 1910), p. 193.

17 Obituary from the *Westminster Gazette*, December 20, 1922, found in Biographical Cuttings, Fawcett Library.

18 Norman and Jeanne MacKenzie, *The First Fabians* (London: Weidenfeld and Nicolson, 1977), p. 99.

19 In *The Flowers of the Forest Being Volume Two of The Golden Echo* (N.Y.: Harcourt, Brace and Company, 1955), p. 249.

20 See letters in Fawcett Library and Garnett Collection. For example, Clementina Black to Richard Garnett, July 21, 1895. See also two letters in Garnett, D., Letters to Constance, 1909–1946, [1917] and Dec[ember] 19 [1923–?], in Garnett Collection.

21 BLPES, uncatalogued materials on Women's Industrial Council, Box D, D-4, Lily Montagu to Miss Papworth, July 13, 1905.

BIBLIOGRAPHY

Royal Commission on Labour, 1894. Reports on Employment of Married Women, etc.

Annual Reports of Factory Inspectors, passim.

PALGRAVE.—*Dictionary of Political Economy*. Article on "Female Labour."

CONRAD.—*Handwörterbuch der Staatswissen-schaften*. Article "Frauenarbeit and Frauenfrage."

Englishwomen's Review, Jan., 1899. Question of Home Work.

BARLOW, SIR THOMAS.—*A School for Mothers*, London, 1907.

BIGG, ADA HEATHER.—*Economic Journal*, 1894, fo. 51. "The Wife's Contribution to the Family Income."

BONEBRETT, J.—*Conditions of Working Women*. Elliot Stock, 1896, 2s.

BULLEY, A. A. and WHITLEY, MARGARET.—*Women's Work*. Methuen, 1896, 2s. 6d.

BURNS, J., Address by. Delivered at the National Conference on Infantile Mortality, 1906.

CADBURY, MATHESON and SHANN.—*Women's Work and Wages*. Unwin, 1906, cheaper edition, 1s.

CAMPBELL, HELEN. *Prisoners of Poverty. Women Wage-earners, their Trades and their Lives*. Boston, Mass. 1887.

CAMPBELL, HELEN.—*Women Wage-Earners*, 1889. Roberts, Boston,

BLACK, CLEMENTINA.—*Temple Magazine*, October, 1901. "Women Factory-Workers."

FORD, ISABELLA O.—*Women's Wages and the Conditions under which they are earned*. Humanitarian League, 1895.

FORD, ISABELLA O.—*Humane Review*, October, 1901. "Industrial Women."

FRANKENSTEIN, K.—*Der Arbeiterschutz*. " Das verbot der Fabrikarbeit verheirater Frauen oder Familienmütter." Erster Theil. A. § 3c. Leipsig. 1896.

GONNARD. *La Femme dans l'Industrie*. Paris, 1906.

GREENWOOD, MRS. F. J.—Reprint from *The Englishwomen's Review*. London, 1901. " Is the High Infantile Death-rate due to the Occupation of Married Women ? "

GREENWOOD, MADELEINE.—*Humanitarian*, July. 1900. " The Economic Position of Women in Trades and Manufactures."

HOLMES, THOMAS.—*Contemporary Review*, March, 1900. " Home Industries and Home Heroism."

HUTCHINS AND HARRISON.—*History of Factory Legislation*. King, London, 1903.

IRWIN, MARGARET H.—*Homework among Women*, 1897.

JEVONS, W. S.—*State in Relation to Labour*.—(Chap. III. Paragraph on Employment of Mothers, pp. 72–77.) Macmillan, 1894.

JEVONS, W. S.—*Methods of Social Reform*. Chapter on " Married Women in Factories," 1883.

KNIGHTLEY OF FAWSLEY, LADY.—*Nineteenth Century*, August, 1901. " Women as Home Workers."

MACDONALD, J. RAMSAY (Ed.).—*Women in the Printing Trades* (esp. Chapter IX. " Married and Unmarried"). P. S. King, 1904. 1s.

MARTIN, RUDOLF.—*Zeitschrift für die Gesamte Staatswissenschaft*, 1896. I. und III. Heft. " Die Auschliessung der Verheirateten Frauen aus der Fabrik. Eine Studie aus der Textil Industrie."

NEWLAND, F. H.—*Leisure Hour*. January, 1899. " Women's Home Industries in London."

RUSSELL, HON. MRS. BERTRAND.—*Nineteenth Century*, December, 1906. " The Ghent School for Mothers."

RUSSELL, HON. MRS. BERTRAND.—*Evening News*, December 29, 1906. " A School for Mothers. The Remarkable Social Experiment at Ghent."

SIMON, JULES.—*L'Ouvrière*. Paris, 1861.

SIMON, JULES, and BLACK, CLEMENTINA.—*New Review*, September, 1891. " Women and Work," Parts I. and II.

BIBLIOGRAPHY xxi

TUCKWELL, G. M.—*The State and its Children*. Chapter on the employment of women after childbirth ; labour protection for mothers. Scribner, New York.

WEBB, BEATRICE.—*Women and the Factory Acts*. Fabian Tract.

WOMEN'S INDUSTRIAL COUNCIL.—*Report on Home Industries of Women in London*. London, 1908.

Note.—This Bibliography is carried up to the date of the Report. For a Bibliography up to 1915 see " A Select Bibliography of Women in Industry," by L. Wyatt Papworth and Dorothy M. Zimmern, published by the Women's Industrial Council, 7, John Street, Adelphi, London, W.C. ; price 1s. or 1s. 2d. post free.

PREFACE

THE enquiries on which this Report of the industrial work of married women and widows was based were made mainly during the years 1909 and 1910. The delay in the publication of the Report has been due to many causes, of which the latest is the European war. This delay is not one by which the book suffers, since up to the outbreak of war the conditions described continued to prevail. These conditions of Englishwomen's life and industry later events have shown to be unequal to the strain caused by the war. It is hoped that a detailed realisation of what these conditions were may be a real help towards that immense social reconstruction which is now seen to be needed.

The thanks of the Council are due to a large body of investigators who have visited personally every case recorded in this book. The remarkable accuracy of their information is evident from the fact that all these separate witnesses tell practically the same story. Nothing has struck me more in going over the whole of the papers than the similarity of the general facts. Of the reports each has been written in complete independence of any other, and their agreement can hardly fail to impress a careful reader.

The very brief account of conditions in Glasgow makes no pretence at being an adequate report. It appears merely as an indication that the problems of married women's work are the same in Scotland as in England.

CLEMENTINA BLACK.

WOMEN'S INDUSTRIAL COUNCIL,
7, JOHN STREET,
ADELPHI, W.C.

INTRODUCTION

IT is a general opinion and especially, perhaps, among persons of the middle class, that the working for money of married women is to be deplored. That such work is sometimes made necessary by poverty will be conceded, and wives who earn because they must are pitied ; while wives who work not for their own or their children's bread, but rather for butter to it, are regarded as at least somewhat blameworthy.

The underlying implication seems to be that a wife and mother who thus works must be withdrawing from the care of her home and her children time and attention of which they are really in need. Pictures rise before the mind of rooms unswept, beds unmade and dishes unwashed, of children hungry, ragged, unkempt and running wild. But when one has personally visited the homes of a good many such women, and when there have passed through one's hands several hundreds of reports, each describing one home and one woman, the real facts begin to arrange themselves and to fall as it were automatically into a classification.

The great mass of married women of the working class now present themselves to me in four groups :—

(A) Those who, although the family income is inadequate, do not earn.

(B) Those who, because the family income is inadequate—whether from lowness of pay, irregularity of work or failure in some way, such as sickness, idleness, drink or desertion on the part of the husband—do earn.

(C) Those who, the family income being reasonably adequate, do not earn.

(D) Those who, although the family income is adequate for the supply of necessities, yet earn.

In Class A (those who, although the family income is inadequate, do not earn) are to be found the largest number of women whose homes and children are conspicuously neglected, and the reason may be sought in the familiar lines of Dr. Watts on the subject of idle hands. A woman who is extremely poor and whose furniture and appliances are reduced to a minimum, has not enough household work to occupy her time, while the fact of her poverty denies her most of the means by which the better-off beguile the dangers of vacant hours. It is from Class A, rather than from Class B—in which wives do earn—that the gossipers at doorways and the frequenters of public houses are recruited. It includes also the helpless, who do not succeed in getting work, the incompetent, who if they get work cannot keep it, and a certain proportion of women whose poor health makes earning impossible. Of course, it includes also—as do all the groups—many steady, industrious women who are the very prop and mainstay of their households.

On the whole, however, the impression left on my mind, and, I find, on the minds also of some other people personally acquainted with working-class life, is that the members of Class A are, generally speaking, inferior in calibre to the members of Class B. Of course, no cases of women belonging to Class A were included in the materials for the present report.

Among the members of Class B—those who, because the family income is inadequate, do earn—are the most overworked, the hardest pressed and probably the unhappiest of working women. Any crueller position can hardly be imagined than that of a naturally intelligent and thoughtful woman, concerned above all things (as are most of the mothers visited) about the future of her children and unable to secure, either by her husband's labour or her own, enough money for their healthy support. No " driving " foreman, no greedy employer, can so spur the efforts of a worker as her maternal affection spurs such a woman, and her too laborious days are embittered by the knowledge that success is after all impossible.[1]

Such a mother will be often sharp of tongue and irritable of temper ; life offers her neither rest nor hope ; she scurries through her household work that she may spend an extra ten minutes at her monotonous toil and receive an extra farthing at the week end ; the premature collapse of a child's boots is a disaster that disturbs all her calculations ; a day's illness is an indulgence that she dares not afford herself. As the children grow up and go out to work the pressure relaxes a little ; if she is fortunate an unmarried daughter remains with her to the end, and if she lives to be 70 years old her pension gives her the gratification of feeling herself rather a help than a burden. She will be anxious still, saying sometimes to herself and her daughter : " What will you do when I am gone ? " But it will no longer be the grinding daily anxiety of bygone years. She will know no pleasures, she will still work ; but she will know intervals of rest, and these—though she will not know it—will be the happiest years of her life.

These women of Class B are numerous, but how numerous no one can tell. We can only guess by review-

[1] One member of the Sub-Committee by which this summary has been revised, considers that mental distress such as is attributed above to some members of Class B is very rare. Scarcely any of these women, she believes, have either the habit of thought, or the time for thinking, and the great majority of them live from day to day without looking forward. That some women, however, are painfully oppressed by the uncertainty of their position, I have learned from their own lips.

ing roughly the many trades in which the wages of a man are insufficient for the support of a family. Such is the case with nearly all " labourers," whatever the occupations subserved by their labour. Until recently there was not one carman in twenty who earned enough, after such of his own meals as were necessarily eaten away from home had been paid for, to support a family. Altogether the army of underpaid men is a considerable one. Moreover, in many trades, employment is irregular ; the money available for a week's housekeeping may drop from 20/- or 18/- to 10/- or even 8/-, or may come altogether to an end, and that for a considerable number of weeks in every year. Then the wife must needs try to supply at least a portion of the needed income, and when experience has taught her to expect the recurrence of such conditions she will probably endeavour to secure employment beforehand, or in other words will take up some occupation regularly ; and the larger her family the more will she find it necessary to spend her hours in wage-earning. The habit of thus working grows upon her ; what was need in times of acute hardship becomes a comfort even in times of regular receipts from her husband. By degrees the pleasure of having money of her very own comes to be dearly prized, and the woman who said : " A shilling of your own is worth two that *he* gives you " spoke the mind of many of her sisters. It is not, I believe, merely the command of the tiny sum to which their earnings amount, but the sense of partial freedom and independence by which their hearts are thus warmed. That wave of desire for a personal working life which forms so marked an element in the general development of modern women touches and inspires even these humble and overdriven toilers.

The question of whether young children suffer in consequence of their mothers being engaged in work for money is one of the most important that arises in connection with such work. Unfortunately it is one to which no generally decisive answer can be given. The percentages of infant mortality are, indeed, usually high in districts where a majority of mothers go out to work, but are scarcely lower in some others where population is equally dense and are as high or even higher in mining districts where wives are mostly not wage-earners but where domestic toil is apt to be peculiarly heavy owing to the prevalence of grime and to the circumstance that members of the same household often belong to different working shifts and have consequently to be fed separately —all with substantial hot meals—at different hours. The only general conclusions derivable from statistics of infantile mortality are that poverty and density of population are unfavourable to the health and survival of babies. But while it is not proved that work for money on the part of mothers is *per se* bad for children, it does appear to be proved that the effects of some occupations (those for example, in which there is risk of lead poisoning) are adverse to the bearing of healthy children and it will be generally conceded, without the need of specific proof, that any employment, whether industrial or domestic, which involves severe muscular strain or the lifting of heavy weights is dangerous for expectant mothers.

It is also fairly obvious that when the mother of a young child works outside her home, the child will be neglected unless some other caretaker can be provided. A good substitute—or indeed any—is not always procurable, and no doubt, many children do suffer from being thus neglected. No doubt also many mothers who would prefer to stay at home beside their children are unable to find work which enables them to do so, and are haunted throughout their working day by uneasiness. Widows with young children dependent upon them who can hardly afford the fees of a *crèche* seem to be peculiarly devoid of relatives willing to take charge. I am sure that a certain number of widows marry again mainly that their very young children may be looked after. Even an unemployed husband will keep toddling children from being run over, tumbling downstairs or setting themselves on fire. In London, where there is a reasonable choice of occupations, it is found that married women do not often, in fact, go out to work while their babies are quite small, unless indeed, circumstances allow of the latter being left in the care of some adult or at least adolescent person.

The assumption, however, that the existence of babies must and should in all cases and for ever prevent the mothers of them from going out to work would be rash. It is by no means always true that a mother is the person best qualified to take care of her infant. It may even conceivably be true that babies would be better off in the charge of an expert and that infant citizens may come to be tended, as boy and girl citizens are taught, in communities by trained persons. Even at present, indeed, it is sadly true that any baby would gain by being removed from a working-class home to the Nursery Training School of the Women's Industrial Council. That some working women are already looking, in the interests of their children, to some such solution, is certain.[1]

Of Class C (women who, the family income being reasonably adequate, do not earn), this enquiry contains, of course, no samples. In it are included a large proportion of the wives of fairly well-paid men, and to it and Class D taken together, belong that great body of intelligent, able and efficient mothers, examples of whom may be seen at meetings, large or small, of the Women's Co-operative Guild. It is safe to say that no country of

[1] See, for example, the able and interesting articles by Mrs. Chew in *The Common Cause*.

the world possesses better citizens than these. They form the very bulwark of national prosperity, in the moral as well as the material sense of the word. A careful study of the lives of women belonging to Class C would be of considerable sociological value and would doubtless cast light upon the real trend of general social development among women. Upon these lives the present volume does not touch ; I can but note in passing that the Women's Co-operative Guild, which so largely represents Class C, is overwhelmingly in favour of Women's Suffrage and of easier divorce.

To Class D belong those reprehensible women who could if they chose afford to live upon their husband's earnings but yet devote many of their hours to paid work. As a rule they are highly skilled and well remunerated ; many of them pay for domestic help ; the great majority buy educational advantages for their children ; very often they are able to provide for health-giving holiday outings. Such women are nearly always conspicuously competent and are marked by an independence of mind which I believe to be derived from the consciousness of their power of self-support. Almost invariably their houses are well kept and the family accommodation adequate. To visit them is to go away encouraged as to the future of the race, and greatly shaken in a prior opinion as to the undesirability of wage-earning for wives.

I may add that they themselves have no consciousness of sin, on the contrary, they are proud of their work and unwilling to relinquish it. Nor, indeed, have I noted any one woman among those whose cases have passed through my hands who has been willing to see any restriction imposed upon the work for money of married women. For my own part I have become convinced that the moral and mental effect upon the women themselves of being wage-earners is good. Wherever the work is well-paid and the total family income comfortable the high charac-

ter of the wage-earning wife is evident enough. Where
the work is ill-paid and the woman suffering from poverty
and from the consequent lack of domestic comfort, the
wholesome effects are masked by the general unsatis-
factoriness of conditions and by the urgency of labour
required to earn the absolutely essential few shillings.
The scandalous lowness of the rates at which many
women, married and single, are paid is a crying evil—
but it is not an evil inherent in the work. It is true, too,
that the underpaid wives of underpaid men bear upon
their shoulders a burden of combined household and
industrial toil far too heavy for any human creature. So
to lighten their toil so as to leave them breathing space
for a little personal life is, surely, a duty which organised
society owes them. But the portion of their toil which
is most onerous, least productive and least in the line of
modern development is not their industrial but their
domestic work. In that direction, I believe, should lie
the course of relief. For a variety of reasons the industry
of housekeeping has not undergone that alteration of
methods which has transformed other industries. It
remains largely (and among the poor wholly) unspecialised ; one person performs all the processes, using for
their various purposes inadequate hand-driven tools.
Even in well-to-do homes the domestic appliances,
although in sum total costly, are for the most part all
primitive ; the broom, the scrubbing brush and the duster
are not yet replaced by the vacuum cleaner, the washing-
up bowl by a machine, nor the individual oven by the
great steam roaster capable of cooking hundreds of joints
cheaply without attention or wastage. [1]

[1] A modern Rip van Winkle coming back to life now, after a
sleep of a century or so, would be totally lost in a big new
modern hospital or up-to-date weaving shed. He simply would
not know the use or significance of most of the objects around
him. But put him in an ordinary kitchen, with its dirty
coal-burning cooking stove, its always unpleasant and often

The poor buy their coal by the half hundredweight, or less, their tea by the ounce, or sometimes by the halfpennyworth ; they are cut off by their poverty from the best cooking, which always means the use of slow and prolonged heat ; in their abodes every defect of spending power has to be made good by the toil of the woman's muscles. Nothing could be more uneconomical, more, in the true sense of the word, uncivilised. Of course, it is true that the middle-class are still walking in the same uneconomical and uncivilised path and getting very little return in comfort for an exorbitant expenditure, but they, after all, have at least the money to spend, while the poor woman pays with her person.

Of the methods by which the burden of unscientific households can be lifted off, it is not my province to speak here, although in theory at least the task is easy enough ; but I should be unfair to my readers if I failed to indicate my own opinion that the wage-earning wife needs to be relieved not of the work which she frequently does well, but of that which she invariably, and indeed perforce does either ill or at quite disproportionate cost to herself.

In saying this I would not be understood to imply that working women are, in general, incompetent in domestic matters. On the contrary, my impression is that considering how very inadequate are the appliances at their command, they do much better than could reasonably be expected.[1] Out of their minute weekly income, the larger part has necessarily to be spent upon food, and

insanitary sink, its pots and pans, brooms and brushes, and he would feel that after all the world had not in every direction moved with such huge strides while he was asleep."—*The Housewife as Bursar*, by MABEL ATKINSON.

[1] A pamphlet by Miss Anna Martin, *The Married Working Woman*, sold at twopence by the National Union of Women's Suffrage Societies, contains the notes of a first-hand observer upon this point and should be studied by any person interested in the lives of wage-earning families.

few are the middle-class women who could make the
sum go so far. But no management can absolutely
make enough of too little ; and where there is an
actual deficit somebody must do without. The man who
is, in theory, the bread-winner, must be well fed to keep
him in earning condition ; few mothers can bear to see
their children hungry, and overworked women are apt to
care little for their food. Thus, in nine cases out of ten,
the mother is the person who habitually goes short, and
she alone is the person who has no time to be ill. Mothers,
in wage-earning families, succumb to illness only when
they literally can no longer keep on their feet ; and the
family disorganisation that results from even a very brief
cessation of their activities is so great that almost every
woman of the working-class gets about too soon after
childbirth. I will not say that there are no mothers of
that grade who have not suffered permanent injury from
this cause, but I do say, deliberately, that there can be
only a minority uninjured. The horrible boast, " I never
missed but one week's wash with any of my babies "—
which has been made to me more than once—tells its
own tale ; and the law which forbids the return of the
mother within a month to factory work, does not prevent
the washing and wringing of sheets, the carrying of coals
and water, the scrubbing of floors or the pushing of a
perambulator. No doubt work for wages has in some
instances been responsible for internal damage to mothers,
but domestic labour is far more largely responsible for
the fact that many thousands of working women have
lost for ever the enjoyment of robust health. If the
maternity benefit of the Insurance Act could be so
administered as to prevent mothers from resuming hard
work for a full month it would indeed be a boon to poor
women. But it is not easy to bring home to the minds
of legislators—nor indeed to those of any persons who
have never known what hard domestic work really means

—the strain put upon a woman's strength by precisely some of those processes which are regarded as pre-eminently " women's work." Few operations performed by women in factories are for instance so exhausting as the doing of the family wash with the appliances to be found in the ordinary poor home. The stacking of jam jars, French polishing, perhaps heavy ironing in a laundry and certainly the carrying to and fro of weights —such as burdens of thick paper for making into bags— may be equally harmful, but light industries, such as box-making, shirt-finishing, flower-making, etc., are not deleterious at all, and any attempt to prohibit the work for money of married women must inevitably result in occupying them more and more in heavier work, such as office cleaning and private laundering.

The grave drawback of much of the work done for money by married women is not that it is injurious in itself but that it is scandalously ill-paid. Many instances appear in this volume of women paid, in London, at the rate of less than threepence an hour. Now, women who earn little per hour are naturally driven to work for more hours, and it is precisely the underpaid women who *must* spend much time at their trade to the neglect of their homes. As a matter of observation the well-paid women in our records have almost invariably well-kept homes and are not themselves overworked. These are often those who are not compelled by necessity to follow any trade and who are working for a better standard of living for their children. All of them, it will be remarked, are working at skilled trades ; and the analysis (on p. 222) of the figures produced by systematic visiting in certain wards of Leicester, shows that in that town the homes of women busied in some regular trade are more prosperous than those of women engaged in work of a more casual kind. Yet the less skilled work no less than the more skilled is demanded by the community, and although it may be just that a period of preliminary training should add something to the remuneration to the person trained, it can never be just (nor in the long run advantageous to the community) that any work really needed should, however easy its execution, be remunerated at rates that do not allow the worker to be in a true sense self-support-ing. Nor, in a civilised society, can it be considered that a level of self-support has been reached unless the worker is enabled to be adequately fed, sufficiently clothed, decently housed, and provided with an extra pound or two per annum for recreation. Now the present enquiry establishes beyond all question the fact that a considerable proportion—probably a very large proportion—of the working people in this country are receiving remuneration for their industry at rates that keep them and their families well below the standard of self-support just set forth. Despite the current theory that the wages of men are reckoned not on an individual but on a family basis, thousands of men are paid at rates which (even if received—as is very seldom the case—regularly through-out the year), are in fact barely sufficient to support properly one adult and one child ; while the wages of thousands of women (based theoretically on the needs of an individual) are wholly inadequate to the proper support of one adult person. The earnings of man and wife together are, in thousands of households, inadequate, however industrious, however sober, however thrifty the pair, to the proper support of themselves and their children. Such are the main facts which emerge from our enquiry.

Thus, until the pay of men is much better than at present, any attempt to prohibit the work for wages of wives would intensify hardships that are already cruelly severe. On the other hand, in households where poverty is not severe, such prohibitions would be without excuse, because in these households the mothers who work are not found to be overdriven, the children are found to be well cared for and the houses clean, comfortable and—comparatively speaking—spacious. In short, the poorer wives must work for money, and when the less poor wives are found to be doing so their houses and families are demonstrably not the worse but rather the better for it. Moreover, it should be recognised that there are women —often admirable and highly intelligent women—who have no natural gift for domestic work and whom neither training nor personal effort will ever teach to keep the rooms around them in a state of real cleanliness and order. Yet such women are sometimes the best of mothers ; theirs is the eye which seems to perceive intuitively what needs doing for the health of a baby, their children are always " good," and always turn out well. They have, generally, also, some turn for industry of a non-domestic kind—not rarely there is an artistic streak in their nature—they make good milliners or embroideresses or dress-designers. We all know women of this type in other ranks of life and never dream of supposing it desirable that they should be restricted to housemaidly duties. It cannot be thought really advantageous that any human being should perform the part of the round peg in the square hole, and since Nature persists in producing a certain number of round pegs, organised society would be ill advised in trying to keep them out of the round holes into which they will, if left alone, fit themselves.

At the risk of superfluous iteration, it must be repeated that what is wrong is not the work for wages of married women, but the under-payment, both of men and women, which compels some women to work who might gladly abstain, and compels those to spend many hours in work who might be glad to spend a few. Under-payment is the evil. If a really self-supporting rate of pay could be secured for men's work and for women's work, the law might with perfect safety leave to working men and women themselves the decision of what sort of work should be done by wives and mothers. But if—even in that better state of affairs—our legislators should desire to weight the scales against the industrial employment of wives, their wiser method would be to endow wives who work solely at domestic duties with a legal claim to a fixed proportion of the family income.

A member of the Sub-committee already mentioned, thinks that the working for money of wives tends to weaken that responsibility for the support of their families which ought to be felt by husbands. On the other hand, it is clear that a man working in one of the numerous occupations which never supply an income adequate for the support of a family can never unaided fulfil that responsibility. To say (as Mrs. Bosanquet, for instance, implicitly does) that these thousands of men should abstain from marriage is merely to shirk the problem. That problem will pretty surely find not one but various solutions. In one direction lies the effort towards the establishment of a minimum wage, in another the tendency to introduce improved methods of child nurture and saving of domestic labour, in yet a third the demand for the endowment of mothers and the right of wives to a fixed share of their husbands' incomes. It is possible that society is evolving in the direction of a family supported financially by the earnings of both parents, the children being cared for meanwhile and the work of the house being performed by trained experts. To me personally that solution seems more in harmony with the general lines of our social development than does any which would relegate all women to the care of children combined with the care of households.

Two observations remain to be made ; the first in regard to the human material of our report ; the second in regard to the report itself.

The testimonies collected bring out very strongly the

sterling qualities of the English working people in the mass. A very large majority of the women visited are evidently kindly, industrious, reasonable, self-respecting persons, emphatically good citizens. About their husbands less information naturally appears, but there is enough to show that in the main the men deserve the same praise. Among both groups there is a certain number of rather weak, thriftless, incompetent though not ill-meaning people ; but the really bad husbands are rare, while the really bad wives are, of course, not found among the ranks of those who earn industrially. Parental affection seems to be the ruling passion of nearly all these fathers and mothers ; they toil and suffer privation with amazing patience in the hope of making their children happy—a hope which can only very seldom be fulfilled and of which the frustration forms the real sting in times of unemployment or of illness.

Of the report itself, produced by so many hands working separately, yet so homogeneous in its character, we can say with conviction that it represents actual facts. What it does not, however, and cannot represent, is the proportion which these facts occupy in the whole field of British industrial life. Some light indeed is thrown upon the point by the Leicester investigation, but we ourselves should hesitate to hazard a surmise as to how far the proportion shown by the two wards of Leicester which were visited coincides with the proportion for the whole country. We can only say that the report presents the true conditions of some thousands—probably many thousands—of married women's lives in Great Britain in this earliest quarter of the twentieth century.

LONDON.

CLEMENTINA BLACK.

LAUNDRESSES.

THE 62 cases of laundry workers in London are scattered widely over different districts. From Notting Dale, Kensal Rise and " North Kensington " taken together come 13 cases; Fulham furnishes 9; Peckham and Camberwell, 5; Harrow Road and Kensal Road, another 5. One woman, not strictly a London case at all, dwells as far afield as Croydon. Of the 62, three women are ironers or pressers of new goods, and, as such, come under the ordinary regulations of the Factory Acts as to hours of work, instead of under the special regulations that apply to laundries in which garments that have been worn are washed. One of the three appears to have been working when visited for longer hours than those permitted by the Act. No such instance occurs among the laundry workers properly so called, a fact which may, perhaps, be attributable to their having mostly been visited at a season when London is comparatively empty.

Thirty-one of these women followed the same trade before their marriage as after; 14 had been in service; 2 had not been working for money; and of 14 the previous employment, if any, was not ascertained.

No difference between the care of the home or of the children seems to be traceable in the case of mothers who have been in service as compared with that of mothers who have worked at a trade; but two of the three thoroughly bad husbands who appear among these 62 women are married to ex-servants. Possibly servants, who live less than other workers among their own class, are worse judges of a man's character. Moreover, it must be remembered that an artisan of the better kind thinks service a calling much below himself socially.

A comparison between 27 cases in which the mothers had been laundry workers before marriage and 14 cases in which the mothers had been domestic servants gives the following results :

Of 27 cases of mothers who had been laundry workers there were 119 children born, of whom 22 were dead, so that 97 survived. Seventeen of these 27 mothers had lost no children, and these 17 mothers had among them 62 children. The 10 other mothers had had 57 children, of whom 35 were alive and 22 dead.[1]

In 14 cases of mothers who had been domestic servants there were 86 children born, and 21 dead, leaving 65 alive. Out of these 14, 5 women, having among them 25 children, lost none, while 9, who had among them 61 children, had lost 21, leaving 40 alive.

	No. of Cases.	Children Born.	Children Dead.	Children Surviving.
Mothers previously employed in laundry ...	17	62	0	62
	10	57	22	35
	27	119	22	97
Mothers previously employed in domestic service	5	25	0	25
	9	61	21	40
	14	86	21	65

[1] These 10 mothers were, on the whole, older women. They had both had more and lost more children.

	No. of Cases.	Children Born.	Children Dead.	Children Surviving.
Mothers previously otherwise or not employed ...	3	8	0	8
	8	41	12	29
	11	49	12	37
Totals	25	95	0	95
	27	159	55	104
	52	254	55	199

There were 62 cases reported of laundry workers, but in 10 of these it was not ascertained whether or no any children had died.

In most of the trades reported the cases are too few to give any importance to such comparisons ; but I have noticed in going through the various reports how largely the total deaths of children are made up of several in one family. There seem to be families in which the hold on life is very slight, and others in which it is very tenacious. Poverty does not appear to be a very strong factor, except in so far as consumption on the part of the bread-winner produces a poverty that aggravates any family tendency to the same disease.

It is impossible not to suppose that syphilis—never stated by a doctor in private practice as a cause of death—is responsible in some proportion of these early dying families, but what the precise proportion may be is diffi-cult even to guess. It is safe, however, to say that many of the infants described as " wasting " or as suffering from " infantile bronchitis " are victims of syphilis.

Wages by the day varied in the laundry trade from 2/– to 3/–, the most usual rate being 2/6. Washers seem to work generally but two days a week, ironers 4 or 4½. The highest regular wage was 14/– a week paid to a young woman who acted as forewoman in a suburban laundry.

Payment by the piece is customary in the case of ironers. Collars were paid for at 1¾d. to 2½d. a dozen. One worker, who was paid 2/- for a gross, thought a gross a good day's work. Another, at the same rate, reckoned a gross and a half. A machine ironer received ¾d. per gross for collars, but gave no estimate of how quickly they could be done. Shirts were ironed by hand at 1/3 a dozen, and a quick worker could do 30 in a day. In large laundries the front and cuffs would be ironed by machinery, the body and collar band by a " finisher," who was paid 9d. per dozen, and whose earnings worked out at about the same as those of the woman who ironed the whole garment by hand at a higher rate per dozen. Two other ironers living in Fulham gave 1/6 per dozen as the rate paid them for shirts. A shirt dresser who ironed new garments for sale was paid 2/- per dozen, and said that a shirt took half an hour to do, or even, sometimes, three-quarters. In another firm of the same kind the rates were 1/3 a gross for collars ; 2/- a gross for cuffs ; and 2/3 for fronts.

A mother with one child or more under 5 to be "minded" in her absence must either find a relative to undertake this charge for nothing (grandmothers come in very handily in this connection) or must pay something to a crèche, a day-nursery, or a neighbour. One woman earning 11/- for four days' work paid 1/2 a day (4/8) to a neighbour for the minding of her two small children ; another whose earnings ranged from 11/- to 14/- paid to a day nursery 10d. on Tuesdays for her two, and 11d. on Wednesdays, Thursdays, and Fridays (she working later and therefore fetching away the children later on those days), 3/7. One baby, whose senior went, at a charge of 4d. a day, to the crèche, was not himself welcome there because he would not accept his food from a bottle but

insisted upon a spoon.   Sixpence a day had to be paid
for him to a neighbour who conformed to his individual
preference.

The following are varying rates paid by different
employers :

(a) Rough body linen, 4d. a dozen; best body linen,
9d ; handkerchiefs, 1½d. ; muslin aprons, 6d. ; flannels,
4d. ; best nightgowns, 1/–.

(b) (Considered to pay very badly, although the terms
seem much the same as elsewhere.)   White petticoats,
1½d. each ; blouses, 1½d. ; skirts, 2d. ; dresses, 4d.—but the
forewoman, if possible, gave out the dress in two parts as
a blouse and skirt, thus paying only 3½d. ; nightdresses
1½d. each, although some nightdresses were declared to
take three-quarters of an hour to do.

(c) Body linen, 4d. a dozen ; flannels, 3d. ; starched
aprons, 6d. ; blouses, 1/6. ; white petticoats, 1/6 ; shirt
backs, 9d.

(d) Blouses, 1d. each ; nightdresses, 1d. ; ladies' body
linen, 6d. a dozen ; maids', 4d.

(e) Dresses, 6d. each (these were said to take 3 hours) ;
chemises, ½d. (said to take 20 minutes).   Unless these
garments were unusually elaborate the woman who gave
these estimates must have been a slow worker.

The habitations visited by those investigators who
collected the facts about London laundresses were spread
over an area extending from Acton to Woolwich, and
from West Croydon to Kilburn.   The lowest rent paid
was 2/– for one room in Peckham occupied by a deserted
wife with two children.   There are two instances, one in
Notting Dale and one in Fulham, in which 4/–, and one
near Gray's Inn Road in which as much as 4/6 was paid
for a single room ; other single rooms cost 2/6, 3/–, or 3/6.
The cheapest habitations of two rooms were in Fulham,
where in one case 3/– and in another 3/6 was paid ;
5/–, 5/6 and 6/– appeared in Notting Dale ;   6/– and 6/6

were common rates ; 7/6 was found once in Kilburn, once near Harrow Road, and once in St. Luke's. Two rooms in Soho and two in a West End court cost in each case 9/–. There were dwellings of three rooms at 6/– in Rotherhithe, 6/6 in Peckham, 7/6 in the Harrow Road district and in St. Luke's. The only two cases in which the accommodation is stated to have consisted of four rooms were one in Dalston at 4/6 and another in Kilburn at 6/6.

Only one instance appears in which a dwelling of six or more rooms was apparently occupied by one family alone, and the report leaves it uncertain whether a married daughter lodged in the house. The high-water mark was reached in Croydon, where a house of six rooms and scullery was tenanted by a husband and wife, one child, a grandmother and one lodger—more than a room apiece. The rent, here, was 10/–.

A house of six rooms and scullery at New Cross, rented at 12/6 a week, was inhabited by husband, wife, child, and three men lodgers, the payments of whom (which covered their board and lodging) amounted to £2 12s. weekly. Six rooms in Notting Dale were rented at 14/–, and three of them let off at 4/6, leaving three to accommodate a man and wife and five children. For a small house in poor repair, one room of which was so filthy that it could not be used for sleeping, the rent was 11/–, two rooms were let off at 5/6 and the remainder—number not specified—served for husband, wife and five children. A house in Fulham was occupied in the lower part by a man who was its responsible tenant (at 11/– a week), with his wife and three children, while three upper rooms were let at 5/6. Another house in Fulham was inhabited by a family of seven, one room being let off at 2/6. Another house in the same street cost 14/–, and part of it was let at 4/6 ; the family here consisted of five adults.

The quality of the accommodation varied greatly and by no means in proportion to the rent ; 6/–, for instance, was paid for a flat of two rooms in a displeasing and not very reputable district remote from the centre. It is true that in this case the flat and the block were both clean. Exactly half this rent was paid for two rooms in Fulham, but in a dirty house ; and in Rotherhithe—no farther from the middle of London—three good and clean rooms were rented at 6/–. The Notting Dale habitations—of which eight appear—are no lower in rent than those in more attractive regions. Soho and an Oxford Street court show most distinctly the dearness of a West Central position, but the worst accommodation at a high price occurs in cases 58 and 60, both of which are East Central. They were visited by a particularly experienced investigator. In case 58, a perfectly respectable man and wife were occupying a single room in " indescribably dirty low class tenements." The stairs were dark, open to the air and devoid of railing ; on each floor were common sinks and water-closets, the doors standing wide open. The rent for a single room was 4/6, and being in arrears the family, when visited, were paying an extra 6d. weekly. The landlord, or agent, was a hard man, who would sometimes break open the door of any tenant whose rent was unpaid and remove all the property in the owner's absence. This treatment had shortly before the visit befallen a young widow with a baby, and the poor creatures spent two nights on the staircase—that unrailed, filthy staircase. The baby had since died and the mother had disappeared. The family visited had taken the room on the recommendation of a fellow-worker, and were horrified when they beheld the place. " My husband," said the respectable and tidy young wife, " swore fearfully when he wheeled the furniture in, and if it had not been so late at night and the children crying, he said he would have tramped back at once." Better if he had, for he fell out of work, and they had spent 18 months in this hated and hateful abode. Of the furniture wheeled in on that unfortunate night only a bed and washstand had been retained. The poverty that had kept them from getting away had devoured all the rest. The tenements, I am happy to believe, are no longer standing.

Case No. 60 was that of a woman with a consumptive husband and five children ranging from 16 years to 9 months old. They occupied at a rent of 6/6 a top flat of two rooms in the neighbourhood of one of the great markets. The buildings were, in the investigator's words, "tucked away down a long passage, each block with a separate staircase leading off—dirty and, I should think, dangerous in case of fire. The postman I asked for directions, who said he had been in the district for 18 years, declared there were no such buildings." The wife, who went out to her work, earned, at the highest, 14/– a week, but some weeks only 7/– or 8/–. Two children between them brought in 10/–, and one of these, being engaged in bronzing, had a pint of milk provided daily at the work place, and looked (on that account, it was presumed) conspicuously well. Two of the younger children were very delicate, and these remained at home in the care of the consumptive father, who could only go out to work in warm weather. It was his custom to go hopping—always to the same farm—every year, and he was paid £1 a week. The whole family accompanied him, and the wife reported of the previous autumn's migration that it "quite set her up" for the winter. It seems difficult to believe, however, that four or five weeks in the fresh and healthy air of a hop garden could do away with the effects upon the babies' health of weeks and weeks shut up in the society of a father possessing but half a lung. The poor fellow was a devoted parent, who among other services cooked midday meals for all his children. But what must have been his reflections during the long hours of tendance upon a pair of tiny, weakly children whose chances of life his very presence was diminishing.

The investigators have in many cases failed to note whether the women were Londoners or from the country. In the cases noted at least three in four are Londoners.

Among these 62 cases the immense majority were evidently those of industrious, decent women who were good mothers. Some investigators rarely describe the worker whom they visit ; some, on the other hand, strike out a portrait in a few words, while most of them give at least an adjective to the general appearance of the woman, house and children. In twelve of these 62 cases there are either no details or none that indicate character —for example, a note that the woman looked very delicate or had a baby of a few days old. Four of the fifty women are described as intelligent, one as " impressive and interesting but most voluble," one as having " a good managing head," one as " most businesslike " one as " very pleasant," one as " friendly," three as " thrifty," six as " dirty " or " rather dirty," and one as " rather untidy." Five or so are noted as being tall, fine-looking or handsome. All of these and all the women called intelligent are also described as clean. Cleanness, tidiness or some similar quality is indeed mentioned in as many as 31 instances ; the report of one woman's conversation indicates a certain captiousness, another was " cross, clean, smart and gloomy," another " depressed," and one is roundly declared to have been " a horrid woman, not very sober, dirty." The steadiness and kindness of several husbands is incidentally indicated ; only two husbands definitely bad appear, and the history of one of these justifies the visitor's remark that he was now quite demented. Some cases showed extreme and un-deserved hardships ; as usual those in which there were consumptive husbands are heartrending. Very few hus-

bands had regular employment ; three or four wives
deplored the necessity of going to work, and about as
many expressed pleasure in their occupation. The level
of health was rather high—washing, of course, demands
strength—but there were some delicate and some few
half-starved women taxed evidently far beyond their
physical capacity.

GLOVEMAKING.

Glovemaking is, as far as London is concerned, a small,
wholly parasitic and local trade. No instance of it
outside of Battersea has come under the notice of the
Council's investigators.

The cases visited in the trade were but eight—all home-
workers—and, of these, four were widows over 50. None
of these widows worked during their married life, and all
but one were glovers previous to marriage ; the fourth
had not worked for money. Three of the widows were
fellers, who finished after the machinist ; the fourth made
the three folds on the back of gloves. The average
weekly takings (piecework) of these four widows were
4/- or 5/-, one had attained to 6/9, another to 9/-. This
last did not devote her whole time to the work, but helped
in a relative's small shop. Of the four wives, one worked
only when her husband was out of employment ; one was
a machinist, the others felled, lined, and finished. Their
respective weekly earnings were given as 5/- to 6/-, 11/-
(with a maximum once reached of 15/-), and in two cases,
5/- to 10/-. The work was fairly regular. Piecework
rates corresponded in all the statements, but varied a
good deal for different sorts of gloves.

	s.	d.	
Lining with fur	1	0	per doz.
When size ticket is sewn in ...	0	10¼	,,
Felling and finishing boys' gloves	0	7	,,
,, ,, larger ,,	0	8	,,

Another worker gave the following prices :

		s.	d.	
One-button gloves		0	8	per doz.
Two-button gloves		0	11	,,
Four-button gloves		1	8	

A third went into smaller differences :

			s.	d.	
Button gloves with tabs ...	...		1	4	,,
,, ,, without tabs	...		1	3	,
,, ,, with tabs ...	...		1	1	,,
,, ,, without tabs	...		1	0	,,

The " tab " is the little " stay " of kid round the buttonhole. The same worker mentioned other gloves at 8d. the dozen.

For stitching folds at back according to type of glove ...	3½d. to 9d. or 10d. per doz.
Machining with thread	3 3 ,,
less 1¼d. per dozen for thread.	
Machining with silk	3 4 ,,
The silk costs more than the thread.	

One feller said she could make five pairs at 8d. in an hour ; another who did chiefly longer gloves, reckoned three pairs to the hour. Rates of pay had fallen.

CARPET SEWERS.

Four cases of upholsteresses appear. Three of these were those of carpet sewers ; the fourth had been trained in various branches of the trade. Of the carpet sewers two were widows, of whom No. 1 followed the same trade before marriage, No. 2 was in service. No. 1 was earning 15/– weekly, apparently at a set wage in a good West End shop, lived in a good flat at a rent of about 10/– a week, and had three children earning, besides one at school. No. 2, an older woman, had but one crippled son, who, however, earned something, and had lost seven children, most of whom died quite young, chiefly of consumption. She was paid at the rate of 2/6 a day.

The third carpet sewer, a married woman, used to earn a weekly wage of 14/- at a West End house, but was now doing jobs and putting her baby at a crèche, at a charge of 3d. a day, but was not altogether satisfied with the management of that institution, where, she declared, the food was given sometimes too hot and sometimes too cold. She had five children and had lost none. Payments had fallen in the trade.

The upholsteress who had ceased to work on account of ill-health learned her trade completely, so completely that she prided herself upon being able to do men's work. At one time she made about £2 a week on piecework. (This trade fluctuates, however, with the seasons.) Afterwards she was paid a standing wage of 16/- a week by a firm that used to send her to customers' houses. Her husband, a railway worker at 24/- a week, was in bad health, and was ill in bed when the investigator paid her visit. They had one child and had lost none.

EIDERDOWN QUILT MAKERS.

Both the women reported upon in this trade were young wives with husbands often out of work

A worked in the trade before marriage.

B made corsets.

A at the age of 27 had five children between five months and eight years old. The youngest two she left at the crèche ; the others were at school, and she came in from work to give them their dinner. She managed to keep the children clean and tidy, but it is not surprising to hear that she herself was " very tired looking."

B had two little children and had lost none. They went to a day-nursery at the rate of 2d. a day for each. During the first two years of married life she did not work, and when it became necessary for her to do so, she did not return to her old trade because wages had gone down. She was machining eiderdown quilts on a power machine ; everything was found by the employer in her case, whereas A had to provide needles at 1½d. each.

A gave the rates at 2d., 4d., or 9d. per quilt, and said that a ninepenny one would be of a large size with frills, and would take over 1½ hours to make, probably 2 hours. The lowest sum she had been paid in a week was 5/–, the highest 17/– or 18/–.

B said that payment depended upon the material of the quilt, not upon its size—a method of payment not uncommon in the sewing trades. Some quilts were 4¼d. each, sateen ones with frills were 6d. She earned from 10/– a week, and said that quick hands can make 15/–. The season in this trade is not a very long one. B eked out the slack times—and perhaps filled in her brief hours at home even in the busy ones—by machining painters' aprons at 5¼d. a dozen, and on the morning when she was visited had made two dozen between 8.30 and 11. She had to hire a machine (1/6 a week) and spent 2/– a week on cotton, so that her profits did not exceed 7/– or 8/– a week.

SACK SEWERS.

Of the four sack sewers reported upon, two were married and two widowed. Two of them worked at home, two upon an employer's premises.

One of the factory workers, a married woman, had been at the trade only a year, and entered it on account of her husband being out of work. She was paid 1/7 for sewing a dozen sacks, and had never made more than 10/– a week. Her hours were from 8.30 to 6, including 1½ hours for meals. Even in her brief experience rates had fallen. 1/9 per dozen was paid, when she began, for the sacks that she was, when visited, sewing at 1/7 per dozen. The husband was discharged on account of slackness of work, about three years before, from the wholesale house in which he was employed, and had never been able to get any regular work since until some two months before the investigator's visit, when he returned to work for his old employers, who were giving him four days' work a week, from 9 o'clock to 5 o'clock, at 5½d. an hour. He earned on this arrangement either 12/10 or 14/8, according to whether he took a dinner hour or worked through that hour. These were superior people, and although they lived in a somewhat unpleasing district, the house was clean. It was occupied by the mother of the wife, who let them three upper rooms at 6/6. There were four children living, whose ages ranged from 12 years to 22 months. The grandmother looked after the children in their mother's absence.

The second factory worker was a young woman who had been five months widowed, and who was herself ill and unstrung, suffering probably from shock, and the investigator did not, therefore, press for details. The work was reported regular ; yet was at that time slack. She earned 9/– a week or less, and received 3/– a week Poor Law relief. Her husband when alive earned good wages. Three children were living, the eldest was twelve, the youngest five years old. Another, a baby, died a month before the father's death. This woman lived in the house of her parents, and paid 4/– a week for rent.

Of the workers at home, No. 1, a clean, superior widow of 50, had lost her husband a year previously. He had worked at a well-paid, skilled trade, in which, however, work is always slack in the winter. When he was unemployed he used to remain at home and look after the children while she worked at her original trade as a paper sorter, which she had pursued regularly during their early married life when his wages were less than at a later period. She had a regular wage of 10/-, her two rooms cost her 4/- weekly, were clean, but scantily furnished, and her children, though untidy, are described as "well-kept." There were five of them; and the eldest was working for his father's employers and earning about 12/- a week; the second was in a biscuit factory at a weekly wage of 7/-, the others were of school age. The mother could not get employment at her old trade; she went for three weeks to a jam factory, but work became slack there, and she had made what she could by sewing sacks at home, earning about 6d. or 8d. at a time, and washing for her neighbours. She had 4/- Poor Law relief and the boys, she said, "were very good to her." Evidently the poor things had a very hard struggle, which, if the sons continue to do well, will become lighter by degrees.

The remaining worker was a married woman of 35, whose husband, after a long illness, had been taken to the infirmary, and would never be fit for work again. This delicate woman, whose youngest child was but five weeks old, had been trying to keep her home together by her work. Before marriage she was a bookfolder, and continued in that trade until after the birth of her third child. Her husband's mother, who lived in the same house, used to look after the children during her absence at work. When she ceased to go out she took small sacks, for years, to make at home at the rate of 1½d. per dozen. Before the birth of her last child she could earn 7/- or 8/- a week, but when visited had earned in the three preceding weeks 5/-, 4/3, and 4/2 respectively. Her rent, 5/6 for two rooms, which were not very clean and were very poorly furnished, had fallen into arrears. Of her four living children, not one was earning anything. She had had seven, but three had died of measles. She was receiving to the value of 8/- in Poor Law relief, half in money and half in kind, and was paying 10d. weekly for her husband's insurance. She could have lightened her burdens by letting one child go to the workhouse school, but was unwilling to part with her. It is clear that the income of from 12/– to 13/– a week was quite inadequate to keep this family lodged and fed. The out-relief allowed, though rather unusually high, served rather to prolong than to remedy their misery.

ARTIFICIAL FLOWER MAKERS.

Sixteen cases were reported of artificial flower makers, and not one of the sixteen was apparently that of a country woman. Ten were definitely stated to be Londoners, and the circumstances point to an eleventh's being so. The origin of four is set down as " town," and in the one case remaining there is no statement as to origin. Ten of these women worked at the same trade before marriage, some of them having begun very young ; three do not appear to have worked for wages before marriage ; one was a cocoa-packer, one a domestic servant, and the previous occupation, if any, of the sixteenth does not appear. Among these cases occur two of the very rare examples of husbands never out of work ; one man was a carman at a wage of about 23/–, the other a printer's assistant at 25/–, a trade union man, who had never been out of work in his 14 years of married life. But although a regular 25/– is opulence in comparison with the horrible poverty of many decent families visited in the course of this enquiry, it is not an income out of which in London, after 6/6 has been paid away for rent, a man, woman and four children can be properly fed and clothed. Mrs. A., therefore, as the family increased, took up the occupation of " sticking and papering " ; that is to say she spent what spare time she could command in affixing little artificial green leaves to stalks

of wire, and in winding around the wire strips of thin
green paper. The leaves, thus provided with stalks,
were packed together in dozens, and the payment for
doing a gross varied from 1¾d. to 2½d. ; the gross took
about an hour. Mrs. A. worked usually from 9.30 in
the morning to the same hour at night, less some two or
three hours occupied by housework, preparation of meals,
etc., and earned—when work was not slack—from 5/- to
7/6 a week.

Let us consider a little the life of this woman and of
her husband. He was away from home probably some
ten hours a day, so that practically he spent only Saturday
afternoon and Sunday with his family. For, let us say
54 hours' work, he got 25/-, that is a shade over 5½d. per
hour. The wife received from 1¼d. to 2½d. for her hour's
work and doubtless (this is not stated) had to fetch and
take back her work, or to employ one of the children for
the purpose. Taking her highest rate of pay (2½d. per
hour), it appears that she must work 72 hours in the week
to obtain as much as 7/6, and must affix and cover
during those 72 hours 3,368 wire stalks. If we add her
average earnings (say 6/3) to her husband's 25/- we
get a weekly income of 31/3 for the family of six persons ;
6/6 for rent leaves 24/9, or 4/1½ per head. Out of that
sum must come firing, light, clothing for six bodies,
and—heaviest strain of all—boots for 12 feet, cleaning
materials, renewal of household goods as they wear out,
the trade-union contribution that goes to keep up wages
and to provide against emergencies, and besides all
these, food for a man, woman, and four growing children.
How can it be done ? What farthing remains for recreation of any sort ? A book is beyond their dreams,
a newspaper, even, would be an extravagance ; a necessary
reel of cotton means the price of a loaf. What does
our civilisation give to these admirable and devoted
citizens ? Not comfort—they inhabit two small and poor

rooms ; not luxury—they have not sixpence a day each for food ; not leisure, not mental development, and, very surely, not the physical pleasure of mere fine bodily health, nor the gratification of seeing their children enjoy such health. The children, though well-kept—and they had lost none—looked pale and delicate. One wealth they had—their love for the children ; the investigator, after describing the small and stuffy rooms, the pallor and delicacy of the children, adds :— " There was an atmosphere of affection and happiness in the home." And this, it must be remembered, is a model pair who did not marry early (the wife at " about forty " had been married 14 years), who had not an improvidently large family (there are 10 years between the eldest and the youngest of their children), and whom the sternest of Charity Organisation Committees could but regard as " deserving."

The trade appears to be one in which rates of pay vary extremely. Nearly all the home-workers reported piecework earnings considerably lower than those of indoor workers, some of whom were on time wages. A colourer of flowers, however, who worked " inside," was reported to be paid no more than 13/- a week. How far the difference is a real difference of rate or how far it is due to the giving of the worse-paid work to the women at home there is no evidence in the reports to show ; but it is safe to guess that the home-worker does, as a rule, get the poorer sort of work.

Although this group of workers is classed as artificial flower makers, very few of those in this report actually made flowers. Most of them were " mounters" who arranged flowers or leaves upon stems, bound them together with fine wire, and covered the stems with paper. The " sticking and wiring " of single leaves is a humble branch of mounting ; the mounter proper receives her flowers and leaves already fixed to their paper-covered stalks, and groups them together.

No. 1 took all kinds of flowers, including " flowers for decoration," by which she probably meant paper flowers ; these were described as badly paid but easy. She thus managed to be busy all the year round and earned an average of 2/- a day, or 12/- a week. She had a daughter working in a factory who did the better flowers and got 25/- a week as a pieceworker. No. 1 did not think there had been much change in the rate of pay.

No. 2 presented the investigator with a specimen of her work, a poor flattened sample of execution. It consisted of leaves which, from their form, appear intended to represent rose leaves, but of which the colour, an unshaded emerald green, belongs to no rose leaf that ever grew. The leaves, made of a sort of calico and waxed, are mounted in four groups, two of three leaves, one of five, and one of seven, and the wire stalks of these groups are then bound together with fine wire so that each spray seems to grow from a main stem. Each bunch thus comprises eighteen leaves, and for making up a dozen branches the worker was paid 2d. For sprays of one rose, one bud, and three leaves, tied up in dozens, she was paid 3/9 a gross. Her highest takings for any week as a home-worker were 10/-, but when in her younger days she worked on an employer's premises she could earn 30/-. Rates had fallen greatly ; thirteen years previously 5/6 a gross was paid for work then rated at 2/-. No. 3 quoted 3d. a gross for buttercups, and said that rates of pay had fallen very much.

No. 5 wired leaves at 3/4 per gross. How much work this represented, and of what sort the leaves were does not appear.

No. 6 did roses at 1/- a gross. What precisely she did to the flowers is not explained. Probably she put stalks to them ; possibly she mounted them, after they had already got stalks, in groups of so many together, and was paid, not by the spray but by the single flower. She said that " prices " had fallen " shocking."

No. 7, of whose work there are no details, also said that payments were lower.

No. 10, who had been engaged in the trade for many years, and now, as an old woman earned about 2½d. an hour, working at home, said that rates had fallen a great deal. At one time, by working extremely long hours, she could make from £1 to 30/– a week in busy seasons, but on the later terms no one could possibly earn as much. She mentioned that leaves were now coming in ready-made from abroad.

No. 11 gave the following rates :—Buttercups, 6d. per gross ; roses, 1/– ; forget-me-nots, 1/3. This woman thought that rates had fallen, but had risen again to about the original level.

No. 12 mounted forget-me-nots at 2/– per gross, and other flowers at 2/6 and 3/–. She earned some 10/– to 12/– a week, and complained that she was kept waiting when she went to fetch her work. On one occasion she was kept waiting for 5 hours.

No. 14, who did not, as a rule, begin work until after dinner, earned 6/– to 9/– a week as a mounter ; and No. 15, working about 7 hours for 5 days a week, earned about 10/– and thought she had nothing to grumble about.

No. 16, a woman of 77, used to be able to earn 18/– to £1 a week, and now earned from 5/– to 6/–. Her old age pension brought her income up to 10/– or 11/–.

Nos. 8 and 9 made paper flowers and sold them to private customers, apparently for purposes of decoration. Flowers of this description may sometimes be seen adorning the windows of hansom cabs. They were sold in penny or sixpenny bunches, the penny bunch containing six blossoms. Two roses were sold for 1½d. or 12 for 6d. The penny bunch took 10 minutes to make, and the two roses about the same time. The other woman said that a sixpenny bunch occupied her for 1½ hours. This woman also made fans which she sold at 2/– a pair; she could make the pair in half a day. Each worker reported her average earnings as 8/–, and each said that before Christmas she could make up to 15/–. One of them said that the trade had gone down because blind children were taught to do it.

The highest rent paid by any of these workers was 8/–. This figure appears twice, but in one case the amount of accommodation was not ascertained; in the other there were four rooms, of which one was let at 2/–, the real rent being thus reduced to 6/–. No. 8, living far from the centre, had a house of four rooms and a wash-house for 7/6, while No. 2, in a crowded and unpleasant district, paid 6/– for two basement rooms, one of which could not be used on account of a vile smell. No. 4 paid 6/– for two dark rooms, and No. 13 for two " very small rooms " paid 6/6. For single rooms (one of them in a basement, but with an outlook into a garden, while another was in a converted stable) the rents were 3/6 (in two cases), 2/6, and 2/–.

As regards children, this group presents one of the few cases in which a woman told the investigator that she had deliberately tried to prevent the birth of her children. Her husband, now dead, was not good to her, the family income was inadequate, and she " wouldn't bring into the world children that she knew they could not keep." The husband was delicate, and of the two children born to them alive, both had died in early infancy.

TENNIS AND RACQUET BALL COVERERS.

Tennis and racquet ball covering is done exclusively, or almost exclusively, in Woolwich. For tennis balls, the rates were the same in almost every case visited, being either 6d. or 7d. per dozen, the worker finding needles and thread. The thread would seem to cost about ½d. in the shilling; 10 needles cost a penny, and the number broken by an unusually hard covering cloth ·might be almost as many. I doubt, however, whether, as a rule, a worker would use more than one packet a week, even if so many. Few women covered more than three dozen in a day; though No. 12, who has supported herself during 16 years of widowhood, could do four dozen a day, thus making 12/- a week. But there were long slack seasons in which she would not get more than two dozen, at the outside, to do in a day. A young niece who lived with her and worked in a factory was earning a regular wage of 16/-. At slack seasons, No. 12 had tried shirt work, and made ten shirts throughout for 6/3; on one occasion she took some shirts from a shop close by to put on the buttons. The two women, working steadily from 8.30 or 9 until 2, found that they earned between 4d. and 6d., a sum which she did not even trouble herself to fetch from the giver-out.

Another widow, not many years under 70, worked steadily, but could only cover two dozen in a day—1/- or 1/2 per day. Happily she had a pension of 5/-, and presumably when she attains the age of 70 her old age pension will raise her income to 10/-.

The cores or centres of tennis balls are made, as most people know, of india-rubber covered with a sort of felt or cloth. Centres and coverings are procured from an employer, the covering being already shaped into the curious lines of junction that may be observed upon tennis balls. The business of the coverer is to make seams along these lines, carrying the stitches about half-way through the felt, and taking great care to avoid putting the needle into the india-rubber.

One worker complained that the smell of the tennis

ball centres gave her headaches ; but it needs the
opinion of a skilled oculist to judge whether the headaches did not rather proceed from her eyes. Any trade
that involves constant sewing puts a strain upon the
eyesight ; the strain is less severe in ball covering than
in either fine white work or buttonholing.

The rates of pay have risen. Several women remembered
receiving 4d. a dozen for the balls now paid at 6d.

Racquet balls were paid for at lower rates than tennis
balls—although in this branch, too, there had been a rise,
due, we believe, to a movement on the part of customers
(particularly in some public schools), who offered to pay
more for the completed article on condition that the
extra payment should go to the coverers. Even in its
improved condition, however, racquet ball covering remained a parasitic trade, but a less irregular one than
tennis ball covering.   3/6 or 4/6 was paid for the covering
of a gross ; some years ago the prices were lower ; the
workers put the rise at 1/- per gross ; but cases appear in
the " Report on Home Industries of Women," published
by the Women's Industrial Council, in 1897, in which
the rates were 1/10, 2/-, and 2/4 a gross. The present
investigator visited perhaps a dozen racquet ball coverers
for that enquiry, and found the rates reported prevailing.
1/10 or 2/- (according to the firm giving out the work)
was the rate for the small kind of balls. If these are now
paid at 3/6 in all cases, the rise is from 1/6 to 1/8. The
three cases then reported were selected as those of women
who worked steadily all day, and it was shown that
half a gross was about a full day's work. This evidence is
corroborated by No. 23 in the present investigation, who
said that a gross took nearly two days. The larger balls
take, of course, rather longer to cover. Of the racquet
ball coverers in this report not one appeared to do
a full day's work. The " cores " and squares of skins
are brought home from the factory, the skins are damped

in wet cloth and the core is pressed into the centre of the damp skin, which is drawn up tightly, any superfluous leather cut off bit by bit, and the seam sewn up with neat stitches close to the edges. After having been sewn, the balls are rolled either under a slab of marble, or, failing that, under a plate, in order to make them perfectly round.

Most of the ball coverers have either followed the same occupation before marriage, or else been in service. One helped in a laundry, and one helped her farmer father in the dairy. A considerable proportion of them were country born, and nearly all seemed to be not only estimable and respectable, but highly superior. Their husbands belonged mostly to the class of skilled artisans ; but even in this so-called aristocracy of labour, much irregularity of work and recurring spells of unemployment are found.

In few of the cases reported could the family spare the woman's earnings. In one case the wife, who had no children, worked chiefly to fill up her hours of soli- tude, her husband being engaged in night work and sleeping most of the day.

No. 21 may serve as an example of the sensible and excellent wives of whom Woolwich seems to furnish many. The family occupied a house of which the rent was 16/- a week, and for a long time a room was given rent free to an old lady who had been a friend of the grandmother, and who had 3/6 Poor Law relief. Lodgers formed a welcome addition when they could be had. The husband had a salary as a salesman, and a commission. Though there were but two children, the income was none too large for the family needs, the standard both of neatness and of health being high. Several pounds—not less, perhaps, than £10 in all—were spent upon a throat operation for the elder child. The husband belonged to the Oddfellows, with medical attendance, better worth having than the Good Templars' benefit of 18/-, without medical attendance. The elder girl was taking music lessons in the hope of becoming a teacher, and the mother was saving to provide a little fund for the future of the younger one. The house of this intelligent woman was, as might be expected, perfectly clean, neat and comfortable, and it possessed a garden. A quaint touch appears in the custom of putting a penny or twopence by in a box to pay for the dog's licence. Mr. A. " doesn't like to be without a dog."

One woman formerly worked in a sort of partnership with a man in a small way of business, who kept the books and carried on the correspondence while she made the balls. The profits were evenly divided, and her share was about 17/- a week. After his death, she took balls to cover in the ordinary way from an employer.

Rents are high in Woolwich. Two cases appear in which as much as 16/- a week was paid for a house, and in no case does the rent appear to be lower than it would have been for the same number of rooms in the centre of London. Probably the accommodation was generally better, and there is mention of gardens. In one case, however, a worker was found suffering from the dampness of her dwelling. The high general character of the families in this report is striking. Among 26 women, not one seems to fall short of a high standard ; and there is only one instance quoted of a bad husband—a man-servant who robbed his employer, and at the end of his term of imprisonment deserted his wife.

WOOD CHOPPERS AND BUNDLERS.

In this poor trade, always slack in the summer, there was found prevailing something like a standard rate of 3d. per 100 for bundling. One employer was paying but 2¾d. Rates had been higher. One woman said that 4d. per

100 used to be paid ; another quoted 3¼d. There was a general opinion that about 100 bundles could be done in an hour, but one woman of experience said that it was impossible to assign a time, because so much depended upon the nature of the wood ; a certain standard of appearance had to be attained by each bundle, and if the wood happened to be rough and untidy much more time was required than when the wood was fairly smooth. Working hard from 9 o'clock to 8.30, she did not believe it possible to earn more than 2/- a day.

Choppers also were paid 3d. per hundred ; in one case 3d. an hour was mentioned, but it does not appear whether this statement represented piece rates or not. No pay is earned during the time of fetching wood and of filling carts. Chopping is clearly hard work for women ; in one of the cases the health of the worker had evidently suffered seriously ; it is but fair to add, however, that she was suffering also from poverty and privation. One woman, not herself a worker, reported that her husband, when dock labour was slack, in winter time, worked in a wood yard, and was paid 3½d. per 100 for both chopping and tying the bundles. Since, however, this woman's own sister-in-law, living in the next house, was paid 3d. per 100 for chopping alone, while other women were habitually paid 3d. for tying, it would appear as if there was some error about this statement, especially as another witness said that men and women were paid alike. This man was said to earn 10/- to 11/- a week, while a quick hand would be able to do as many as 900 bundles in a day—that is 2/3, or 13/6 per week.

The information about this trade came from many different parts of London ; most workers believed that the trade had suffered severely from the competition of the Church Army and the Salvation Army, and one woman used to take 4d. per 100 instead of 3d., but another

(in the south of London) said that wages had risen
" since the strikes."

On the whole, the women of this group were rough
and of a low social grade. Two, at least, lived in a
street of bad character. None of them had a husband
whose work was sufficiently regular to keep the family,
although it is not alleged in any of the cases that the
husbands were unsteady or idle. Several were dock
labourers, but, as it happens, none of these belonged to
the large East End docks.

FUR SEWERS.

The work done by the four women in this group
was too dissimilar to yield any general earnings. Three
of them were Londoners, and three of them worked
in the same trade before marriage. No. 1 and No. 3
both worked upon muffs and lappets, but it was not
quite clear what processes were performed by No. 1. She
was paid by piecework rates, and working from 9 to 7
earned 12/- to 14/- a week. No. 3 lined, wadded, and
finished muffs at 1/9 per dozen, and could do one muff in
twenty minutes, thus earning at the rate of 5¼d. per hour.
For necklets—presumably lined and wadded—she got
2/- a dozen, and used formerly to get 3/-. This woman
treated her work as a regular trade, working from 7.30 to
8.30, with an hour and a quarter taken out for meals.
She had a servant to do her housework, and in the previous
week to that in which she was visited had received 16/-.
When her mother helped she could earn 25/-. A third
woman worked with her husband at covering and lining
fur boots, and the two together earned about £1 a week.
Another, now widowed, used to work with her husband,
and now worked with an uncle, doing the best class of
work. She was unwilling to be communicative because
in this very good work patterns are carefully guarded,

but said that they earned " good money " and sometimes had many pounds' worth of skins in the house. Her children, grown-up, and doing well, were living with her in a house rented at £48.

Although none of these women said so, fur sewing is admittedly an unhealthy trade, the hairs being drawn in by the breath, and causing, sometimes, very serious illness. It is a trade that ought never to be carried on in a room where food is eaten. Fur pulling, a trade in which such evils occurred in an aggravated degree, and of which an appalling account, by the late Mrs. F. G. Hogg, was given in the Women's Industrial Council's " Home Industries of Women in London," 1897—is not now allowed to be carried on at home.

The husband of one worker—a superior man who, having been a sailor, had probably a high standard of cleanliness and tidiness—objected to his wife's work, complained of the hair being over everything, and considered the work only fit to be done in a workshop. One of these women was afflicted with a brutal husband, to whose ill-treatment she attributed the deaths of two of her children.

FEATHER CURLERS.

Of the three feather curlers visited, one worked only for private customers ; a second worked in a factory and had done so before marriage. She was paid 1d. or 2d. per feather, according to size and quality, and earned an average of 12/- a week, upon which she had to live, her husband not providing even the rent money. This poor young woman, who married against the advice of her friends, had evidently known little but misery in her married life, and had had, and lost at birth five children. She was not quite certain even of her husband's occupation, if indeed he had any, and she, a superior woman, was looking for some occupation to fill her lonely evening hours after she came home from the workshop. The third feather curler, a widow with three children, kept herself hidden behind her door while she spoke to the visitor, and gave little information about her trade ; 9d. to 3/6 a dozen were the prices, and she " made her money."

MILLINERS.

Several women worked at home in various millinery processes. One visited made bandeaux (shaped pieces to place inside hats), which she wired all round ; 4d. to 6d. a dozen was paid her, and a dozen took about an hour and a half. Her average weekly wage was 9/– to 10/–. Another tucked chiffon for hats, and earned 10/– to 12/– a week. A third made straw shapes at an average rate of 5d. each.

One old lady went to work for a firm which had employed her for 40 years. She earned 9/– to 10/– a week, and said that rates had fallen greatly within her remembrance. One woman, with some assistance from her husband, made the mysterious, cylindrical frills that may still be seen at the edges of widows' caps and in the interior of widows' bonnets. A machine, described as resembling a miniature mangle, was employed, and the frilled tubes, after having passed through it, were threaded on sticks, exposed to steam and carefully dried. 1/6 for a dozen strips seems to be a low price, but the woman managed to earn about 9/– a week. The trade, she said, was dying out.

An unusually high wage was earned by No. 15, a maker of sunbonnets, but the trade was, of course, a seasonal one. She could earn, being a very quick hand, £1 to 30/– a week ; and since she had seven dependent children and a husband who, although he earned 30/–, handed but 20/– weekly to his wife, her earnings were absolutely needed. The remaining 10/– seems to have been devoted to the pleasure of the husband who, to use his wife's expression, " likes a bit of life." " But," she added, " he doesn't treat me badly on the whole."

No. 16 also was able to earn £1 a week if she had some other person to look after her house and child. She generally, however, preferred to do this herself, and her earnings in that case were about 12/– or 13/–. These figures are interesting ; it would appear from them that the domestic labour of a wife in a household of three members (one a child of 2½ years old) reduces her power of wage-earning by from 7/– to 8/– a week, or, in other words, that she gives about a shillingsworth a day of unpaid service to the household, Sundays included. A larger family and more rooms would increase the work in proportion.

In these small groups conditions are so various that any comparison of rents could have little value.

JAM MAKERS, PRESERVE MAKERS, MINERAL WATER WORKERS.

Of the 19 women in this group, all worked away from their homes in factories of various kinds. Some of them lifted pans of 56 lbs. weight, some washed bottles, some pulped fruit or stacked jars, or put fruit into bottles. One was an " onioner " ; one packed tea ; one prepared skins for sausages ; two bottled mineral water ; and one worked in a meat preserving factory.

Work in jam factories and mineral water factories is seasonal, and in most cases the full time wage was but 10/– or 11/– a week. One woman, working for a well-known firm, earned 13/9 time-wage when busy, but at the time of the investigator's visit was peeling oranges, receiving 1½d. for ½ cwt., and, working short time, was earning 5/– to 8/– a week. One bottle washer gave 4/6 to 9/6 as her weekly earnings; another " washer," who may have washed either bottles or fruit, said she earned from 2/– in slack times to 10/– when busy. A tea packer, filling packets by means of a machine, and receiving 1/– for every 3,400 packets, earned from 7/– to 9/– a week. An "onioner" and fruit bottler set down her earnings as 10/– to 12/– in busy seasons and 3/6 to 4/– in slack ones—and the slack season in this trade is the winter time.

Two mineral water hands each said that they might earn up to 11/– a week, but in winter not more than between 6/– and 7/–. Thus the earnings of the women in this group—all indoor hands—seem to average roughly 9/– to 10/– a week for perhaps three months in the year, about 4/– to 5/– for another three months, and something about half-way between these two extremes during the remainder of the twelve months. The figure of 7/6 a week, which Miss Mary Macarthur's experience leads her to assign as the average wage, taking the year through, of a London factory worker, seems not far out as regards this group of workers.

The highest rent paid (after subtracting that of rooms let off) was 8/– for two rooms in a central position. Particulars of the rooms do not appear, but in them were housed a grandfather, grandmother, mother and two children aged 10 and 12. A good deal of overcrowding appears in several of these cases.

The work done by "stackers" and "lifters" is often very heavy; it is difficult to believe that the carrying or piling up of pans or trays weighing half a hundred-weight each can be suitable for women who are expecting the birth of a child. Yet of the two women who expressly mentioned this lifting as their work, neither had lost a child; one had six, and the other four.

SHOPKEEPERS AND HAWKERS.

The nine cases of shopkeepers and street sellers seem to be fairly typical ones, and to present, among them, samples of the lives generally led by women who work at home in the humbler branches of shopkeeping, or who go out to sell in the streets.

No. 1, a widow, had for 20 years worked in a little coffee-house in a central district of London. The house, though small and old, was rented at £60 a year, and the rates and taxes amounted to between £20 and £30 more. Her six living children (she lost three in infancy) were all " doing for themselves in business." Her kitchen was spotlessly clean, and its mistress, clean and tidy, was reading the paper, while her two helpers (who live in) were washing up and cooking. The business, she said, had gone down sadly, because firms, in building new premises, provided canteens at which men could get their meals. She now furnished from 100 to 150 dinners daily, at 6d. each ; and spent quite 1/- a day upon coals and gas. Supposing her profits, after paying expenses, to have been 2d. per dinner, she would have been making about a guinea a week. Her rent and taxes, amounting to a total of £85 a year, seem exorbitant, but the street in which she lived, being largely occupied by factories and workshops, had, no doubt, a high site value.

No. 2, also a widow, kept a little shop in a poor street in a residential district, and sold domestic stores, sweets, etc. She also did needlework. Her rent was for many years 9/-, but had been reduced—she did not tell the visitor by how much. Of her four living children, one was crippled, and one had defective eyesight. She was not able to say what she earned, but the sales of the shop were chiefly in pennyworths and halfpennyworths, and seemed barely to cover expenses.

No. 3 kept a sweet shop in a part of London that is

near to suburbs, but has ceased to be suburban. She said that she made very little, about 2/– a week, but the shop did not take up much of her time. For a house of four rooms, old and dirty, the rent was 6/–. Her husband was a labourer whose earnings she did not know, and there were four children, one of whom was earning.

No. 4, with her husband, son and daughter, kept a greengrocery shop in the same neighbourhood. The rent of the house and shop was 14/– a week, but a back room was let for 3/–. The husband went on a " round " with vegetables. Of her nine children she had lost four, and another son was in consumption, while the daughter (wife of a man who had just got work after seven months' unemployment, and mother of a baby) looked almost as ill as her brother.

No. 5 was a Russian Jewess who came to London with her relatives about 21 years ago, and whose imperfect English made it rather difficult to gain information from her. Her husband, after being a foreman in the employ of a firm for which he had worked for many years, lost his post by the bankruptcy of the firm and could not get another. Until that time the family had been happy and prosperous. They set up a fried-fish shop, which failed ; and the wife took to keeping a little general shop—although one would suppose her imperfect English and her very poor health to be severe handicaps—by which she could not make a profit of so much as £1 a week. The shop seemed to be languishing for lack of replenishment. The rent was 14/– for the small shop, and (as the visitor understood) six rooms. Of the five children (none were dead) only the eldest girl was earning —a wage of 7/–, less 1/– weekly for fares.

No. 6, a widow living in a poor working-class district, rented a house at 12/–, and let one room at 4/–. Of her five children (none dead) two worked at a factory and earned, one from 10/- to 20/-, the other from 4/- to 12/-. She herself sold in the streets from 10 to 1 daily. Very tantalisingly the investigator has omitted to note the nature of the wares ; but the statement " Buys fresh goods in the afternoon, comes home and mends and cleans them " suggests second-hand goods of some kind. This woman said that she earned nothing at all—perhaps a penny a day, but she looked very comfortable, and it is obvious that six persons do not live with an appearance of comfort and pay 8/- rent upon an income that is sometimes but 14/-, and never more than 22/-. Under the head of *Remarks*, the visitor notes briefly :—" A regular virago."

No. 7, a married woman between 40 and 50, had been a fish hawker all her life, and went out with her husband, her son, and the barrow. Their takings might come, she said, to £1 per week, or they might lose £1. A clean, tidy woman, much troubled by the failure of her eyesight. Rent 10/- for four rooms, three children dead, and six still at school.

No. 8 had been an artificial flower maker before marriage, and when her husband fell out of regular work she got some roses to do at home, but found that a gross, for which only 10d. was paid, occupied her all day. Being a good hand, she could not do what she scornfully called " slop work " badly enough to make it pay her. The husband, after having a post at 32/-, with a firm for whom he had worked many years, was dismissed when they cut down expenses, and, being unable to get work, set up a barrow, and began to sell at a street stall. A helper being needed, she began to work with him. As usual with street sellers, she either could not or would not name a figure for the average earnings. A brother-in-law gave them stock ; they paid 2/6 for the barrow, and 2/- for shed money weekly. This was a capable, thrifty woman whose philosophy, as she explained it, was to keep on smiling, and not to tell other people her troubles.

No. 9 was a young widow with two small children, of whom the elder was at a Poor Law school. She lodged in a very old house in a central district, and paid 3/- for a room of which the floor was shaky and rotten, and which possessed only an ordinary bedroom grate. The room was fairly clean, and she herself a strong, tidy young woman. She was a Londoner born, and said definitely that no offer of good work and better pay would induce her to live out of London. She sold flowers in the streets, and had done so all her life ; went out early to buy her stock, came home and " made up," then went forth to sell, and finished her day's work at about 4.30. In August it was her custom to go hop-picking. Her trade, she declared, had fallen off so much that there was no longer a living to be made at it. Formerly she had earned " good money," but now people bought seeds and grew things for themselves. She was anxious to give up her flower selling, at which she never made more than 1/6 per day, and sometimes only 4d. to 6d., and take to office cleaning or charing, at which she believed she could do well. Moreover, she was expecting to have her elder child back on her hands. There had been a question about the " settlement " of the children, and it had been decided that they belonged to the district from which their father came—one in which, according to her story, assistance was not given to widows unless they had as many as four children. The husband, also a Londoner, had been a window cleaner, and had died two years previously of " chest trouble."

Among these nine women, not one seems to have been a country woman. Of No. 4 the origin is not stated. No. 5 was born in Russia. Of three others it is stated that their place of origin was " town," which may or may not stand for London ; the other four are Londoners,

of whom No. 9 (and possibly also No. 1) had never lived
beyond a radius of about half a mile from King's Cross
Station.

They form a group that is interesting and picturesque,
but too heterogeneous to have any clear economic significance. Their cases are recorded at some length, because
they and their like are elements so characteristic of
London life, with its infinite variety of types, that their
very differences must form part of any true picture.

PAPER BAG MAKERS.

The majority of women whose cases are reported
are Londoners. There was but one widow among
them, and she was the only indoor hand. For two
reasons, however, she cannot serve, as the widowed
worker often does, as a standard for a full day's work.
She was ill and unable to work at her former speed, and
she was not a bag maker but a paper sorter. In former
days, when wages were better, she could earn 20/- a
week; now, she said, she could, if well, earn about
12/-. Her illness—she was consumptive—she attributed
to the dust which came from the paper, to over-work,
and to insufficient food. This consumptive woman
was inhabiting two dirty rooms, shared by her own three
children, her niece, and her niece's two children. The
poverty which comes of a breadwinner's consumptiveness
seems to lead almost invariably to a degree of over-
crowding particularly likely to cause further infection.

Not one of the bagmakers (six of them) in this report
was working a full day, some because they could not get
work, some because their time was taken up by home
duties. Some of them received the paper in sheets—a
heavy burden—and made the bags throughout, fourteen
separate processes being required, according to the statement of one worker. Another, who was working with her

husband, said that each bag passed six times through her hands. No doubt the other processes were performed by the man. This woman said that he and she together could do from 4,000 to 6,000 bags a day. No other woman claimed to be able to do more than 4,000. A very common rate of payment was 6d. per thousand ; one woman, who worked only after her children were in bed, and made only from 1,000 to 2,000 each week, received from 1/1 to 1/3 for tea bags. Another, making drapers' bags, had 5d. per thousand for what she called " half-quartern " bags (meaning presumably of the size that would hold a half-quartern of flour), 6d. per thousand for " cap " bags, which were larger, and 1/– for large hat bags. She earned from 6/– to 8/– a week ; but by working hard could have made as much as 12/–. Wages, she said, had fallen about a penny per thousand in the course of the last twelve years. Another worker, who had been a bag maker for 26 years (seven years in the factory, and 19 years at home), made chiefly bags for fruit, and for tea, at 6d., 8d., or 10d. per thousand. She said that a thousand took her 1½ to 2 hours, according to the size.

No. 4, working 7 or 8 hours for five days a week, earned 6/– to 7/– when the trade was busy, and had earned up to 8/–. She received 6d. per thousand.

No. 5, also getting 6d. per thousand, said that she could do 4,000 in a day, but could seldom get so many to do. Sixpence per thousand was the rate named by No. 6, who was working with her husband.

Rates had evidently fallen, but not, it would seem, very greatly. On the other hand, it was clearly more difficult to get enough work, and the difficulty was attributed on all hands to the use of machinery. A machine, it was stated, could turn out 50,000 bags a day, and hand-work in homes was being superseded.

That the health of women, especially if they are mothers, should suffer from carrying home a ream at a time of large-sized and sometimes thick sheets of paper seems inevitable.

No. 4 in this report ..ad had five children, one of whom was born dead, and had been in the habit of working up to the day of birth, and then resting for a month. At the time of her last child's birth she was not working, but was exceedingly ill, and was obliged to go into a hospital. The doctor said she had probably been over-lifting. During the earlier months of her pregnancy she had been fetching her work—carrying backwards and forwards a ream of paper, and bringing that weight up several flights of stairs to the flat in which she lived. One would suppose, although no complaint appears on this subject, that the presence in the home of some hundreds of bags pasted with damp paste, and in process of getting dry, must conduce neither to health nor to comfort.

These cases show no great divergence of rent. The highest figure is 8/9 for three rooms and a kitchen, the lowest 6/- for two rooms and a kitchen. This represents rooms in an old street. They were not seen by the investigator, but there was reason to suppose them not very clean. The wife, her consumptive husband, and apparently two children, both earning, occupied these rooms.

Every woman but one in this group is stated to have worked at the trade before marriage, and of that one nothing is stated, so that she also may have done so.

Evidently this trade as a home industry is destined to disappear.

TIE MAKERS.

The very small number of tie makers—six, of whom one seemed to be irresponsible—renders it impossible to say with assurance anything more general about the trade than that it is a poor one.

No. 3, who was said to get 2/6 a gross (probably for slipping, but the work is not particularized), and who worked but six hours a day, was able to make 10/-. On the other hand, No. 4, who did tie-slipping, declared it impossible to make more than 6/- a week, working from seven in the morning to ten at night. Her piecework rates could not be elicited.

No. 2 got 10d. a dozen, out of which she paid for slipping and knotting. "Slipping" I believe to be turning inside out after machining. "Knotting" is presumably fixing on the cross-piece of a "made" tie. No. 2, who had been employed in the trade for years, declared that it was formerly a well-paid one, but had been killed by the German knitted ties. Other women, also, said that rates had fallen.

BOOK-FOLDERS.

One of the women in this group worked but one month in the year, just before Christmas, when she was engaged in folding and stitching what she called "calendars" and explained as resembling "Old Moore's Almanack." For the two processes she was paid 1/0½ per thousand sheets. She had been a folder before marriage, and was glad to make these little extra sums at the slackest time of the year. Strictly speaking, this case is not one that should come into this report at all.

No. 2, an indoor hand, had worked 17 or 18 years in the same firm, with a break of six or seven years from her marriage. Her husband had poor health, and, as she said, "How can you lay out a pound fairly to do justice to your children—rents, boots, insurance!—then he falls ill and gets out! Three months he tramped the streets last year, and now he never knows from day to day when he may go out on the street He'd barely strength to crawl to the shop when he found this." The husband was a printer's labourer, but had the appearance and

manner of a clerk. Of the four children three were
earning, two girls in the mother's trade, the younger
earning 2/–, the elder paid by the piece, but working
only three-quarter time at the period of the visit, and
taking therefore but 7/6 or 8/– a week ; and one boy, who
gave his mother 7/– out of his weekly 9/–. The youngest,
twelve years old, was away on a holiday. The firm for
which No. 2 worked was turning out 6d. novels, and paying sometimes 1/3 a thousand, whereas " the real price,"
according to her, was 1/4½. Only three-quarter time was
being worked (at the end of July), and her earnings were
but 7/6 to 8/–, but in the winter employment would continue during the full number of hours allowed by the law.
There had been, she said, a considerable drop in wages
of late years. Old hands were being dismissed, and young
ones coming in on lower terms. These new arrivals did
not know " the trade and the prices like we women do,
and so it's easy to beat them down—it is not done in big
drops, only ½d. and 1d. on the thousand, but it tells in the
long run." It was therefore of great advantage to the
workers that there should be some experienced married
women among them who would " speak to the foreman "
and resist reductions. The home and children of No. 2
were patterns of what home and children should be, and
she herself a most superior and intelligent woman. She
was indignant at the idea of married women being forbidden to work, a proposal about which she had read in
papers, and heard at meetings.

No. 3 belonged to the interesting class of jobbing book-
folders who have a more or less regular group of employers,
and went at intervals to various firms who summoned her
by post-card according to the pressure of work in different
branches of the trade. She learned her trade in all its
branches before marriage, and her husband proving to be
an intemperate man who had had and lost two businesses,
she returned to her work. He then took to " busking "

(*i.e.*, playing the violin in the streets). He brought home little or no money ; she fed him and expected him to look after the children in her absence, and, when not drunk, he did so. Like most jobbers who have secured a good connection, she was well paid, reckoned upon 5d. an hour, and in the previous week had earned 29/–. Generally she earned 38/– during two or three weeks of each month, two weeks on one and one on another periodical, and the fourth week's earnings ran down to 15/– or less. She folded only, did not wire or stitch, although she was competent to do both processes. This was a pretty, very superior woman, not yet thirty. She left her husband once, taking her children with her, but when she saw him " swelling about the street with a cigar in his mouth, and jingling money in his pocket " while she was working hard, she was moved to try and place part of the burden on his shoulders.

No. 4 was receiving 10d. a thousand for folding, and did 200 or 300 sheets an hour, but could do 500, she said, if the work were there to be done.

No. 5 worked regularly as an indoor hand, one and a half days every week, and ran in from her workplace, close by, to get the children's meals during the mid-day hour, and the afternoon half hour. She earned 6/– for the day and a half at 10d., 1/–, or 1/3 per thousand, and could do 500 in an hour, if she could get them. In her opinion, machinery was ruining the trade.

No. 6 was a young widow with a child of eight months old, who was paid only 4d. per thousand, and took over an hour to do that quantity. She was living with her mother, and both were superior people. Probably the solution of this young woman's problem would be re-marriage.

Bookfolding is, for some not very easily definable reason, a trade looked upon as especially respectable, and women who practise it are nearly always of a comparatively high social grade. Yet it has not, within the investigator's memory, been generally well-paid, except in the jobbing branch, and is subject to considerable intervals of partial or total slackness.

BOX MAKERS.

The covering of cardboard boxes is entirely a woman's trade ; and some women are employed in factories upon machines that cut and nick the cardboard or paper ; no such workers appear, however, among the 42 box-makers visited in London. In the case of fairly solid boxes, the corners, as they are bent up, are strengthened by a strip of paper or of calico, but small boxes are held together merely by the paper covering. A coverer requires for her work a certain space of table, and a square, smooth board upon which she spreads an even surface of liquid glue. The various pieces of shaped cardboard and paper are ranged in order on each side of her.

Let us suppose that she is about to cover a soap or candle box. She will bend up the sides with one motion of her practised hand, will draw across the glue-board the long strip of paper meant to cover them, holding away from it as she does so the one or two fingers that she allows to become touched by glue, and applying the paper without wrinkle or bubble, will be in an instant tucking and smoothing down (with the gluey fingers) the inside borders. A similar treatment will be applied to the lid, and so swift and dexterous is the manipulation of an experienced box-hand, that the paper seems to cling of itself to the board and requires none of that smoothing out that demands much of an amateur's time and attention. No speck of glue will appear upon the satiny white surface either of box or lid, and there will be neither lack nor superfluity of paper at any edge or angle.

The speed and skill attained by some women is amazing. One among those reported upon made three gross of small boxes—roughly 430 a day—besides attending to her household. But the occupation is one of those in which long years of work bring incapacity. The hands of older women grow cramped and rheumatic. Some of us have seen poor old distorted hands bent almost into claws, and incapable of ever opening out again into flatness. This being so, the calling ought, in equity, to be well-paid during the years of maturity ; but it is not. The fact that the work is, generally speaking, not heavy, and demands but little outlay for apparatus, encourages home work, and it is a commonplace that trades in which home work prevails tend to become ill-paid. Within the experience of the present writer, the average indoor rate has fallen from 14/– or 15/– to about 10/– weekly. How far the box trade, like the paper bag trade, suffers an extra pressure of competition on account of its providing articles which are often nominally given away with other goods, rather than sold, it is impossible to decide.

Of the 42 women visited, all but two worked at the same trade before marriage, but the majority were, when single, employed in a factory or workshop, and afterwards became outworkers ; only 9 of the 42 were indoor hands at the time of the enquiry.

Piece rates are almost invariable for women's work throughout the trade, and only one exception, in the case of a pattern card maker, appears in this group. She was receiving 12/– a week, and working from 8 to 7 for a large West End shop.

Pattern mounters are not infrequently paid by time, the probable reasons being that the jobs are brief and various, and that great care and neatness are required. There seems to be (as usual) no difference between the *rates* paid to indoor and to outdoor workers, but the former are more regularly employed, and the highest paid work is generally given to them. Moreover, the home-worker probably loses more time in various small ways ; so that the week's takings of any worker inside the factory would almost invariably work out at a higher average than the takings of the same woman working at home. But where there are children who are put into a crèche, the difference in earnings will generally be less than the payments thus made, and the mother will be apt to stay at home. Widows who have acquired the habit of doing so seldom return to the factory—where, indeed, they will probably not be accepted if they have at all passed middle age.

All home workers provide their own glue, and, as a general rule, all factory workers either provide it or pay for it. It is, of course, very difficult to estimate the earnings per hour of a home worker ; not only are her working hours variable, but the rate of interruptions in each hour is variable too. We turn, therefore, to the few indoor hands for trustworthy figures, and find that one woman who only went to work when her husband was not fully occupied, and who never left home on Monday or Saturday, earned in her four days an average of 12/-, whether gross or net is not stated. She was making large boxes for artificial flowers or feathers at 7d., 9d., or 11½d. per dozen, according to size. She was able, therefore, apparently, to make four dozen of the 9d. boxes in a day, and was evidently a particularly quick hand, as might indeed have been divined from the circumstance that her employer was willing to have her at work for a portion of the week and at intervals to suit her convenience. She paid 7d. a day for the care of her three children at the crèche in her absence.

Another woman who went out to work, and covered hat-boxes at 7d., or 10d. a dozen, earned from 10/- to 14/- ; the latter figure perhaps representing a week in which there was overtime

Among home workers, women living alone furnish the best comparison ; there are two widows without dependants in this group, one of whom, a woman of 50, said that she was a quick worker, and could make 9/– a week or more ; the other, who was 63, and had worked at the same trade for 50 years, used to earn 15/–, but was earning now only 6/– to 7/– a week. Her three surviving children, all married, helped her a little.

There does not appear to be one woman in this group whose work was not necessary if the family was to be kept above the barest level of subsistence ; and there were several without whose earnings even that could not be attained. Not one family attained a weekly income of £2, and the highest wage of any husband was that of a shunter at 27/–. This man's wife added 10/– to the total income, and, as they had but one child, this family knew something approaching to comfort, and paid as much as 8/6 for five rooms and a scullery.

A bacon curer was receiving 26/–, and his wife's work brought the total income to an average of 33/– or 34/–, out of which a rent of 6/9 had to be paid, leaving 26/9 to clothe, feed, and keep warm five persons.

No. 11 was the wife of a carman who received a regular wage of 23/–. She, working as an indoor hand, earned from 10/– to 14/–, so that the average weekly total was 35/–, out of which 5/6 was paid for rent, leaving 29/6 to keep father, mother and four children. Moreover, carmen have to take their meals away from home, and their work makes them hungry, so that they cost more to feed than men in many other callings. The wife in this case was an intelligent woman who expressed herself clearly and performed the miracle of working in a factory, and at the same time keeping clean herself, her four healthy children, all under twelve years old, and her three well-furnished rooms in a block.

Rent is a heavy item. Two families—comparatively

prosperous and not numerous—spent as little as one-sixth of their total income upon their lodging, but some poor people spend as much as two-fifths (one poor woman as much as two-thirds, and two households as much as one-half) of the whole income on rent. Hardly any family has really room enough—probably only that which pays 8/6 in rent is able to enjoy those decencies of privacy which middle-class people consider essential.

UMBRELLA MAKERS.

In the small group of six women employed in umbrella making, four different operations were represented.

No. 1 machined covers to be afterwards fixed to the frames, and received 8d., 1/–, 2/–, or 3/– a dozen, and had made not more than 6/– a week for many months, but said she used formerly to get as much as £1.

No. 2 sewed on the covers, and was paid a penny for each umbrella. She could do a dozen in two hours, therefore the rate of pay was comparatively high, but she got only 5 or 6 dozen to do in a week—sometimes she would have three dozen in one day, and then perhaps none for three or four days.

No. 3 both machined and finished. This was a superior woman who compared the real values of the West End and the middle-class trade, which latter, she was convinced, paid better in the long run. As an instance of the expense caused by having to use cotton of various colours, she said that for a special West End sunshade she spent 2½d. for cotton to match, and never had occasion to use the same coloured cotton for six years. She received from 2/– to 4/6 a dozen. This woman, like most of the others, said that the rates were lower than they used to be. They seem to be lower than some with which the present writer was familiar a good many years ago. She does not seem to have worked for many hours a day, and her earnings were from 7/– to 10/–. Working as an indoor hand, she used formerly to make from 15/– to £1 weekly.

No. 4 was an indoor hand, a finisher paid by time, 12/– a week, her hours being from 9 to 8. Two shillings were paid out of this each week for rooms, and, as she lodged over the workshop, she took her meals at home. As her husband was a casual labourer at the docks, earning irregularly, but always less than £1 a week, her regular 12/– (or rather 10/–, since 2/– was paid away each week for having the baby " minded ") was essential for the family support.

No. 5 made silk rings to be attached to umbrellas for convenience of carrying them, and, when slack, made bead ornaments for trimming blouses. She was a Pole, a superior woman, who took up work at the beginning by the doctor's advice when she was in a state of great depression at the loss of her first child. Later on, her husband's wages fell, and the family needed her contribution. For the little silk straps she was paid from 2/6 to 5/– a gross, according to the quality. The rates worked out to about the same total—roughly 3d. for an hour's work. She earned about 11/– a week.

No. 6, who before marriage did not work for money, made elastic bands for umbrellas. The elastic (and no doubt the other materials) was given to her ; she cut it into lengths, fixed a button at one end and a little tab of silk at the other, then tied up the bands in dozens, and then in bundles of six dozens. She received 8d. a gross, and said that nobody could possibly make more than one gross and a half in a day, and that all the people who worked at this occupation regarded it as supplementary to some other source of income. The question suggests itself whether this parasitic little industry might not be abandoned without any serious disadvantage to the carriers of umbrellas.

In this group, again, every woman's earnings were

required by the family, and no husband earned enough to keep the household going.

BOOT AND SHOE MAKERS.

Six out of the ten women in this group followed the same occupation before marriage and the two deserted wives are among the four who did not do so ; one of them was a servant, and it certainly appears in these London reports as though servants were particularly apt to be unfortunate in the matter of husbands.

Among the whole ten there is not one woman who is not ill-paid, and it would hardly be a rash generalization to declare that there are no well-paid sewers or finishers of shoes. Almost every worker spoke of the fall in rates— the most glaring example perhaps being the payment of 8d. a dozen pairs for soling babies' leather boots or shoes in place of 1/– a dozen for boots, and 10d. a dozen for shoes.

The fullest report in the group is that of Case 5, a woman of 38 who had lived all her life in London, and worked in the trade ever since she grew up. She inter-mitted her work for some months after marriage, but resumed it within the first year. She had five children, varying in age from 2 to 9 years, and had lost one. Her husband's wage, though regular, was small, and in addition to the expenses of her own household, she had an old father and mother, the former nearly blind, and a widowed sister for whom she did what she could. Her house, person, and children were all clean and neat. The husband was evidently a steady man and had worked all his life for the same firm, to the members of which he was devotedly attached.

Her industrial history is interesting ; her mother, sister, and herself had long worked for an employer whose business had now passed into the hands of a former subordinate, who, announcing that he would not be so long in getting rich, had lowered his rates of pay. Impatient of this treatment, Mrs. W. sought work elsewhere, and obtained employment for a couple of years with a better firm, which, however, at the end of that time, became bankrupt, and she had some difficulty in getting back to her old place. During her absence shoes paid at 1/6 a dozen had dropped to 1/3, and the 1/3 had since become 1/-. " I could fair cry sometimes," she said to the investigator, " when I think of the 2d., 6d., and 9d. that have been knocked off our work." Incidentally she described the hot weary tramp of herself and her mother seeking work at every boot-making factory or workshop from Clerkenwell to the " Salmon and Ball," at Bethnal Green, and finding none.

When visited, Mrs. W., was busy upon babies' shoes of blue ribbed silk ; she stitched on the soles by hand, an operation always performed inside out, and necessitating the turning of the shoe to its right side afterwards ; then she pasted and inserted the stiffening at the heel, and finished off the inside. She was paid 1/- per dozen pairs, and could not do more than three dozen in a day, even if she sat at work from 9 to 11 or 11.30. One evening her husband timed her unawares, and reported that she had earned 2d. an hour—presumably four shoes. At that rate she would have taken 18 hours to do the 72 that she described as barely possible between 9 and 11.30. The discrepancy is probably to be explained by the fact that she would work quicker at the beginning of the day than at its close.

The numbers that she actually did make are shown by her wage book, from which she allowed the visitor to copy the figures of eleven weeks.

Here they are :—

						s.	d.
Week 1—36 pairs at 10d.	...	...	...	2	6
36 ,, 10d.	...	...	...	2	6
6 doz.	...	...	...	5	0
Week 2—24 pairs at 1/–	...	...	...	2	0
23 ,, 9½d.	...	...	...	1	6
30 ,, 10d.	...	...	...	2	1
12 ,, 1/–	...	...	...	1	0
12 ,, 10d.	...	...	...	0	10
8½ doz.	...	...	...	7	5
Week 3—12 pairs at 1/–	...	...	...	1	0
12 ,, 10d.	...	...	...	0	10
24 ,, 10d.	...	...	...	1	8
36 ,, 10d.	...	...	...	2	6
7 doz.	...	...	...	6	0
Week 4—18 pairs at 10d.	...	...	...	1	3
18 ,, 9d.	...	...	...	1	1½
36 ,, 10d.	...	...	...	2	6
36 ,, 10d.	...	...	...	2	6
9 doz.	...	...	...	7	4½
Week 5—18 pairs at 1/–	...	...	...	1	6
18 ,, 10d.	...	...	...	1	3
30 ,, 10d.	...	...	...	2	1
24 ,, 10d.	...	...	...	1	8
7½ doz.	...	...	...	6	6

							s.	d.
Week 6—24 pairs at 10d.	...	...	...	1	8
12	,,	1/-	...	...	...	1	0
12	,,	10d.	...	...	...	0	10
18	,,	1/-	...	...	...	1	6
18	,,	10d.	...	...	...	1	3
33	,,	10d.	...	...	...	2	3½
9¾ doz.	...	...	...	8	6½

Week 7—3 pairs at 10d.	...	...	...	0	2½
36	,,	10d.	...	...	...	2	6
36	,,	1/-	...	...	...	3	0
12	,,	1/-	...	...	...	1	0
24	,,	10d.	...	...	...	1	8
9¼ doz.	...	...	...	8	4½

Week 8—24 pairs at 1/-	...	...	...	2	0
12	,,	10d.	...	...	...	0	10
36	,,	10d.	...	...	...	2	6
13	,,	1/2	...	...	...	1	3
18	,,	9d.	...	...	...	1	1½
8₁₂⁷ doz.	...	...	...	7	8½

Week 9—18 pairs at 10d.	...	...	...	1	3
18	,,	9d.	...	...	...	1	1½
18	,,	1/-	...	...	...	1	6
18	,,	9d.	...	...	...	1	1½
18	,,	1/-	...	...	...	1	6
18	,,	10d.	...	...	...	1	3
9 doz.	...	...	...	7	9

						s.	d.
Week 10—36 pairs at 1/–	...	...	...	3	0
36 ,, 10d. (35½)		...	...	2	5
36 ,, 1/– (35)	...	...	...	2	11
9 doz.	...	...	...	8	4
Week 11— 1 pair at 10d.	...	...	...	0	1
1 ,, 1/–	...	...	...	0	1
18 ,, 10d.	...	...	...	1	3
18 ,, 9d.	...	...	...	1	1½
36 ,, 10d.	...	...	...	2	6
36 ,, 1/–	...	...	...	3	0
9⅙ doz.	...	...	...	8	0½

Her fares (going three times a week to fetch work) amounted to 9d., and she had to provide thread, paste and needles—often, she said, using a halfpenny worth of needles in soling a dozen pairs.

One room of the little house (for which they paid 11/–) was let off for 4/– (with attendance)—but the investigator had her doubts whether the young man whom she saw smoking a cigarette over the fire at half-past ten in the morning paid his 4/– with any regularity, and strongly suspected that, when he was not at work, his meals were taken with the family. Another 6d. a week was earned by Mrs. W.'s taking an old man's washing to do with her family's. This industrious and capable woman showed with pride (as well she might) a neat and tidy frock made for the child of two out of the husband's old trousers. In the course of her talk she mentioned that she often put on buttons for an uncared-for little family whose mother never lifted her hand to a job. Like several of the boot-workers, she had suffered much at the births of her children, and attributed this to sitting so much. At the birth of the youngest she worked to within some hours of the event, and in six days was making shoes again, propped up in bed with pillows. And with all her heroic industry the family income does not attain the height of 30/–.

The lowest rate of all seems to be that of No. 6, a Polish Jewess, who had lived in England for 16 years, and who sewed on buttons and did " trimming," a mysterious term that indicates possibly the sewing on of a pom-pom. Even taking into consideration the sketchy manner in which buttons, bows, etc., are generally attached to shoes, three farthings per dozen pairs must be a very inadequate payment.

The boot trade would appear to be one in which the Trade Boards Act might wisely be applied.

SOME CLOTHING TRADES.

BLOUSE MAKERS.

In this trade the competition between power machines and hand machines makes itself felt, and has, of course, an adverse influence upon the payment of home workers. There exist also very great differences of rate between one employer and another ; for practically the same work women may be receiving 2/3 or 3/3 a dozen, and some-times more work is demanded by the worse-paying employer.

The number of women in this group is small but representative. It includes three women who worked for private customers, and two who had tried to make money as middlewomen, employing other workers ; the majority, however, did work at home for fairly large firms. None of the women enumerated were described as working for either of the two firms who are known in the blouse-making trade as the pioneers of low rates, and who elsewhere have been declared to be in a large measure responsible for the excessive under-payment that has for some years prevailed. One woman, however, was as ill-paid as though employed by one of these.

No. 1 worked for only one firm, and did all the making (except buttons and buttonholes) of cut-out garments of the best kind, made of muslin or other fine white material, generally embroidered. These blouses she had to shape as well as to sew, and was paid 7/– to 15/– a dozen. Her earnings averaged 14/– to 18/–, although she did not sit steadily to work all day. The trade was slack at two periods of about two months each every year. Rates had fallen. Articles at 9½d. used to be 1/–.

No. 3 received print blouses cut out. For quite plain ones she was paid 2/3 a dozen ; for some that had a little piping on the collar and cuffs, 2/6 a dozen, and for some with more trimming, 3/–. In a day of eleven hours she could complete nine of these more elaborate garments, thus earning 2/3, or about 2½d. per hour. The blouses at 2/6, she said, paid best. Her average takings were 12/– a week.

No. 5, who before her marriage worked in one of the best factories in London, used to earn from 11/– to 19/– a week, and was subject to none of the insidious deductions that prevail in so many work-places. Her work there was the making of costumes, those of cotton (zephyr) being paid at 2/3, 2/6, or 2/9 each, and rates ranging up to 3/4 for a cloth dress. Power machines were, of course, used. This firm removed to a more expensive part of London, and the workers complained of the extra fares, whereupon rates were raised to the extent of 3d. to 7d. for each costume. When seen No. 5 was machining blouses at home for another firm at from 2/3 to 2/9 a dozen, of which she could do about a dozen in a day to a day and a half, and had recently made some at 5d. each, of which she could do nine in a day. For these (but not, apparently, for the cheaper ones) she had to provide cotton. Her previous week's earnings had been 12/-. Her two nieces, who worked as indoor hands for the same firm, made from 15/- to £1. She was emphatic in her declaration that cheap work paid best because it could be done so rapidly. It is certainly true that some practised workers can run cheap work through their machines at an amazing speed, and with very little apparent attention.

No. 7 was making tucked blouses of cheap silk, with two strips of insertion down the backs and one down the fronts and yokes, at 4d. each.

No. 10 was making blouses of similar material, but with much less work (four half tucks and a strip of insertion), at 6/- a dozen. For these the rates had actually risen, having at one time been 5/6. No. 10 did not work many hours a day, and earned about 8/-.

No. 8, who again was making blouses of cheap silk that in addition to tucks and insertion required shaping at the waist and fitting to a basque, was paid 4d. each.

No. 12 was busy upon fine garments of lawn and nainsook, embroidered, and with insertion. One took her three hours to make, and she received 9/- per dozen. She " took in " her work three times a week, the return ticket costing 1/2 each time, paid 1/6 a week for her machine, and spent 1/- for cotton. The expenses of her work were therefore :—Fares, 3/6 ; machine, 1/6 ; cotton, 1/- ; and her net earnings 5/- or 6/-. Her rates had fallen.

No. 14, who had a mother to help her with housekeeping, worked daily from about eight in the morning to about nine in the evening, taking half an hour off for dinner. She was making embroidered and tucked blouses of cream-coloured delaine, buttons and buttonholes included, at from 2/- to 3/9 a dozen. A dozen took the whole day and two hours over to make, even with the assistance of the mother, who sewed on the buttons. Rates had fallen greatly ; it took longer, No. 14 declared, to earn ten shillings than it took formerly to earn a pound. She herself used to make 23/-, working for the same employer. This woman sent her boy to take the work (three times a week), so that her time was unbroken.

The blouse makers working for private customers were Nos. 4, 6, 11 and 16, of whom one (No. 4) was, before marriage, a bodice and coat hand working in the West End, earned " always over £1 a week," if she chose, and often 27/-. She was a woman of 31 living with her husband and two children in two rooms ; the husband, a railway carman, had a standing wage of 24/-, raised by extra duties to an average of 29/-. Thus the average family income was about £2 14/- weekly. Of the two children, one was staying with a grandmother ; the other, aged four, was at home. When seen, Mrs. W. was making " an elaborate and apparently well-cut silk blouse," for the making of which she proposed to charge 3/-. She remarked that she often charged less to poor customers, but never more, and that she probably got so much work because her prices were low. She also remarked that she " could not do it " if she were dependent upon her own work for a living. She put out her washing, worked all day on Saturday, and devoted her Sunday mornings to cleaning up for the week. Her day's work occupied her, she said, from 8 a.m. to 10 p.m., and she appeared to enjoy doing it and to do it well.

No. 6, a young woman who before marriage had been an umbrella maker working for a West End firm that did not give out work, was engaged in making blouses " for friends " at 6d. each, and got about eight to do in a week. Her three children, all under school age, she sent to the local nursery. The husband was a skilled artisan in one of the smaller trades, and had lost his place after nine years owing to a feud with a foreman, since which time he had not regained any regular work. The

one room—in a house of good appearance—for which
they paid 6/-, was not seen, nor did the appearance of
this worker incline the visitor to press for admittance.
This lady, an investigator of experience, described the
dirtiness of No. 6 herself as "appalling," and expressed
wonder that any person could be found to give her
garments to make.

No. 11 worked for neighbours, making blouses at 4d.
each and pinafores at 2d.   She had been twice married,
the first husband having been a veterinary surgeon, who
left her £500, which she "lost in the *Liberator* ' smash.' "
The second, an engineer's labourer, had been thrown out
of work by the bankruptcy of his employers, and had
had only casual jobs since.   Of her eleven children,
eight by the first, three by the second marriage, only
three survived, two married, and one at school.

No. 16, a Jewess, made blouses at 1/- each for private
customers, when she could get the work, her husband's
earnings being small.   Her employment was irregular
and uncertain, and her earnings about 2/- to 8/- a week.

The two workers who had attempted to be middlewomen were No. 7 and No. 15, and their experiences do
not indicate that there is much profit to be made in that
much abused capacity—not, at any rate, for people
without capital.

No. 7, an intelligent woman of over 50, who worked to
eke out her husband's low wage and to cover his slack
times, lived in a six-roomed house in a decent road.
The family must have been numerous, for there were
five still unmarried and several (the investigator did not
succeed in ascertaining precisely how many) married.
The daughters were apparently employed—one as an
indoor hand in a blouse making factory, and made
"good money."   One son of 16 had passed a Civil
Service clerkship examination, and was earning 15/-,
which barely kept him—"There's his clothes, fares, and

no cheap place for food in the Strand—not much on that." The other son, of 18, had begun work at 16/-, and in hopes of " bettering " himself had gone to an art dealer's in the West End, where he was paid 21/- (of which he must have spent at least 5d. a day in fares) and was " slaved to death," so that he had to leave. He was working temporarily for a firm of carriers by whom his father was permanently employed as a clerk. No. 7 set up a workshop " when blouses first came in " and engaged some " hands," including, apparently, her own daughters, but found that when the wages, hire of machines and cotton had been paid for no profit remained.

No. 15, a widow of over 60, had worked since her husband failed in business, about 25 years previously ; a few years later he had a serious illness, and although he had lived until about a year before the date at which she was visited, had never again been strong enough to do any work. Mrs. Z. rented a whole house at 9/6 a week, one room of which was used as a workplace for herself, her daughter and three girls. Of the fourteen children born to her, eleven had died under two years of age. One of the three survivors was married, the other two, a son and daughter, lived with the mother. The daughter, a capable looking woman, superintended the workroom in place of the mother, who had now grown too old, and the son was a clerk, earning £1 a week, of which he paid the mother 10/-. Mrs. Z. was somewhat hazy as to her balance of expenses and earnings, but said that she thought they took about 8/- a day. The wage bill for three girls amounted to 23/- ; cotton (two dozen reels) to 4/6 and fares for fetching and returning work to about 2/6—in all 30/——without reckoning heat, light, machine needles or repairs. Eight shillings a day for five and a half days would be 44/-, and the profit remaining (for the work of mother and daughter together) is 24/-, a wage which the daughter alone could probably earn as a forewoman. The mother was not able to do much, any longer, but she went " to shop," and so saved the time of some more active worker.

No. 14, a superior and able woman with a husband who had given way to drink and lost his post, but was now steadier in a humbler one, allowed the investigator to copy from her wage book the figures for the whole of a year. They are as follows :—

	s.	d.			s.	d.			s.	d.
Jan.	10	4	May	...	14	9	Sep.	...	11	10½
	5	9			16	2½			8	9
	13	7½			3	9		No work.		
	11	1			11	0				
Feb.	... 13	2	June	...	15	10½				
	17	1½			5	10½	Oct.	...	6	9
	11	8½			12	10½			9	4
	11	1			8	7½				
March	... 12	7½			6	5½		No work.		
	9	9	July	...	2	9				
	17	0			6	9	Jan.	...	9	10
	11	3			10	9			10	3
April	... 14	8			12	9			11	7½
	14	2			11	3				
	8	3	Aug.	...	11	10½				
	7	6			11	11				
					12	3				
					7	6				

UNDERCLOTHING MAKERS.

This group of workers presents an instance of a wife who was working, not because she absolutely needed to do so, but because she was anxious to keep up a good standard of life for her family. Particular attention should be called to the case of this woman, because it

exemplifies home work at a not wholly inadequate wage
—or home work as it might be if minimum rates were
fixed by a Trade Board.

No. 16 was a London-born woman, 50 years of age,
living in a house of two floors in a suburb, her four or
five rooms comfortably furnished. She belonged, and
was proud of belonging, to a family of teachers ; her
husband was a clerk earning " a regular income." For
14 years before her marriage and one year after she was
employed in a city showroom, and did not take up home
work until her three children were growing up, when
she became anxious to give them educational opportuni-
ties and to provide books, possible expenses of illnesses,
and various extras. The elder girl of 18 was a pupil
teacher ; the boy ($15\frac{1}{2}$), still at school, was intended for
a clerk, and his mother was hoping that he might be
employed by the L.C.C. or perhaps in the Civil Service,
2nd Division ; the younger girl, aged 13, who was also
to be a teacher, was at a secondary school. None had
died. The mother's work was the machining of camisoles
(the modern name for the garment known in former
days as " petticoat bodices ") at 3/9 a dozen, and she
earned " apparently quite easily," says the investigator,
about 18/– a week ; and said that she would not do the
work if it were not worth her while. It was sent to her,
whether at the employer's expense or hers does not
appear. She was of opinion that married women should
be allowed to work, " as you never can tell when it may
be necessary."

Now in what interest, public or private, is it desirable
that such a woman as this should be prevented from
earning that 18/–, which it is her pleasure to earn ? Her
children would not be better off, nor her husband, nor
herself ; as to her house, that is well kept as it is—
better kept in all probability than if she were debarred
from this source of income. Nor is there any economic

injury being done by her to her class. She is receiving the highest payments per piece of any worker in this group, and, apparently, working for comparatively short hours. Her case shows, conclusively, that what is wrong economically with the work of women done at home is not any special evil depending upon its being done in one place rather than another, but the same great evil—under-payment—that affects almost all the industrial work of women, and much of the industrial work of men. That the evils which often accompany home work, and are supposed by hasty generalizers to be involved in it, are absent in this instance arises mainly from the fact that both husband and wife are decently paid. Cut off the regular salary of the husband, cut down the price of the " camisoles " to 2/3 a dozen, and all the familiar painful features of home work will reappear in this home too.

The case of No. 18 presents some interesting points. She was an elderly woman who had worked before marriage in the same trade, and when she married set up a business of her own and employed six hands. But the firm which supplied her with work closed, and she found it difficult to obtain enough to do for more than one person. She therefore gave up her workroom, retaining, however, three machines, and continued, single-handed. Her husband, a sealskin dresser, was always unemployed or half employed for some months in the year, but used to make £4 to £5 a week when busy. With the advance of years the slack time lengthened and the payment shrank until, at the date of the investigator's visit, he was earning but £2 a week, and that for only four months in the year. The wife's work was limited by the fact that all her machines were chain-stitch ones. She made aprons, caps, and fancy collars, and when seen was busy upon maids' aprons at 2/- a dozen. She saved a little time by keeping one machine adjusted for gathering, one for hemming, and one for plain stitching. When out of work her husband helped her, and their earnings together would amount to over £1 a week ; hers alone never reached £1. It must be remembered that a chain-stitch machine consumes considerably more cotton than a lock-stitch one. On the other hand, some makes of chain-stitch machines run singularly easily, so that work is very rapid.

Of course the articles still made by No. 18 are fast ceasing to be made by outside workers, and are being more and more passed over to power machines.

Another woman, No. 19, also machined caps and aprons, probably at a lower rate—the figures were not ascertained —and could barely make 15/- to 16/- a week by working almost night and day. Her usual takings were about 8/-.

Among the other workers of this group are to be found the following rates of pay : —

Chemises, from commonest unbleached calico, at 1/- to 1/6, 1/8, 2/6, and 2/9. At the last two prices the garments have to be feather-stitched, and threaded with ribbons. The woman who made these said that no person could possibly earn more than 1/6 per day, and that the cheapest work took more time because the machine resisted the material. She attributed the low rates to the fact that City firms will give work out only in large quantities, whereby the middlemen command the market and pay badly.

Another woman, working for small shops, made little pink flannelette chemises (which she had to cut out) at 9d. per dozen, and—when she got the work—could, by sitting close, make two dozen in a day. She also made large unbleached chemises at 2/- a dozen, and could make seven in a day. These did not pay so well as the others. She managed to earn 5/- to 7/- a week.

Camisoles, finished entirely with buttons and buttonholes, 1/4 to 2/9 per dozen. Those at the latter rate had little sleeves to be put in, a good deal of lace trimming and ribbons to be threaded. When this worker entered the trade the price per dozen was 4/– ; and the sleeves had been a recent addition without extra pay. No. 16, it will be remembered, received 3/9 per dozen.

No. 15 was a middlewoman making " underbodices," presumably the same sort of garment, at 2/9 a dozen. Her profits, which used to be 35/– a week, had fallen to £1, and she had to work hard to reach that figure.

Knickers (the term applied by the workers—the garments are really drawers), ladies' and children's, of flannelette and cotton, were made by No. 10 at from 8d. to 1/2 per dozen, according to size, for a shop. Of the eightpenny ones, she could do a dozen in two hours ; of the shilling ones, a dozen in three hours. She seldom got as much work as she wanted.

No. 12, a buttonhole machinist, sometimes (presumably when she could not get enough buttonholing) made girls' knickers at 1/1 a dozen, being 3d. for the holes and 10d. for the making.

No. 11 made nightdresses at 8d. or 9d. a dozen, and said that 1/6 a day was the utmost that anybody could earn working hard all day.

No. 17 made nightcaps, as her mother did before her. The trade is a dying one, and she made only about a dozen in a week at 1/3.

The two buttonhole machinists (who, of course, have had to buy their machines) were among the best paid of the underclothing makers. No. 12 received 3d. a dozen pairs for girls' knickers (which presumably had either four or five holes in each) ; No. 13 was paid 9d. a gross of holes, or ¾d. a dozen, and could do about four dozen in half an hour, according to the material. She earned about 14/– when she got work enough, but sometimes only 8/–. By buttonholing, she said, a single woman should be able, if she sat very close, to keep herself.

One of these two, after speaking of the continually

falling rates of pay, her husband's irregular work and low wage (he received but 18/- when at work), enunciated her own philosophy to the effect that whenever she got the " blues " she comforted herself with the reflection that things could not be worse, and therefore one might as well look as cheerful as possible.

Looking back on this score of women, what is to be seen ? One, No. 16, living a reasonable, human life, working perhaps rather harder than is quite healthy, but not starved, either physically or morally. One, No. 18, still keeping above the level of swamping poverty, but with an unpromising future ahead. One, No. 15, snatching a bare livelihood for her solitary self out of her workshop—in which, although the report does not say so—it is almost certain that she " drives " her hands. All the rest toiling for wholly inadequate pittances, with the wolf always at the door, the rent that, as one of them said, " is always with you," the recurrence of unemployment that breaks the heart of a decent man, the impossible effort to keep whole boots upon the children's feet, and, amid it all, the heroism of a woman who will not apply for school meals for the children because " there's others need it more."

Almost every worker told the same tale of lowered rates. None of these women showed evidence of being undeserving ; all were industrious, nearly all were toiling for the sake of their children ; not one complained of having to work. They complained, and justly, of being horribly underpaid, and of the underpayment of men, which makes it impossible for two industrious people to keep a family properly nourished—to say nothing of properly clad and properly housed.

Yet the selling price of the garments which they made was almost always high enough to allow a margin of profit out of which they might receive more. A rise of a halfpenny on each garment would often make all the differ-

ence between cruel hardship and comparative comfort ;
the difference of a penny would transform most of these
women's lives.

SHIRT, COLLAR AND CUFF MAKERS

This group contains 23 cases, four of which are those
of soldiers' widows at Woolwich engaged in the making
of army shirts, and thus not subject to the ordinary
conditions of the market.   Three women are indoor
hands, one of whom gave up working at home because
the liveliness of her youngest child—two years old at the
date of the visit—prevented her from getting anything
done.   So she had placed the vivacious one in a crèche
at 3d. per day and gone into a neighbouring factory.
As usual, no sort of standard rate emerges, but a
persistent tendency to reduction.

No. 7 told of Oxford shirts (which, however, she herself
was not making) at 2/6 and 3/– per dozen. No. 8 machined
quite plain Oxford shirts at 1/5 a dozen ; double-stitched
ones with a front pleat at 1/8 ; double-stitched with a
yoke, 2/8.

No. 13 had machined shirts, kind not specified, at 1/–
per dozen.

No. 22 made double-lined Oxford shirts throughout
for a shop at 4/6 a dozen ; she also machined shirts
for a middlewoman at 2/9 and 3/9 per dozen, from which
8d. a dozen had to be paid to a buttonhole machinist
for the eight dozen buttonholes. Sitting very close
at work a dozen of shirts at 2/9 could be machined in a
day.   Of those at 4/6 half a dozen could be made in the
day.

No. 23 machined and finished Oxford shirts for boys
and men, the boys' at 3/6, the men's at 5/– per dozen,
and could do a dozen of the cheaper ones in a day, if she
worked steadily, or nearly a dozen of the dearer.

No. 9 machined common shirts of white fancy material at 1/5 a dozen, and could do a dozen in about 6 hours.

No. 10 worked for two middlewomen, one of whom did, and one did not pay for extras, gores, etc. No. 10 had resisted a reduction at the worse paying employer's, but her fellow workers had weakened, and the reduction had come. She was making flannel tennis shirts at 2/2 per dozen, had been working from 5.30 to about 4.30 upon two dozen which were then nearly finished. 1d. extra was paid if an initial was tacked upon each shirt to mark the size. Cotton, provided, of course, by the worker, cost 1/- a week.

Four button-holers appear. No. 14 worked for a middlewoman, and was paid 5d. for a dozen shirts described as containing 35 holes—a number which appears to be impossible, and should perhaps be 36. Six shirts took her an hour. No. 16 was also paid 5d. per dozen shirts, but said that there were 7 holes to each shirt, and that she never earned more than 1/3 a day. No. 17, who was a buttonhole machinist, working on her employer's premises, used formerly to earn £1 a week, but of late could never exceed 14/-.

Of the four collar workers, No. 18 was a machinist receiving 1d. or 1¼d. per dozen ; her rates had fallen. No. 19 was engaged in " running " and " banding " collars ; she received 4d. per gross ; 6d. per gross if there were little fronts attached, 9d. if she did the banding as well as the running. She had worked at the trade for 20 years, during which time rates had become lower by 50 per cent. It took her an hour and a half to do a gross at 4d. No. 20 worked indoors as a collar " turner," and received 9d. a gross for bands and 1/3 for " overs." " Turning " is turning right side out the band or collar after it has been stitched ; the corners of the " over "— i.e., of the collar as distinguished from the band—are troublesome, and most workers use a little bone imple-

ment to poke them out neatly.   Formerly in a City workroom (she was working, when seen, in a poor district of
South London), she used to be paid 2d., 3d., and 4½d. a doz.
for similar work.   Rates, she reported, had fallen very
much.   No. 21, a widow also, was an indoor hand,
a collar machinist in a City place where she had been in all
for 21 years, but had not worked for money during her
married life.   She little thought, she told the investigator,
when the firm gave her a wedding present, that she would
be back in the same shop at her time of life.   She was
forty-four.   Her earnings were from 10/- to 12/-.   She
appeared to be employed to a considerable extent upon
samples, but sometimes machined collars at 1d., or 1½d.
a dozen.

The four soldiers' widows, who made Army shirts, all
complained that although the comparatively high rate of
7½d. per piece was paid, they were unable to support
themselves by the work because only ten shirts were
given to each of them in a fortnight.   One woman reported
that she could make four shirts in a day by working from
7 in the morning to 11 at night—say 13 hours.   A skilled
and active woman would be able, it is thought, to make
one shirt in 2½ hours, or less.   6/3 a fortnight is obviously
no livelihood for even the thriftiest widow, and none of
these four mentioned the receipt of any pension.

There are few prosperous families in this group, but even
a larger proportion than usual of women who exhibit
remarkable force of character.   Take, for instance, No. 1,
who was aged about 32, and whose husband was in New
Zealand.   She worked indoors for a City firm, and had
apparently done so before marriage, since she said her
husband had wanted her to take up work at her trade
again, and she had refused to do so while they lived
together.   His social gifts—she reported him able to play
any kind of musical instrument—seemed to have led him
to bad company, and finally she had to sue him for

deserting her (such is the wording of the report, but probably it was the Guardians who sued him for leaving his family chargeable). Six months' imprisonment had the unusual result of bringing him to a better mind; he had emigrated, was working well, and trying to get together a home for the family, who in a few months' time were going out to him. Her children, twins of 7 and a baby between 2 and 3, were delicate but well-cared for, and evidently devoted to their mother. She washed the children and gave them breakfast before going out each morning, left the elders in bed to get themselves dressed in time for school, and took the little one to a crèche. The twins went for dinner to their grandmother who lived hard by, and who received 1/– a week in payment. In order to get the school dinner, they would have had to cross a road full of traffic, and she was afraid to let them do so. For a short time she had worked at a neighbouring factory—the same at which No. 20 worked as a collar turner—but when she, one week, earned 12/– (of course at piecework) the manager observed that 10/– was enough for any woman, and she received notice the next week. She was now paid 3/9 a dozen for machining and finishing (*i.e.*, for making shirts completely), and, trade being slack (she was visited early in January), had earned but 7/4½ that week.

MAKERS OF CHILDREN'S CLOTHES.

Of the 15 women in this list, eight worked at the same occupation before marriage; in four cases there is no information as to previous employment.

So small a number of cases is not sufficient for generalization, but, on the whole, the earnings ran high for a sewing trade. No. 1, for instance, who machined children's frocks at 2/6 per dozen and upwards, said that she could earn 18/– if she had not her children (7 of them), and her house to look after. Having these other calls upon her time, she managed to average 10/-.

No. 5 made children's blouses at from 2/9 to 6/9 per dozen, and reported that she could make a dozen at 3/9 in the day ; of dresses at 5½d., 6d., or 7d. each she could not do more than two in a day. Her wage book showed the figures 13/-, 10/-, 13/-, 15/- (the highest figure she ever attained) and 6/- (the lowest to which she had ever dropped).

No. 9, making navy serge kilts affixed to bodices of lining at 2/9 a dozen, said that she had earned up to 30/- a week, but did not now reach £1. This young woman declared that she did not believe " all these tales of sweating," that it was impossible to get anything nowadays without working, but that it was no good telling her that a woman who worked hard could only earn 5/- or 6/- a week ; she wouldn't believe it. Against this opinion may be set the experience of No. 2, who had worked for 40 years in the trade, and said that 25 years earlier the rates were double. She was making cooks' aprons at 1/9 per dozen ; black sateen overalls with strappings and flounces at 3/- a dozen ; and children's print pinafores trimmed with lace at 9d. a dozen. Her average earnings were 9/- a week, and she could have done more work if she could have got it. The dozen aprons at 1/9 took her 14 hours to do, which works out at 1½d. an hour ; the overalls took 21 hours— about 1¾d. per hour ; the dozen pinafores, seven hours— 1¼d. per hour. Perhaps being an elderly woman (about 60, says the investigator), her speed was less than it had been, but I doubt whether even a very rapid worker could make the dozen overalls in less than 18 hours, and the rate in that case would be but 2d. No. 2 attributed the fall in rates to the introduction of steam power in factories ; No. 3, however, who worked in a factory, and for long hours, earned but an average of 11/- weekly. This was a widow of about 30, who was paid 1/6 to 1/9 for machining children's costumes and 1/1½ for children's coats. In very busy times she had taken as much as 17/–; but in slack times dropped to 5/–. Another woman, making children's costumes at home, and not working full time, earned 12/– to 13/–. All these are, of course, gross earnings, fares, cotton, and often hire of machines must be deducted.

Nos. 13 and 14 were middlewomen in a small way. The former, who had always made babies' bibs, worked before marriage in a factory. On her father's death she took to doing her work at home to keep her mother company. The mother took up the same employment, and by and by they took apprentices and " enlarged their scope." On the daughter's marriage, she lived in half her mother's house, and ceased her work for money. The mother continued to make bibs with the help of apprentices, and, on her death, four years later, the daughter resumed " rather than let the business fall to pieces." Her plan was to employ four girls, one of 15 and three of 14 years of age. They received 2/– a week to begin with, and 3/– at the end of two months. The eldest was getting 6/– and would be kept until she rose to 10/– or 12/–. The employer received material from " the warehouse," and cut it out herself, and the bibs were made entirely by herself and her assistants. The machines were provided by " the firm," a somewhat unusual circumstance. In her busiest times, No. 13 reckoned that she made a profit of about £1. She apparently included among the outgoings of her workroom the hire of a charwoman once a week for housework and the putting out of all the family's washing. Taking the year through, she estimated her net weekly profit at 10/6. Clearly, her enterprise, although it satisfied her, and helped to keep a comfortable household in which there was a fairly well-paid husband, and but one child, was a parasitic one and depended for its continuance upon a succession of partly supported employees.

No. 14 married at 18 from a comfortable home, having previously done " a little dressmaking." The husband, a superior clerk, lost situation after situation owing to drink. His family got tired of helping him, and she, at the age of 25, began a private dressmaking business. After the birth of her last child she gave up dressmaking, and for sixteen years had been making babies' robes and frocks for a City firm, receiving the material, cutting out the garments, and being paid 3/6 a dozen for the frocks, and 5/– a dozen for the robes. She employed one girl, to whom she paid 7/6, and her daughter of 16. The hire of three machines came to 4/6 a week, and although these payments were supposed to purchase the machines she found that these were worn out by the time that she had paid for them, so that the expense was a constant one. Cotton cost from 1/– to 1/6 a week, fares, three or four times a week, 2/3 or 3/–, and rent of room used as work-room, 2/6. The average expenses therefore were 18/4½, while the average takings were 40/–. The only son paid 10/– for lodging and breakfast, and one room was let furnished to a young woman who took her meals with the family. Yet, as the husband had long done nothing more than occasionally fetch and carry back the work, it is difficult to understand how the family maintained its high standard of living—unless, indeed, she had saved or inherited some little income. It seems fairly clear that even an able woman cannot, as a rule, make more money in her own workroom than she could earn as a forewoman—and that only by employing the cheap labour of girls can she make as much.

PRIVATE DRESSMAKING.

In addition to the 13 cases in this group, many of the women visited have done dressmaking for private customers in a more or less desultory and spasmodic manner. Of the thirteen, several did no work before marriage ; one was in service, and all the others did dressmaking. Only three seemed to be earning anything like a living wage, and the family circumstances in some cases were deplorable.

No. 4 was, before marriage, a tea-gown hand in the West End, and found herself unhappy without something to do. When visited she was busy on the reparation of an elaborate Paris gown, and was sewing sequins upon white net for the trimming. She was going to charge 10/- for the whole job, and reckoned that it would occupy such spare time as was left from her household duties for a week. Sometimes she earned 18/- or 19/- in the week, but thought her average was about 12/-. Considering that she had two small children—one delicate—this seems a high rate. She said that she had no difficulty in getting as well paid as before marriage, and that she had as much work as she wanted. She and her husband (whose earnings are but 24/- to 27/-, and irregular at that) were supporting an orphan niece of 13.

No. 3, who before marriage worked with her mother, their joint earnings being about £4 a week, was living in an East End court (quite a clean and comfortable abode), and found the locality unfavourable. She now took from 15/- to £1 or 30/- a week, and the family—there were two young children—was mainly supported by her. Her husband was a hawker whose only certain earnings were 4/- for minding a barrow in a street market on Sundays. The wife made no complaint of him, but her sister confided to the investigator that he would not take a regular job, but preferred hawking, and relied upon the profits of the dressmaking.

Mrs. B., No. 6, performed all sorts of casual jobs— charing or washing in neighbours' houses, sewing or dressmaking at home, and selling flowers in the streets on Saturdays. She was married at 17, and at 32 found herself the mother of six living and five dead children, three of whom died of convulsions, and two, in one week, of consumption. The husband, a rag and bone man, was consumptive, and able to earn but very little. The family inhabited a little basement flat of three rooms and a scullery, and, under pressure of poverty, one room was let off for 3/– a week ; the rooms were ill-ventilated and ill-lighted; the passage is described as being " pitch dark." A daughter of 14 minded the younger children when the mother was at work, except on Saturdays when both went out to sell flowers, and the father remained at home to look after the children. This is one of those cases that proclaim the ineffectiveness of our social arrangements. The poor man was a source of danger to his family, and the circumstances in which they lived cultivated that danger. The wife—herself a strong and healthy person— was working too hard, and the children could not possibly have proper food or clothing. Proper air and space we know they had not. Surely it would be cheaper for the country—to say nothing of common humanity—that the invalid should be removed to proper surroundings in which he might possibly recover, and that enough assistance should be given to the industrious wife to save her remaining children from becoming invalids also.

No. 7 was a woman of over 50 living in the same very poor part of the town as No. 6. She too was not employed before her marriage, and was now doing odd jobs of sewing and dressmaking ; she would have done charing or washing if she could get the work. She often had none of any kind. The husband, a bricklayer's labourer, earned but 24/– when in full work, and was often " out " for weeks at a time. If only he were regularly employed she could manage comfortably. They had nine children, all strong and healthy, and had lost none.

Two daughters were married, and one son—out of work at the time of the visit, and the father of four children. A machinist daughter, living at home, was out of work ; another, earning 9/- in a factory so far off that her fares cost 2/9 a week, paid 5/- weekly for her board and lodging ; a younger one, working nearer, earned 4/-, and gave all to her mother. A boy of 17 who had passed the Cambridge Local examination, but had been unable to get a good post (on account, as the family believed, of being a labourer's son), was engaged all day in a warehouse, receiving just enough to keep him, and he spent all his evenings learning shorthand in the hope of by and by getting a clerkship. Two younger ones were still at school. The labours of No. 7 were very inadequately paid. Her best customer, she said, was a fruiterer's wife, who sometimes gave an order for two or three blouses at 1/6 each ; only one could be made in a day. Most customers paid 6d., 7d., or 9d. for a plain blouse that could be made in half a day. No. 7 showed the visitor an old skirt out of which she was making a child's coat and a pair of knickerbockers ; she was to receive 1/- for each garment, and would take two days to finish the two.

This family, living in a clean but necessarily crowded flat—eight persons : father, mother, three daughters, one son, and two children of school age in three rooms and wash-house—was evidently on the very verge of destitution. Any breakdown in the health of the admirable mother, any accident to one of the three young wage-earners who were keeping themselves, and the household must fall to pieces. Regularization of employment for the man was the desideratum here, and surely it ought not to pass the power of humanity so to organize the building trade that a man may know beforehand how many weeks he will be wanted in any year, and may be supplied during the other weeks with some supplementary work of a useful sort to save him from being a burden upon his family—or in other words upon the community.

This group of cases does not lead to any general conclusions, unless it be the obvious one that a woman has not a chance of earning what she would call " good money " if she works at a trade that she has not learned properly in her early years.

WAISTCOAT MAKERS.

The tailoring trade varies so much in its diverse departments that it may almost be said to comprise three or four trades. The cases in this enquiry have been placed in three divisions ; namely ; waistcoat makers, mantle machinists, and a general group headed " tailoring." Of these, the most prosperous section, waistcoat-making, has been set first.

Every woman in this group seems to be clean, respectable, industrious, and a good mother. All but two are stated to have done the same work before marriage, and of one of these the previous employment does not appear. In most cases it is stated that the worker made the whole garment ; but in some this was not made clear. The investigator inclines to think that No. 4 only machined. Several family histories are full of interest.

No. 1 married at 18 a man who was earning only 17/- as porter in a warehouse. Apparently he never received much more, although he remained for 17 years with the same employers. She herself was then earning 18/- at waistcoat-making in a good West End firm, and had made waistcoats for royal personages. Children came fast—there were five living, and eight dead—and the wife's work was absolutely indispensable. She received 7d. or 6½d. for each waistcoat according to size ; six or seven years earlier the price had been 8d. ; the work was fairly regular, but slack for about three weeks in every quarter; in full work she made about 14/- a week, the husband pressing, and a married daughter sewing on buttons. Her working days extended to midnight, even on Saturdays, and the husband generally fetched and took back the work. He, having become too old for heavy work, lost his place, and after some time got employment as a scene-shifter at 12/- a week. There was, however, a good deal of slack time for him. Being at home by day he now cooked and looked after the house. In former years, when the wife worked away from home, she had a woman in to help. Two daughters were married, two others and a son lived at home; the son, of 23, paid 10/- for his board and lodging: " but he eats all that; " the daughter, of 21, earned 8/-, gave her mother 5/- and clothed herself. A little girl was still at school. Of the dead children one, the eldest boy, was run over at 12 years old; the others died under five years old, chiefly of colds or bronchitis, their chests being delicate. The mother, about 50 years old, was beginning to feel worn out, and had been at a convalescent home in the previous year—her second absence from London in 20 years. She had bought three sewing machines on the instalment system during her married life, and was becoming unable to continue working at such high pressure. She seldom went out except to do a little shopping, and remarked that it seemed hard to have to work so ceaselessly to keep a roof over their heads. The husband belonged to a club for many years, but was unable to keep up his payments; she, however, nearly always managed to scrape together a few shillings to get the children sent away on the Country Holiday Fund. She thought their delicacy might be due to her working so hard; she usually continued to the time of her confinements and was often up on the fifth day, or, if not up, working as she sat in her bed; she herself, she thought, must have had a very strong constitution. Her room was perfectly clean and neat, though bare. What a heroine !

Another woman of about the same age—No. 4, made fancy waistcoats at 5/6 a dozen, with the help of an apprentice to whom she paid 5/- a week. The output was from 8 to 9 dozen a week, and the hours about 60. Cotton cost 2½d. for every nine garments ; fares about 1/- a week ; her net takings, therefore, were from 36/6 to 42/- a week. Moreover the work was regular throughout the year. She employed a girl at 7/- a week to do household work, and the family paid 12/- for a whole house. The husband was an artisan earning £2 a week, and the mother's aim in working was to apprentice her sons to good callings. She, like No. 1, was the mother of 13 children, but only two—twins—had died of whooping cough as infants. Those who were seen by the visitor were well-cared for, and looked healthy. Two sons were following their father's trade, and earning each £2 a week ; a daughter, aged 24, was earning 22/- a week when in full work ; a younger girl was learning waistcoat making at a friend's house, and receiving 3/- weekly ; a younger boy had been nominally " apprenticed " to a craft, but, not being indentured, had been dismissed on account of slackness ; 5/- a week was paid him when in work ; yet another boy, also apprenticed, received 10/- ; and five children were still at school. The income of this family of seven earners ran to fully £10 a week. All three men were trade unionists, and all were (in January) out of work but receiving " unemployment benefit " from their union.

No. 2, aged 48, was the wife of a man subject to intermittent madness who had been in an asylum " on and off for several years." His trade being, moreover, a declining one, he found it difficult to get employment during his lucid intervals. Six children had died in infancy ; three were living ; a son of 19 earned 14/-, a girl slow, and perhaps slightly defective, earned about 5/- for four days' work each week ; a child of school age was very delicate, and attending the hospital. The mother made waistcoats at 5d., 6d., or 7d. each ; paid 1/6 for machine and of course, provided cotton. Her average earnings (net, presumably) were 3/- to 5/- ; 9/- was her highest. Work had been slack through the winter, and she had had to sell most of her furniture.

Other workers are paid at the following rates : No. 6, 2/3 to 2/9 each waistcoat (" bespoke " work), could make two in a day when she had the work, and 5/- to 10/3 a dozen (fancy waistcoats) ; No. 7, could make 30/- a week when busy ; No. 9, indoor hand, 3/- a day, time wage ; No. 5, 6/- each garment, formerly 7/6, West End ; No. 3, 2/6 each, could do a dozen in a week when she could get them, but work was irregular.

There are signs in this report of a tendency to lower payments even in the West End trade.

MANTLE MAKERS.

The making of coats and mantles is perhaps the most " seasonal " of all the clothing trades, every firm seeming to have a long slack period in every year, although apparently the time of year at which this period occurs differs with different firms. In all cases, however, the late autumn provides little or no work for the mantle machinist, and most women must expect a marked diminution, if not indeed a total cessation, during three months at least of the twelve ; some speak of a slack time extending from January to June. Quite evidently no woman who wants to live by her work should undertake mantle machining unless she can (like No. 7 in our list) have some other employment during her off season.

The mantle makers do not present, like the waist-coat-makers, a homogeneous group of clean, superior women. On the contrary, there seems to be a sharp division into two sets ; the one conspicuously and even repulsively dirty in person and abode, the other as remarkably clean.

Considerable variations of payment appear. For example, No. 8, a clean industrious woman, who had worked 7 years for the same employer and previously for another, received 8½d. for a plain, three-quarter length coat, which she could machine in two hours, and 1/- for one which takes three. She said that a person who could sit close could earn £1 a week—supposing work enough to be forthcoming ; she herself, who had household work, washing, etc. to do—there were two daughters at home—did not earn much more than an average of 8/-, taking the year through, though at busy seasons her rate was a good deal higher. She thought that in her 34 years' experience payments had not altered very much. Rather higher finish was demanded, and the amount paid was slightly better ; she instanced a set of coats at 2½d. each, which she had once made, and declared that such rough, cheap work was now never seen. Yet No. 1, living in the same district, and visited by the same investigator, was actually making coats from 2¼d.

No. 1 was a woman of fifty who before marriage was a domestic servant, and taught herself this trade when her husband fell into ill-health. The investigator was not invited to enter the house, which was dilapidated and situated in a wretched street, but the woman and the passage are described (by an experienced investigator) as " filthy." Yet she had lost none of her five children. She made jackets at from 2¼d. to 5d. each, the cheapest kind taking her 20 to 30 minutes, the dearest 1½ hours. But she said that working very hard she could earn but 10/- a week, so that probably she greatly underestimated the time required.

In the same postal district, but in a poorer part of it

lived No. 3, a young woman of 27, who was already the mother of five children. She had worked before marriage at the same trade, and was still doing what she could in her few spare moments. Besides her own flock, she had a little orphan sister living with her and going to school. The husband was a " navigation labourer " and, at the period of the visit, working only three-quarter time. Whether his wage of 25/- is the full or the three-quarter figure does not seem clear, but it is probably the former. She made sets of six children's coats at from 2/6 to 2/9 per set, and women's coats at 4d. or 5d. each. A five-penny coat represented two hours' work. Rates had fallen ; she used to get 3/- for the two-and-ninepenny set.

The case of No. 11 is a curious one. She was a widow of 75, living with her married daughter in a repulsive street and receiving Poor Law relief. She was by no means clean, and an experienced visitor thinks that she probably " takes a little to drink." Her circumstances had formerly been good ; her husband was a skilled artisan, and she formerly had a mantle-making and dressmaking business, and employed 14 hands, but her husband became an invalid, and she gradually lost her business. She was at work on a long cloth coat of medium quality, with double stitchings and two pockets, for which she would get 6d. Three years earlier the payment would have been 10d. She provided machine—1/6 weekly—and cotton. About her average earnings she was vague, but they were evidently never high. This woman had lost ten children out of twelve, and hers is one of the few cases in which it seems pretty clear that the children suffered actually from the mother's work, and not from her poverty or privation. She had, she said, the best attention and a proper midwife, but the infants were weakly at birth, and " popped off soon after." She thought the machining was bad for her, as probably it was. It must be remembered, however, that the father was apparently delicate. The married daughter had a large family of intelligent children ; one son had taken a scholarship of the L.C.C., and had become a chemistry demonstrator ; a little boy of seven whom the investigator saw was clean, well developed, and remarkably clever-looking. There seemed to be a curiously mingled strain of descent.

Other rates are (No. 2) 1/6 to 2/4 per coat, formerly 1/9 to 2/9 (No. 4) 3/6, 4/-, 4/6 per dozen, those at the highest rate being full-length, and having been paid, some fourteen years earlier, at 9/-. The work did not differ much in the worse and the better-paid garments ; a dozen took from 1½ to 2 days, of long hours ; (No. 5) 4d. for a child's, 5d. for a woman's coat, the one taking an hour and a quarter, the other an hour and a half ; payment reported as going down every year ; (No. 6) 4d., 4½d. per garment, about the same amount of work in each, sitting close, a dozen could be done in two days ; formerly the same coats were 1/- each ; (No. 7) 5½d. per coat, plain, half length, with raw seams, to 11d. per coat, long, braided, or trimmed. In the slack season No. 7 makes coats and skirts at 2/6 each, for her employer's friends. Coats now paid at 6½d. used to be 10d. or 11d. No. 9, an indoor hand at a small tailor's, working from 8 to 8, with no tea interval, from 8 to 4 on Saturday, with no dinner interval, and often kept late on Saturdays without extra pay, 18/- time wage. The absence of meal interval during periods of over five hours, and the overtime on Saturdays (except after notification to Home Office) were, of course, both illegal. No woman in this list seems to have had a bad husband. Two, at least, of the husbands were exemplary.

TAILORING (GENERAL).

In this group of 23 cases, there are instances of women working indoors by the day, of wives helping middlemen husbands, of a woman making uniforms for postmen, of outdoor workers doing comparatively well-paid West End work, and of other outdoor workers paid at far below a living rate. They represent among them almost every part of London, except the extreme West and North. In two cases the report was too inadequate to be of any use.

To take first those women who worked with relatives.

No. 4 was a Polish Jewess who worked with her husband, he cutting and felling trousers (*i.e.*, putting together the various pieces), and she sewing. 2/- a pair was paid them, and they could make five or six pairs in a day if they had them, but they never got so many.

No. 3, a German, in very poor health, made trousers entirely at from 1/- for the very best kind, 5½d. and 2½d. for some others. She and her husband (a presser) worked for his brother-in-law.

No. 6 made and repaired trousers, working " with " her husband, says the report, although it rather appears that their work was quite separate. For repairs she was paid by time at 6d. per hour ; for a plain pair of new trousers she got 2/6, 6d. extra for a hip pocket, and 6d. extra if the garment were lined ; dress trousers 3/6. These rates were lower than she had known them ; the 3/6 trousers had been 5/- ; the 2/6 ones, 3/- ; indeed, No. 6 said that the trade had gone down so much that she should not put her daughter to it. Husband and wife together made a clear profit of about 28/- a week, after payment of all expenses.

No. 13 was, like her husband, a Russian ; they employed two hands, and the prices paid them were as follows :

Waistcoats, 1/6, 1/9, 2/-, 2/3, 2/9 each ;

Trousers, 1/6, 1/9, 2/3 ;

Coats, 4/-, 4/6.

There was five months' slack time in the year—in other words, tailoring is done but little when London is "empty."

No. 17 was the wife of a man with whom she worked for a local shop ; 2/9 each was paid for waistcoats—which presumably formed her share.

No. 18 worked at home with her father and husband, partly for a shop, partly for private customers. 10/- or 12/- was paid for each costume by the shop, and no additional money was paid for the extra braiding which had become fashionable ; £2 10s. or £3 3s. was paid by private customers.

Of indoor hands there were eight, and nearly all worked for the longest hours allowed by the Factory Act—as is indeed customary in this trade. No. 1 was paid 3/6 a day, and made riding habits. Work was slack when she was seen. No. 2, a coat hand, who also made button-holes, received 3/- a day, or in slack times, less. No. 7, employed by a middleman, was paid 1/- a pair for trousers (as a machinist, I think), and earned 10/- or 11/- when busy, but in slack times only 5/- or 6/- or less still—sometimes nothing at all. When there was a great deal of work, she brought it home and sat up " till all hours " doing it—a practice which is illegal. Hers was a very hard case. She was a widow with a delicate looking daughter of 12, and a son of 15 who earned 2/6 a week and all his food. Her husband had had a small tailoring work-shop, and having seen so much of the trade she took it up when she was widowed. While the boy was at school she had Poor Law relief, which was stopped when he went to work. The three were living in one room—the boy, however, was expecting to be taken indoors by his employer shortly ; the mother and daughter were both re-fined, superior people, spotlessly clean ; neither seemed strong. The eight years of this poor woman's widowhood must have been a time of terrible struggle and hardship. No. 8 made trousers and breeches at 1/3 for trousers, and 2/- for breeches. In the busy season she earned £1 a week ; in slack times from 5/- to 10/-. Her husband having lost his place as a coachman had great difficulty in finding any other employment, but had at last been engaged as potman in a public house, where he worked from 8 to 5, and from 8 to midnight for 13/– a week.

No. 19, a Polish woman, worked for 1/6 a day, which day is the usual long one of this trade. In slack times she earned but 3/– or 4/– a week. No. 20 " felled coats," *i.e.*, put in the linings, in a Jew's workshop. This was a young woman, very unfortunate in her marriage ; her husband, a " coalman," not only made the whole place extremely dirty, and drank, but also ill-treated her, and had the singular and unpleasant habit of deserting her whenever she had a child. She had had four, and lost three during the five years of her wretched married life, and when visited was living with her one surviving baby at her mother's.

No. 12 worked in the Royal Army Clothing Factory at a time-wage of 15/– a week for a shorter working day than generally prevailed. No. 21 made postmen's overcoats at 6/9 a dozen, in a factory from which workers were discharged if they failed to earn a minimum of 13/9. She herself made about 14/6 ; 2/– to 2/6 was deducted weekly for cotton.

Homeworkers were generally doing poorer varieties of work ; and the usual custom is to pay according, not to the amount of work done, but to the quality of the material.

No. 5 was paid 10d. or 1/– per pair for trousers, the cheaper ones taking about three hours, and the dearer ones a little longer.

No. 9, a Jewess, finished trousers at the appallingly low rate of 6d. per dozen. A daughter of 15 helped the mother, and another girl still at school worked with them when at home. The efforts of all three could not achieve more than a dozen in from 2 to 3 hours. Their utmost earnings were from 8/– to 9/–, and 6/– their average.

No. 10 finished knickerbockers at 4d., 8d., 1/–, or 2/6 a dozen. She could not devote much time to the work on account of household duties—she had a paralyzed husband, and four sons and daughters at home—and never earned more than 6/–. The variations of payment were according to quality, not according to the work required. No. 11, a finisher of coats and trousers, received 6d., 8d., or 1/– a dozen. No. 15 earned 10/– a week, when busy.

All but two, or perhaps three, of these women were economically compelled to work for money. One, a young woman, worked with her father and husband, both tailors, because she liked to have something to do, and to help them. She had learned the trade from her husband and liked the work. As is usually the case with women who take up this attitude, she was a superior person, intelligent and energetic. A girl was kept to look after her one little child while she was busy.

It is painfully clear that miscellaneous tailoring offers no prospect of a comfortable livelihood. A coat hand or perhaps even a trouser hand in a very good place may, in the West End, hope for more than a mere subsistence wage during the busy season, but in the slack will barely earn the necessarily heavy rent which she pays for living within easy reach of her employer. On the other hand, the hours of tailoresses are excessively long. To work from 8 to 8, and from 8 to 4 on Saturdays, is to have no personal life left, except on Sundays. If it were not for the slack intervals, tailoresses who work on a master's premises would be worn out early in life ; but the recurrent fluctuations are trying and demoralising. By February, nine families out of ten are in debt and men and women work feverishly to pay off arrears.

EMBROIDERY, TRIMMINGS, Etc.

In this group of 8 workers there were no two who did

the same kind of work, and their earnings varied as much
as their employment.

No. 1 made policemen's armlets at 2/6 a gross ; work
was slack, and she had made but 3½ gross in a week,
earning 8/9. No. 2 was a maker of " conduct stripes "
for the Navy, but the supply of work had ceased, and
she had done none for months. The stripes were stencilled
on a sheet of cloth, and braid had to be sewn over the
markings. 2¾d. was paid for each sheet, and the work
was, therefore, not ill-paid, if only the supply had been
adequate.

No. 3 did " worsted " lettering for railway uniforms,
and took work from two firms ; for a cloth collar upon
which three letters (the initials of the company) were
embroidered twice over she received 1¾d. ; the work
occupied her half an hour. She earned about 8/- to 9/-
a week, but said that a person sitting close for ten hours
a day could make 16/- or 17/-. Rates had fallen ; she
used to be paid about ½d. per hour more. The work
is done in a frame ; and half-an-hour for the six letters,
even though they are small, strikes me as being quick
work. This woman was working partly to help support
an afflicted sister.

No. 4 did cross-stitch marking, generally lettering
for handkerchiefs, at rates that varied with the size
of the letters. The only rate named is 3d. a dozen.

No. 5 made trimmings of every description ; employing
braid, beads, or chenille ; she was always paid by the
piece, and the variations were, naturally, great. For
some gimp ornaments of difficult design which took a
whole day, she received 2/6 each ; for some others as
little as 1¼d. ; her average takings were 15/- a week.
Rates had fallen slightly.

No. 6 was a " chenille spotter," that is to say
she received lengths of plain net and transformed
them into spotted veils. Chenille has a backbone,

as it were, of very fine soft wire, and the worker slips a short end under a mesh of the net, and with a small pair of pincers twists it into a spot. Regular intervals are left between one spot and the next ; for a veil in which nine spaces were missed ¾d. was paid, and a veil of this sort could be spotted in a quarter of an hour. A veil in which but three spaces intervened between spots took an hour to do, and 3¼d. was paid for it. A sevenpenny veil, which was spotted very closely all over, took three hours, therefore, in this case the work that was worst paid by the piece was the most remunerative to the worker, and that which was best paid least remunerative. Rates had fallen 2d. per yard in the course of 12 years.

No. 7 was an able and superior woman who, with her daughter, embroidered children's garments, making their own designs. She did not begin to work till she was 40 years old, when the family circumstances became impoverished. She designed her own patterns, and made samples which she sent to her employers, assigning a rate for each. The manufacturers generally gave her an order for the pattern they preferred, and usually accepted her rate. Rates varied from 2/- a dozen for small collars, to 18/- a dozen for pelisses. No. 7 provided the embroidering silk, which she bought from her employers by the pound, at a cost of 1½d. for a skein of 14 threads. She showed the investigator a cape embroidered from a design of hers by her daughter. It had taken two hours, and just over two skeins of silk. The payment was to be 9/- a dozen, and the deduction of 3d. for silk leaves a net total of 6d. per cape. The mother thought her takings—which varied from 5/- to 20/- a week—averaged about 12/-, taking the year through. Fares were a heavy item ; she lived far from the centre. She said there was great competition even for work so skilled and responsible as hers, and that the garments were sold so cheaply as to produce underpayment. She had learned the trade by helping a young woman whom she knew, and when her instructress married, had inherited her business connection.

No. 8 did gold embroidery and had served four years' apprenticeship before her marriage. She valued her trade and would, on no account, give it up. She had always earned " good money," the precise totals were not ascertained, but she laughed at the idea of getting no more than 30/–, and it seems probable that she did not make less than £2 a week. She had in the previous year made an apron for an Eastern potentate which had three pounds of gold upon it, and made all kinds of elaborate things for Freemasons. The family inhabited a large, old-fashioned house of seven rooms at a rental of £50, inclusive of rates and taxes. Her husband was an artisan in good and regular employment, and there was but one child.

No. 8 lived easily and comfortably, and spent pretty freely. She said she had paid 12/11 and 18/11 for ready-made blouses for herself, but she often made her own clothes, and considered that any one with a grain of commonsense ought to be able to make clothes. About this case the investigator remarked : " Mrs. X. helped to confirm an impression I have gained that the continuation of work after marriage would probably become a much more widespread and generally recognised thing if there were more scope for women in skilled and well-paid industries."

Women working at the sweated industries, such as brush-drawing, box-making, blouse-making, etc., or laundry work also, perhaps—take little interest or pride in their work, find it exceedingly irksome and arduous, and thankfully relinquish it on marriage if possible. When asked why they are working, the answer is almost invariably that, for one reason or another, the family cannot get on without it. The few who can command a high wage at skilled work—such as fur-stitchers, gold embroiderers, and the more expert mantle-makers—seem to view the matter from an entirely different point of view. Their work is only thoroughly mastered after years of apprenticeship and experience. They perhaps are only just entering into their full wage-earning capacity when they marry. They are proud of their ability and specialised skill, find pleasure in their work, and would regard it as the height of folly to throw aside all they have gained. They appear to marry workmen of a higher grade, earning proportionally good wages and live a very comfortable life. Many of them employ servants or charwomen to do their house work, and enjoy their position of freedom and independence.

CHARWOMEN.

L. Wyatt Papworth.

The Census of 1901 gives 111,841 as the number of charwomen in England and Wales. Of these 25,378, among
whom are included daily servants, are returned as
unmarried, while 86,463 are married women or widows.
Charwomen in 1911 numbered 126,061, an increase of 12·7
per cent. upon the number enumerated in 1901, against an
increase of only 6·7 per cent. between 1891 and 1901.
The unmarried women so employed increased from 25,378
in 1901 to 26,900 in 1911, or by only 6·0 per cent., while
the married or widowed increased from 86,463 to 99,161,
or by 14·7 per cent., the number of widows at the latter
census being 61,720, or nearly half the total.[1] For the
purposes of its enquiry into the work and wages of married
women the Women's Industrial Council has investigated
the cases of 215 families selected at random, and has
besides over a period of 14 years been in close touch with
some 1,300 women who are on the books of the Association
of Trained Charwomen and Domestic Workers founded
by the Council in 1898 for the sake of securing better
conditions and higher wages for this class of work. It is
therefore probable that there are not many problems
connected with the life and labour of the charwoman
which have not at some time or other come before the
Council. Of these, the more salient will be discussed here
in the light thrown upon them by the Married Women's
Work Enquiry, but it must be premised that there are
as many grades of charwomen and as many problems as

[1] Census 1901, Vol. X., Pt. I., p. xxxi.

there are among workers in any other industry, in addition to those peculiar to charing.

The first point to note is that the charwoman's work shares in the grave disability that attaches to all work, but particularly to the domestic work done by women. It would appear that this aspect of the problem of women's work has not so far met with the attention it deserves, and that it is only now beginning to be perceived that the fundamental problem of women's work is just this : that woman's fundamental work—her work as wife and mother, nurse and homemaker—is and has always been unpaid—in cash. The result is inevitable. In a commercial age work which is unremunerated and a worker who is unpaid are alike of small value and little esteemed. But all women, or with exceptions so few as to be negligible, have been, or are or will be engaged as unpaid workers in unpaid work, with the consequence that all work done by women and all wage-earning women are paid at a lower rate than would be the case if their work were not cheapened, and it is cheapened because either they will later engage in domestic work, so that they are not worth training for anything else ; or they are, in fact, doing unpaid domestic work all the time, and to their employer their value in other work is therefore less ; or they have been spending their life in domestic work and cannot therefore claim proficiency in the new industry they may be compelled to turn to.

While admitting that women's judgment of the value of their own work is as much affected as men's, and while granting that the low value attaching to that work is one of the results of the sex handicap, there is no reason to deem the position irremediable. The lines of woman's fundamental work were laid down in an age when agriculture, like the domestic work of women, also mainly unpaid or the work of slaves, was the staple industry. It has not advanced as other more recently developed industries have done, but the stirrings of the scientific spirit are already visible, and there is no reason to doubt that organisation and legislation will complete the reform which training and method have already begun, as has been the case in other industries.

Secondly, domestic work, charing especially, is just the work that every woman with the usual complement of arms and legs and a mind above that of an imbecile is able to perform ; hence its value is the result of work performed by ordinary muscular movements apart from directing intelligence, which is, in the case of a man, the slave value, and in the case of a woman is something less.

In its most widespread form domestic work is untrained, unspecialised and unpaid. In a country like England, where the standard in cooking and cleaning is notoriously low, and where women are in a considerable majority over men, it has not been thought worth while to avoid the drudgery of human beings by the introduction of labour-saving appliances, as is increasingly the line of development in every other industry. Hence it follows, inevitably, that the domestic work of women, being in a stage of development anterior to that prevailing in other industries, is despised and considered of little worth even by women themselves. It follows also that no remedy can be brought to bear on any section of domestic work, whether that of charwomen or servants, until the question of the domestic work of women, as a whole, including the unpaid domestic work of women in their own homes, is brought into line with present day economic development. One of the lessons which that development has most plainly taught is that (rarity value apart) where payment is exacted for services, training and specialisation are required in return in direct ratio to the wages paid. The problem of the charwoman is then in the first place part of the fundamental problem of woman's work (the solution of which has been indicated above) and can only be reached successfully as part of that problem.

And, thirdly, it has to be admitted that the work, nay, the very fact of the charwoman in anything like present day numbers, is due to the gravest problem of men's work—their irregular earnings. If low wages are bad, irregular earnings are worse, and it appears that women whose husbands have regular wages, however low, do not go out to earn money by charing unless exceptional circumstances, such as a large number of children or other dependent relatives, force them to do so. On the other hand, the woman whose husband brings home even comparatively high wages half the year, and nothing the other half, does earn money by charing because, as she says, you cannot make both ends meet when you do not know what you'll have from week to week. The army of charwomen, far in excess of the work available for them, is thus seen to be part of the " pool " of unemployed and partially employed men, the existence of which at our present stage of industrial evolution in the present conditions and with our present population is admittedly inevitable. Long experience has shown that the number of charwomen fluctuates with the amount of unemployment, and may be temporarily increased, as women have themselves stated, even by a strike. Thus the charwoman is a by-product of the irregular employment combined with low wages of men, and the problem of the charwoman will only be satisfactorily solved by the settlement of this fundamental problem of men's labour.

To the charwoman herself, the most visible difficulty is not any of the above, but the fact that the supply of labour of this class is in relation to the demand inexhaustible. This work every able-bodied woman can after a fashion perform ; therefore in her hour of direst need every able-bodied woman turns to it, and, if the need be great enough, will accept a wage of a few pence. It is, therefore, shortness of cash that sets them seeking to add the domestic tasks of other women to their own ; while it is increasing shortage of money in the middle class, who are their principal employers, which is steadily diminishing the demand, already too unequal to the supply.

It is evident that the work of charing offers striking advantages over any other occupation open to the married woman or widow who has children on her hands. Over and over again the women say that it is better than the trade they followed before marriage, which means that it is possible to earn as much, or more, with less expenditure of time ; that one can regulate the amount of work one does in a week without losing the job ; that the hours admit of far more attention to one's own housework and children than do those worked in any factory, and that you do get for yourself good food, and often something to bring home to the children as well. Last and greatest of gains, there is the fiction of doing the work " to oblige a lady," which saves one's dignity, glorifies the relationship of employer and employed, and preserves appearances before neighbours. For it is quite clear that married women in London, at any rate, do not go out charing unless driven thereto by necessity.

Of the 215 cases investigated in London, Leeds and Liverpool, 72 have been omitted as, being widowed, separated or deserted, they were in the natural course responsible for their own and their family's support ; 78 have had to be discarded owing to insufficient detail in the report and a further six cases where the husband was an invalid and the wife was supporting him. The remaining 59 cases have been used to show the considerable difference made by the wife's earnings to the income per head of the family, and that without such earnings it would have been in many cases impossible for the family to exist without recourse to the Poor Law. This cash difference is expressed in the appended table, and the following cases have been selected to illustrate the principal causes which have led Mrs. Jones and her friends to go out " to oblige ladies."

The family circumstances under which married women go out charing are as follows :—

1. When there are no wages, because the husband is out of work and only picks up odd jobs. These families are practically destitute, and even with the wife's earnings, they only have about 1/6 per head per week to live on.

2. When the wages vary greatly in amount because the husband's earnings are irregular. This is the main reason why women go out charing. It is quite clear that among the very poor if the housewife knows what she will have to spend, she can make both ends meet and will therefore stay at home.

3. When the wages are actually insufficient, although brought home regularly. These cases appear to be rare in the families of charwomen for the reason given under No. 2.

4. When wages are rendered inadequate by the size of the family. Over and over again the mother said she had resumed work only after the births of several children.

5. When the wages are inadequate because the wife has a higher standard of living. It appears from the cases that the standard of living depends on the wife, who, when she is superior, shares the point of view of some women in the professional class in thinking it better worth while to increase the family income by going out to work than to make a possible saving of expense by staying at home.

The following cases illustrate the above five groups :—

Case No. 45 (husband out of work).—Mr. Jones was a barge-unloader at Fulham and Mrs. Jones stayed at home, where she had plenty to do looking after her eight

children. But changes came, wharves were cleared away
to make room for the large electric generating station,
and goods are brought up to town by train ; instead
of seven busy wharves there is now only one, where sometimes not more than one barge moors in a month. Mr.
Jones still goes out to look for work diligently, but there
is hardly any for him to do. So Mrs. Jones has to help
earn the family income instead of spending it ; she works
from 6 a.m. to 12.30 every day as a cleaner in an institution
near at hand, and brings home 13/- a week, the only
regular family income. Her place at home is taken as
well as possible by the eldest child, a fine-looking girl of
15, who will be sent to good service, as soon as her place
at home can be taken by the next girl, who is just about
to leave school.

Case No. 38 (husband's irregular earnings).—Mr. Brown
is in the Post Office service as a mail-driver. He is
paid by the job, 1/- each time ; it may come to 24/-
a week, but " it's all according to the number of runs you
go, strictly in turn," and country work has been superseded by motors. So Mrs. Brown turns out to work also,
for her husband's income is so uncertain, and " it's
difficult to lay out what you are not sure of getting."
She was in service before marriage, went out at 11 years
of age, and spoke feelingly of having to clean 14 pairs of
boots before she had breakfast. After a time she went
into the confectionery trade, learned it thoroughly and
got into the fondants and jellies, the best work, and had
12/-, but " you could not get that now." She also used
to do nursing, but gave that up as she wanted to be at
home on Sundays. Now she has a regular charing job at
a boarding-house four days a week from 9 to 6 at 2/- a day.
She washes for 25 people on Monday for that money, and
it is heavy work, as they all wear flannels. There are
three children, a delicate girl of six, in need of a country
holiday, a bonny little girl of four, and a boy of five, who

is looked after by an old woman upstairs for 6d. a day. The father is in at meal times and can attend to the little girls then, for the mother is away four days a week. Undoubtedly she is " the grey mare," an active and not-to-be-beaten sort of woman, who makes the most of her husband's and her own earnings.

Case No. 85 (husband's earnings insufficient though regular).—Mr. and Mrs. Robinson live in Deptford, they have four boys ranging from eight to a baby of two, who is cared for in a crèche, and another is expected. Mr. Robinson is a labourer at some gasworks and is in regular work, and out of his wage of 30/- he does not think 4/- is too much to keep for his private needs. As Mrs. Robinson cannot keep the necessary expenditure on the needs of her growing family within the 26/- left to her, she herself attempts to earn what she can to provide for boots and clothes and for the fresh arrival. She does any odd jobs she can get, scrubbing, charing, washing, mantle making (that is finishing at piece rates that work out at 2d. an hour), in fact anything that will bring in any money ; her ambition is to earn three shillings a week. She is a delicate woman, and is not really equal to the task of both providing for and looking after her family, yet her only complaint is that she cannot get enough work to do.

Case No. 84 (husband's earnings insufficient for size of family).—Mr. and Mrs. Smith have each been married before, and there are children by the former marriages as well as by the present one, making eleven in all ; consequently the 20/- brought home by Mr. Smith and the 13/- earned by the two eldest boys is not sufficient to supply the needs of them all. So the baby is sent to a crèche, the older children look after the younger ones, and Mrs. Smith goes out daily from 6.30 to 9 or 10 in the morning, and again from 6.30 to 8 at night to earn another 12/- to increase the family income. She is a clean, tidy, intelligent woman, thoroughly capable of managing her large family with thrift and economy, and fond of them all, though a chance caller may sometimes find Tommy putting the baby unwashed to bed, while mother " has gone down the road," or the same Tommy is sent out to look for her " in the corner house." But she has only lost one child, from convulsions ; another of six seems to be defective.

Case No. 60 (woman with better standard of living). —Mrs. White is a country woman and was in service both before marriage and again for 12 years after being divorced from a bad husband. Her present husband is a " horseman " in the service of a railway company at £1 a week, and " you cannot keep yourself respectable and your family as it should be on that without going out." So she works in a coffee-house from 8 to 12, and all day on Saturday for 7/– a week, of which 1/– is spent in fares. She has only one little girl, but has an orphan girl living with her, who earns 6/3 a week in a sweet factory. This hardly pays for her keep and clothes, but " she's a friend, that's all ; it's so hard on a girl to be left like that, I've no father or mother myself." Though she finds the constant standing very trying and being a " homely woman of the motherly type," would much prefer to look after her house, which is in a nice quiet street ; she feels she cannot afford to give the work up.

NOTE —See Table at end of book, shewing the differences in family income per head with and without the Mother's Earnings.

WAGE-EARNING WIVES IN A SLUM.

L. D.

OUR modern urban civilisations can only remain wholesome at the expense of effort, labour and organisation
Where these essentials are absent, corruption sets up a
horrible social decomposition more frightful than any
mere primitive savagery. Few large towns are without
some such festering spot, larger or smaller. In London
considerable areas have been reclaimed, some of which had
been vile for centuries; and reference to Mr. Booth's map
of poverty published in 1899 will show a large proportion
of black streets that would be more hopefully tinted in a
similar map to-day. On the other hand there are some
old-established black spots that have persisted and that
have extended, and these seem to be traceably connected
with some inadequacy of communication. As the disreputable gravitate to *culs de sac*, so does the lowest section
of a city's population gravitate to a district devoid of
great main roads. " Opening up " is no mere official
catchword, it is the motto of a sound municipal policy,
and owing largely to the application of this policy the
black patches have, as far as inner London is concerned,
diminished both in number and in extent during the last
twenty years. But in outer London new black patches
have arisen, some of them so new as to have become
slums almost before the building of the houses was
completed, some of them old residential areas that have
fallen from their creditable estate. Of a suburban area
of this kind, an investigator engaged in this enquiry has

sent in a vivid account which here follows. The names
of the streets are of course fictitious.

There exists an old-fashioned London suburb which
seems to have been altogether passed over in the rapid
development of recent years. I can remember it myself
as long as twenty years ago, and I do not think it has
grown much in the whole of that time. When I went
back to make my enquiries, I found that there were no
new streets, no new houses since I left it eight years ago
—only an air of general depression and shabbiness, and
a number of familiar houses uninhabited. At one time
it was the home of well-to-do middle-class families, but
with increased facilities for travelling these have long
since gone further afield. I can find no other reason to
account for the degradation of the place than that its
railway facilities do not compare with those of many
places twice its distance from town. The train service
is slow and infrequent, and the fare is high. There are
no large factories or works for several miles around
The " working " population is employed chiefly in supply-
ing the needs of middle-class residents ; hence the exodus
of so many of the wealthier of these has meant ruin to
tradespeople and workmen alike. Within recent years an
electric tram service has been run to a neighbouring centre,
but it does not seem to have brought prosperity in its
train.

My investigations were to be conducted in the neighbourhood of a certain school, where it was reported to
us that the children were unusually dull, and that the
mothers worked in the fields. This district lies about
three quarters of a mile off the route of traffic on a main
road. It consists of three thickly populated streets
with houses varying in size from 4 rooms to 6, and in
rent from 7/– to 10/–, in the midst of large middle-class
houses, still fairly well-to-do.

The population of the three streets is roughly estimated by the Medical Officer of Health at 1000.

This peculiar district is said to have originated in
the first place through a mistake of the landowner's
agent, who let the land without making stringent building
conditions, and, as a result, this small property was
erected about 35 years ago. Some of the first inhabitants
were coachmen and gardeners, dependent on the larger
houses, but there was also a brickfield which afforded work
for a good many ; this, however, I gather, was closed so
far back as 25 years ago.

I am told that the reputation of the place as regards
respectability used to be worse than it is now.

The three streets form three distinct social grades—
Florence Road being the most respectable and the shortest ;
Genoa Street coming next, and Verona Street being the
poorest and roughest as well as by far the longest and
most crowded. None of the streets, however, appear
from the outside to be of an unusually low type, and most
of them have little front gardens, with some attempts
at cultivation.

"The sanitation of the houses," says the Relieving
Officer, "is fairly good since the Guardians have had
power to report to the sanitary authority."

This district ought to be a fairly healthy one—it stands
at the top of a hill (most of the district lies rather low)
and all the streets open at one end on to potato fields,
while the land for several miles round is cultivated by fruit
and vegetable growers, and nursery gardeners.

The present occupants are, with few exceptions, casual
labourers. Some have found temporary employment
about a mile away, where a great deal of building development has taken place during the last ten years. How
most of them get a living it is difficult to say—many
are casuals and loafers of the lowest type. A few are
entered in the directory with their occupations, as

follows :—3 gardeners, 1 wheelwright, 1 carpenter, 1 chimney cleaner, 1 bricklayer, 2 house decorators, 1 dairyman, 1 upholsterer, 1 grocer, and 1 carman. These, together with a few railway men form the *élite* of the place.

None of the women have learned any trade, and the place is too inaccessible for any homework to be done there.

Before marriage, the women were either in service or in a laundry. I found it very difficult to estimate what proportion of the married women were wage-earners, certainly less than I expected, and in any case, the principal occupations were charing and laundry, not field work, as had been stated to me. And certainly it was not possible to trace any connection between dull children and wage-earning mothers ; on the contrary, in some striking cases of dullness, the mother was not a wage-earner.

What details I was able to obtain as regards particular cases, I will add later. All this detailed information is second-hand, *i.e.*, obtained not by actual visits to the homes, but from experienced District and Care Committee Visitors, who gave me much valuable help.

I found that the people of Verona Street were so rough that even the policemen did not visit it alone after dark ; also I found that the regular visitors there were more willing to give me information if I would give them the assurance that I was not going to make personal inquiries myself, thus possibly creating suspicion of them among their people. Taking into consideration also the very doubtful accuracy of any first-hand information I might get, I decided to rely altogether on what other visitors could furnish me with.

Some of the married women are working in laundries (of which there are two) ; some as charwomen, a few in the fields.

Some of these are widows, but many work because there is no continuity of work for the men, and their husbands are so often out of work. Social workers in the neighbourhood seem almost unanimously of the opinion that many of these men deliberately live on their wives, and make no effort at all to find work for themselves. The self-reliance of the people has not been increased by the fact that until the establishment of a voluntary committee for school feeding about six years ago, there was no attempt at co-operation among charitable agencies (which are numerous) and many families were receiving assistance from three or four sources at once.

Besides those women who are driven by necessity to work, there is also a small class in which both husband and wife are wage-earners, because their standard of living is higher, and the wife prefers to work to add a little more to the comfort of the home.

The charwomen are the aristocracy of female labour in Parma Road. They have to be women of a certain standard of neatness and cleanliness, or they would find no employers, and these it is who combine wage-earning work with their household and maternal duties. Most of them have husbands in regular work earning 20/- to 25/- a week. They seldom go out every day of the week, and often make arrangements for their babies to come to them to be fed.

The laundry workers are of a distinctly lower grade. Their homes are generally ill-kept and dirty, their children improperly fed, or underfed and neglected. They have only an hour in the middle of the day to get to and from their homes. To prepare, cook and clear away a meal for the family is an impossible task ; and consequently among the laundry workers very little attempt is made to cook decent meals. Very few of them know how to cook. Bread and dripping is the main diet in the middle of the day, while some mothers give the children a penny to buy what they fancy, and never trouble themselves how it is spent.

The main meal of the day takes place about five or six in the evening, or even later, when both father and mother are at home—far too late to be of much benefit to the children.

The fare is generally very inferior fried fish or cooked meat from a neighbouring shop. Infants are fed on the cheapest kind of condensed milk.

The laundry workers do not work on Mondays, and they earn about 11/– a week, unless they happen to be fine ironers, when they can get from 16/– to 18/–.

They all drink, more or less—many of them a great deal, and vice of every description is rampant.

The Medical Officer remarked that for some unknown reason laundry workers seem to be the most immoral of all classes of women workers. Certainly the neighbourhood has a universal reputation for vice, and is known to the public health department as, with a single exception, the blackest spot in the borough. About half a dozen women in Verona Street are strongly suspected of adding to their income by prostitution—and such is the lawlessness and violence of the place, that even the police never venture there alone after dark. There are only about six women who are employed in the fields regularly all the year round ; these would do potato sowing in the early months of the year, fruit-picking of all kinds later, and potato gathering in the autumn. They get 1/6 a day (9/– a week) and work from 7 a.m. to 5 p.m. six days a week.

During the fruit season the number is augmented to 20 or 30 women and girls, who (according to the largest employers of this kind of labour) can earn from 30/- to £2 a week.

Some of the women leave the laundry in the fruit-picking season and return when it is over. The type of woman who does this work is very low and rough.

The mothers who go out leave their babies with older brothers and sisters, or give them to a neighbour to mind for a trifle—one woman, rather feeble-minded, gets five or six babies every day, and is paid 3d. each for them. She does keep them clean, but they are tied up in chairs all day long, which must be bad for their backs.

The only crèche is about three-quarters of a mile away, and is only used by one or two of the most respectable. One woman has been known to shut a small child up alone in the house all day.

The registrar of births and deaths, who has been a rent-collector in the neighbourhood for many years, says : " The wonder is that the infant mortality is not much higher than it is, for mothers will bring infants to the door half-dressed in the bitterest weather, and many a time have I seen babies in perambulators left outside public-houses on Saturday nights until midnight."

At childbirth, most of the mothers are attended by an old woman who has served in the capacity of midwife for twenty-one years. Some get maternity letters from a local hospital, which sends out certified midwives.

There can be little doubt that the children of the district as a whole are underfed and neglected. Out of 204 examined by the school doctor a few months ago, only 70 were pronounced to be in normal health. The rest were all suffering in some way. At the time of writing out of 174 on the books, 28 children are having breakfasts of bread and butter and milky cocoa, but the headmaster is of opinion that at least twelve of these need dinners too.

The head-master, while taking a great interest in the well-being of his children, is apparently satisfied with the number of children being fed, and is rather fearful lest too much food should make them as difficult to teach as too little. The Secretary of the Care Committee considers that more children are necessitous, and is doing her best to get the breakfasts replaced by dinners.

It is extremely difficult to get at how far the bad condition of the children can be put down to the fact that the mothers work.

Underfed and neglected children are to be found in homes where the mother is not a wage-earner.

The Secretary of the Care Committee remarks : " There are few, very few, who understand the laws of hygiene and feeding ; they are appallingly ignorant. I should think 80 per cent. of the children are underfed and improperly fed. As regards lack of cleanliness, that certainly is often because the mother is away all day, and has not time to look after the children. Sometimes as many as 60 children at the school have been found to be in a verminous condition, and it is generally worse after the holidays.

" Then again it must be remembered that the parents start life with no physique of their own—and marry far too early. I know a case in the district of a boy of 17 who married a girl of 16. She is now 29 and has 10 children."

The headmaster of the school also lays stress on the number of early marriages as an important factor in the problem. He also told me that six years ago, when he came to the school, the condition of affairs among the children was appalling. He had to make it " an offence punished with the utmost severity for a boy as much as to look at a girl." One girl became a mother while she was still at school, and he subsequently found that, with the knowledge of her parents, she had regularly run the streets. She is now 16 and in a rescue home. Another of his school girls has been in gaol, and is now in a rescue home. Cases of consanguinity are innumerable—it is impossible to follow the relationships of many of the children in school. Teaching according to the recognised curriculum is impossible, most of the children are below average intelligence, and many of them little more than animals. He has made a point of open-air lessons whenever possible, and cricket, football and other kinds of organised games and outdoor sport have been greatly encouraged ; he has succeeded in developing a certain amount of self-respect and corporate pride through athletics. They have done so well in sport that they have been classed with the Intermediate Schools in the borough, and take a very high place in inter-school sports. But the problem is an appalling one, and the good that is done at school is undone immediately at home—parents and children alike seem utterly devoid of moral sense.

The Medical Officer considers that married women's labour as a factor in the problem of race degeneracy is infinitesimal compared with the four main causes—drink, epilepsy, the marriage of persons with hereditary disease, and the marriage of the feeble-minded—all of which features are prevalent in the Parma Road area.

These are the problems which have to be courageously dealt with before we can hope for much improvement in national health. To this may be added the testimony of the school attendance officer (an old soldier) :—" I am certain," he says, " that one child of 15 dying of phthisis is the child of her own mother's father. Another girl I know to be taken regularly out by her father for purposes of prostitution. One knows of innumerable cases, which however, one can rarely prove."

A lady living near, who has supplied information about several families, gives separately a notice of this black patch. " The people," she says, " are nearly all over-worked and underfed, and in nearly every case the woman works to keep the man and big family—an arrangement," she adds, " that tends to make the man lazy and the children delicate." The men " being for the most part unskilled workmen, or men having no trade whatever " do not get regular employment. The boys go out as errand boys until they are about 18, and then, having no industrial training, " drift into the regular lazy, bad work-men so common in these parts." The girls on leaving school go into inferior places as servants, their lack of proper clothes debarring them from getting good places. " The drinking and gambling and bad living in both men and women here is almost impossible to do anything with." " We have on the other hand, many most respectable families, the men are railwaymen, postmen, carmen, gardeners and good labouring men, builders and coach-men. The women don't go out to work in these cases, and the children are therefore nicely brought up and the houses are comfortable."

The lady, we perceive, believes that it is because the mothers stay at home that the children and homes are well-cared for, but it may be suggested that the presence at home of a mother who is not sober, not reputable in her way of life, and not industrious, does not lead to comfort in that home, nor to good conduct in her children. The factors required to produce these effects seem to be good character, good sense and fairly good health on the part of the parents, and an average income that renders possible a civilized standard of life. Where the wife and mother is a thoroughly worthless woman, the less she stays at home the better for her family.

Here are some sample cases reported by one or other of two ladies who work in this district.

Mrs. A., Verona Street, about 40, was born in an English town, and is married to a labourer who drinks, and is described as " a cruel man." She has worked regularly throughout her married life and previously, as washer-woman at a steam laundry and earns about 4s. 6d. a week, " often more " ; she is a delicate woman who really ought not to work and her health is probably the worse for her habits, since she is described as given to drink and living a bad life. The pair pay 7/6 for four rooms which are very dirty and contain little furniture. They have had 10 children, of whom 7 died in infancy. Of the three survivors—all delicate—one is at work.

Mrs. B., Verona Street, is a country woman, aged about 36, who was in service before her marriage, and who now does charing three days a week in private houses. Her husband, described as an agent, is by no means honest, and never retains one post long. When at work, his earnings average 15/-. In the earlier years of their married life his work was more regular, and she did not then go out. Their rent is 8/6 for 5 or 6 rooms, which are kept clean and are neatly furnished. The seven children living look healthy. Three of them are at work ; the eldest son when employed earns 18s. a week, but is not honest, and consequently gets dismissed ; the second, a milk boy, receives 4s. a week and one pint of milk daily ; the third is a boot boy who gets 1/6 a week and his breakfast every morning. Two children have died, one of scarlet fever, one of inflammation of the brain. Mrs. B. is a thoroughly respectable, very clean woman who has brought up her children well, and to whom the conduct of her husband and eldest boy is a great trouble.

Mrs. C., Florence Road, is the wife of a gardener who has always been in regular work, and who earns 23/- a week, besides getting from his employer a certain amount of foodstuff. She has always done a little work, charing, when she could do so without neglecting her home, and says that she works in order to see her children decently dressed. She has always nursed her children, and if she went to work while she had a young baby, made arrangements to have it brought to her. She occupies a beautifully-kept house with a best parlour, and the lady who gives the information describes the family as " of intense and overwhelming respectability." She has eight children living, whose ages vary from 20 to 3½, besides a son by a former marriage ; and has lost two or three. Two girls are

in service ; one boy of 18 is learning a trade and earns
about 8/– ; another is a telegraph messenger, and hopes
to be kept on later as a postman. The daughters all
go to service as they grow old enough. But the intensely
respectable Mrs. C. has a darker side to her family history.
In a mews, a few yards away from her " beautifully kept "
home, lives D. E., the son of her first marriage, married
himself and the father of five children. The lady who
reports the case says that she does not think he has ever
in his life had regular work ; he drinks and is an utterly
disreputable person. At the time when the report was
given he was undergoing three weeks' imprisonment for
assaulting a policeman. The wife, Mrs. E., works regularly in a laundry and will not say anything against her
husband, idle though he is. Their rent is 5/– and their
two rooms are very dirty, the state of the beds being
described as disgusting. The children are aged respectively
8, 6, 5, 3½ and one year. The child of eight has to take
the baby to the crèche, about a quarter of an hour's walk
away, and to fetch bread before going to school in the
morning. When she arrives there, she is too tired to learn.
If, as happens sometimes, the mother has not the necessary
3d. or 4d. for the crèche, the three elders are kept at home
to look after the two babies, and the five are left alone in
the house all day. The children are visibly underfed,
but are not permitted to go regularly to the school breakfast. The parents said they could feed the children themselves, but do not.

Our informant thinks that they are provided with
clothes by their grandmother, Mrs. C. The earnings of
the mother are 11/– to 12/6 weekly, and upon that income
the family of seven persons has apparently to subsist.
This is a hard-working woman, but drinks sometimes.
The officer of the Society for the Prevention of Cruelty to
Children tells the Council's investigator that several complaints have been made to him about the neglect of

these children, and that he has visited the house and warned the parents.

Mrs. F., of Genoa Street, goes out as a charwoman, rather because she likes to do so, and for the sake of procuring luxuries than because of any actual need. Her husband is in the employ of a railway company, and earns 28/– a week. They rent a whole house at 8/6 a week ; it is nicely furnished and clean. Of their four children, two boys of 14 and 16 are at work, one as an errand boy, and one on the railway. A girl of 13, who is always nicely dressed, and a younger boy, are at school. This family is not idle, not dirty, " there is no evidence of drink, they save money and draw out for holidays," but there is a moral and perhaps a mental taint somewhere. The father and mother are said to have no idea of morals, and the elder boys, young as they are, have already a bad reputation, and the eldest has been charged before the magistrates with offences of an indecent kind. The lady, who is one of our informants, thinks the mother " not quite right in her head." That this family, with its outward respectability and inner depravity should be described as typical " of the top middle class of this district," is shocking. Such families exist here and there in many districts, but only in very vile quarters can they be called typical.

Mrs. G.'s is one of the many slum households that would in the present conditions of life, be decidedly better off if its so-called head could be permanently eliminated, although, in a perfectly well-ordered condition of society the peculiar habits of Mr. G. might be treated more rationally than by repeated doses of imprisonment. This man has a propensity, apparently incurable, for stealing horses. His practice is to hire a stable, possess himself of other people's horses, and keep them there ; he has been known to have as many as 12 to 14 at a time. Of course this procedure does not remain long unobserved, and he gets sent to prison, where his good conduct invariably leads to a reduction of his sentence. His latest sentence—in course of being worked out when the report of the family was written—was for seven years ; heavier and heavier sentences having been (quite futilely) imposed at each repeated offence of this monomaniac ; and, of the last 12 years, he has spent but 18 months at home. Mrs. G., a most respectable woman, keeps her home excellently and has lost none of her three children. These are now 13, 8 and 7 years old. The eldest earns 1/6 a week as boot boy, and receives in addition his breakfast and tea daily. The mother does rough washing at home, and works in the fields, earning, in fine weather, from 7/– to 8/–, and in wet 3/– to 4/–. She has also relief in kind to the value of 6/– weekly from the parish ; the total income being thus from 10/6 to 15/6 a week.

The mother and the children are not very bright, and the little girl is very hysterical. Mr. G., in his rare intervals of home life, does not behave ill to his wife, and his children are devoted to him. Mrs. G. declares that she would have had a judicial separation long ago, but was afraid that her husband would find her and kill her if she did—a fear that hardly seems justified by his previous career. This fear is said, however, to be common among the women of this district, many of them wishing for a judicial separation but dreading the violence of their husbands if the men afterwards discovered their place of abode.

YORKSHIRE.

B. L. Hutchins.

PART I.—INTRODUCTORY.

The chief occupation for women in the manufacturing towns of Yorkshire is the woollen and worsted trade. This trade employed altogether, according to the Census of 1911, the following numbers of women, omitting for the sake of simplicity a very small number of women sorters.

Carding and Combing	...	...	5,373
Spinning	...	...	...	...	41,235
Weaving	...	...	...	...	60,595
Other processes	...	...	...	4,831
Undefined	...	...	...	...	1,288
Total	...	...	113,322

Out of the total, 79·2 were single, 17·1 married, and 3·6 widowed.

It is obviously impossible within our limits to give any full description of the woollen and worsted trade on its technical side. The work varies greatly from district to district and from mill to mill, according to the nature of the fabric produced, the character of the firm, the development of machinery and technique, the organisation of workpeople, and other factors. For us an interesting feature is that in at least some sections of the woollen trade we do find that rare phenomenon, direct industrial competition between the sexes. In the Huddersfield and

Colne Valley woollen trade women work in direct competition with men in weaving and warping, and in competition with boys in piecing. The effect of women working in the weaving has been to reduce the wages of men weavers to such a point that it is a matter of indifference to the employer whether men or women are employed. The position has much changed in the last 30 years. In 1883 men were the standard weavers and women were paid something less than the men's scale. To-day, women are the standard weavers, and men are paid something more than the women's scale. To understand the change, we must look back a little further still. The year 1877 was the highest point of the " boom " in the woollen trade. Practically every man, woman and child available was absorbed by the industry. Irish workers in Yorkshire sent for their friends and relations. Generally speaking, good wages were earned without difficulty. In 1883 the " slump" had begun. Trained workers were abundant, and a move was made by the manufacturers to reduce wages and to standardise prices. The operatives resisted the reduction and a strike took place. The manufacturers won, and the price list was enforced which still forms the basis of calculation for wages.[1]

The 1883 list is based on the 50 pick loom, that is, looms running 50 picks per minute. A new loom was then introduced working 70–80 picks per minute. The original list was therefore reconsidered, and the manufacturers enforced a reduction on the 50 pick loom prices. In recent years further improvements have been made in machinery and one further reduction in loom prices has been enforced. It has been calculated by a statistical expert, who has kindly provided us with this information, that while the output of the loom since 1877 has practically doubled, the wage of the operative

[1] This list can be seen in a Board of Trade paper, Cd. 144 of 1900.

has remained almost stationary. It is estimated, in fact, that whereas the average earnings of weavers were 23/9 in 1877, in 1910 they were 23/10. Thus the whole of the advantage of improved machinery and increased output has in this particular trade been divided between the consumer and the manufacturer. Closer investigation however, shows that the present position of the operatives is somewhat more favourable than at first appears, for between 1877 and 1886 wages declined, the average dropping to 18/-. Since that date there has been a steady upward tendency.

The 100 pick looms now in use give more scope for efficiency in the operative. The weft runs out more quickly, the efficient weaver will shuttle quickly and thus gain time on the slower operatives, and at the end of the week will draw a much higher wage, so that while the average wage for women may be 20/6 to 21/-, and the average wage for men 27/6 to 28/-, the range is much greater, namely : women from 16/- to 25/- and men from 21/- to 35/-. These figures are based on full time employment, women working 55½ hours per week, men 58 hours per week. In short, the wages are now equal to the "boom" year of 1877, with the advantage to the efficient operative. The inefficient operative is no better off than in 1877. The manufacturer argues that there is no more work for an operative on an 80 pick loom than on a 50 pick loom, and that he should therefore have all the difference to share between himself and the consumer. The operative argues, however, that greater speed involves greater nerve strain, and claims that he should be paid in proportion to the output.

The reasons for the differentiation of women and men weavers are stated to be :—

(1) The women's wage would not attract men to the industry, and the manufacturers must have men for overtime and night work.

(2) Men can earn more per unit of time ; that is, the productivity of the machine is greater with men weavers.

(3) The men require less help from tuners. Men usually tune their own looms.

Some firms will not have women weavers, others will not have men weavers, or as few as possible. In the heavy woollen trade there is said to be no special advantage in employing women rather than men. It is not uncommon to find a woman and her husband working side by side in the same shed on identical looms. In the making of woollen stuffs for men's clothing three conditions may be noticed. In the woollen trade proper men preponderate in some mills, women in others. In the fine woollen or cloth trade men preponderate. In the lower class, worsted, women are in a large majority.

For warping, in some mills men and women are paid exactly the same. The best women will earn as much as the best men, but the average woman will earn less than the average man. In worsted warping, a higher standard of skill is required, and men are mostly employed, at an average wage of 34/-. In the woollen warping it is more a question of the amount to be done, and women predominate, their average wage being 26/- to 27/-. Speaking generally, where men and women are paid on exactly the same wage list, the men will earn an average of 3/- more than the women. Warping is considered the alternative to weaving as a skilled occupation for women The numbers employed in warping have increased, and the number of women has increased at a greater rate than the number of men. This increase is due mainly to modern warping machinery.

In spinning the masters are considering the advisability of substituting women and girls, as piecers, for men and boys. The supply of male labour is inadequate, and " piecing " is a blind alley occupation, with no prospect of advancement. Although women are in competition with men in weaving and warping, and with boys in piecing, it cannot be stated that they are ousting the men from either of these processes. All boy labour is running short.

It is not uninteresting to note that in Bradford, where the leading industry is the making of dress stuffs for women's wear, employment is much more unstable and irregular than in the Huddersfield district, where cloth for men's clothes is made. The difference is due to the fact that in the Huddersfield trade the employers combine to dovetail work, so as to lessen the seasonal fluctuation. In the manufacture of women's wear the caprice of fashion, it is said, makes any such arrangement difficult or even impossible.

The competition between men and women weavers noted in this district is a rare phenomenon,[1] and as such we have here given it some space. It is not, however, a constant feature, even in the Yorkshire weaving trade. Thus from a mill at Bradford we learn that the work done by men and women is distinct. The men work the broad looms, and some of them work the old hand looms in pattern making, while the women work the ordinary power looms. In this mill the proportion of women had increased. Again, in woolcombing there appears to be little if any real sex competition. We learn from information supplied by one firm, that in their business no men do the same work as women, except those who work on the night turn. The women's wage is the standard rate for one kind of work, and " if it were possible to deal with the quantity of work available for combing in the daytime only, we should not have to pay men for

---

[1] See " Problems of Modern Industry," by S. and B. Webb, pp. 94-95, and Report on Women's Labour to the Economic Section of the British Association for the Advancement of Science. Southport, 1903.

doing this kind of work." A somewhat more detailed account of work in another woolcombing mill is given. The first process—sorting—is done by men. The second process—washing—is done by machinery tended by men. The wool is then dried by hot air and carded, after which it is " back washed " in a machine constructed on the same principle as that used in the former process, but much smaller. These machines are tended by women. After the second or " back " washing, the wool is passed through three or four machines, each finer than the last. This is called " punch-balling." The long ropes are then " boxed," and women are employed in this process, which consists in uniting 10 or 12 strands into one. Two young men were, however, working on two of these machines, but only for the reason that the wool had to be brought downstairs in bales too heavy for the women to carry. In some other cases men are employed on the same kind of work as women, but they card a heavier wool and work heavier machines. They are able, also, to keep their machine running more continuously, so that the actual output per hour is more. The master of this mill admitted, however, that the difference between men and women's wages was partly due to custom and tradition, and could not be entirely accounted for by difference of work or output.

FAMILIES OF MARRIED AND WIDOWED WORKERS.

The material obtained by an investigation such as the present, initiated and financed by private persons, lends itself only to a limited extent to statistical methods. The numbers are too small, and the classifications used are apt not to be sharply defined, but to merge gradually. In the preparation of the present chapter it is found possible to reduce only certain very simple relations to statistics, and in these cases considerable qualification is necessary in using the results. The cases examined numbered 95, and in these 95 families there were 213 living children, and 103 dead children were mentioned to the investigator. This gives a proportion of 3·3 children (living and dead) per family, and of the total children no less than 32·6 were deceased, exclusive of still-births.[1]

If we tabulate the mortality according to industry, the results are as follows :—

CHILDREN.

Occupation.	No. of Women.	Children.		Stillbirths.	Mis-carriages.
		Living.	Dead.		
Weavers ...	26	55	42	3	3
Woolcombers	18	50	4	5	—
Spinners ...	14	25	6	—	1
Warpers and Winders ...	11	15	2	—	—
Ragpickers...	10	27	30	3	5
Sheffield Trades ...	9	32	15	—	2
Miscellaneous	7	9	4	—	—
	95	213	103	11	11

It will be observed at once that the cases are too few to give a fair basis of comparison between industries. The weavers and ragpickers appear with a conspicuously heavy mortality of children, but this is partly due to the fact that one weaver on the list had lost 11 children and reared none, and one ragpicker had lost 9 and reared one, and these two cases have considerable influence, the numbers being small.

[1] The information as to still-births and miscarriages may be incomplete.

Reasons Given for Going Out to Work.

It is not possible to find a perfectly clear classification of reasons for going out to work. But on the whole, although the information given is not always adequate, the motives given seem to fall into the six classes given below. It is true that some of the classes rather overlap.

In every case the cause has been assigned to that motive which appeared most important and compelling.

No. of Women.	Per cent. of total.	Reasons for going to work.
6	6·3	Widowhood.
60	63·2	Insufficiency of husband's earnings.
4	4·2	The husband not giving enough of his earnings.
5	5·3	Drinking habits of husband.[1]
8	8·4	Desertion or separation.
6	6·3	Preference for outside work.
6	6·3	No definite reason.
95	100·0	

We thus find that in an overwhelming majority of cases where the wife works she does so because she otherwise cannot get enough money to pay her way and feed her household, and these figures, small as the numbers are, give, I cannot but think, a just view. There is the small group where the husband is callous and selfish, keeps his money himself, or drinks it, or deserts his wife. There is also the small group of women who go to the factory because they like it. But in the majority of cases the

[1] In a few other cases it is mentioned that the husband drank, but not apparently to such an extent as to constitute the wife's main reason for seeking employment.

woman is driven to the factory by the economic cause, although, as will appear below, among those who work because their income is otherwise insufficient, there is some divergence of opinion as to the nature of industrial employment itself, some women viewing the necessity with great dislike, others with tolerance, or even pleasure. Inadequate as is the material from the statistical point of view, the cases described at the end of this chapter will be found to give a good deal of insight into the working woman's point of view.

There is first the extreme exertion involved in the combination of industrial work for nine or ten hours with the duties of nurse, cook, housemaid, and maker of clothes, which begin and conclude the day. It is also still usual in this class and locality to bake bread at home. We read that Mrs. A. (No. 8), for instance, on occasion, has stayed up all night to get her washing, cleaning and baking done. Again, Mrs. E. (No. 10) thinks that industrial work alone, or housework and child-bearing alone, would not be too much, it is the combined strain that is " wearing her out." Every night in the week (save Sunday) has its allotted household duty, baking, cleaning, washing, etc. Again Mrs. D. (No. 17) says her work doesn't hurt her, it is having to set to work again, doing two women's work, that is " wearing her out." Mrs. D. (No. 7) owns to having sat up all night to make or mend children's clothes, and says she gets " run down with overwork." Indeed the extraordinary pluck, industry, and tenacity shown by women who under such a strain continue, as some do, to keep house and children clean and tidy, is worth commending to those arm-chair pessimists who discourse of the " decadence of the race." [1]

---

[1] A pathetically ironic phrase current among the women is " going to Blackpool," which means neither more nor less than going home for the arrival of a baby. " Blackpool " is West

Another grave evil is the almost inevitable neglect of children, from babyhood upwards.

In old times, we learn, women were permitted to bring their babies to the mill and put them in a basket near the loom, but this is no longer permitted. The necessity of taking the baby out early in the morning and leaving it in a neighbour's charge till evening is bitterly resented by some women. Some, also, though feeling no injury to their own health through work, own that it involves neglect of their home and children. Economic pressure may demand this sacrifice, but some of these women consider that great discomfort is caused by the absence of the mother at the mill, others dilate on the anxiety they suffer from the thought of the children going uncared for, and running risks from fire, etc. Sometimes the unemployed husband is pressed into the service and strictly forbidden to leave the house until the breadwinner wife returns.

In only one of these cases is there anything like evidence of the husband's character being demoralised by the wife's working. Mrs. F. (No. 3) inherited a small business from her mother. Her husband had a good business of his own, but gradually took to drink, idleness, and dissipation. She ascribes his degradation to her having continued her own work, instead of throwing the whole responsibility of the household on his shoulders. In several cases, however, the husband is described as doing his best, when out of work, to help the wife tend the children, and even wash the clothes and so on. In the cases where the husband is described as bad or neglectful, there is no evidence to show whether the wife's employment had affected his character in any way.

It must be said, however, that while many of these

Riding for a holiday; but the nearest approach to a holiday some of these poor women ever have is the fortnight in bed on the occasion of their confinements.

cases demonstrate the employment of married women to
be an evil, it appears not so much as an evil *per se*, as
the effect or result of evil circumstances.   As Mrs. A.
(No. 23) says pathetically, she " does not work for pride,"
or for dress, or for savings, but to obtain some measure
of comfort for the children.   Again, Mrs. A. (No. 24)
thinks no woman would go out to work, if she could afford
to stay at home.   Mrs. A. (No. 25) does not believe in
married women working for wages, but thinks it worse
to get into debt.   Mrs. A. (No. 2), who stayed at home
with her children when they were babies, and had at times
to manage on 17/– a week, when it was all her husband
could manage to give her, now thinks she might have
done better to go out more and earn some money.   Mrs.
A. (No. 8), who also stayed at home with her babies, but
lost no less than 11 children in infancy and babyhood,
thinks she may have been mistaken to stay at home with
them.   She was badly nourished, and thinks she might
have done better to earn money for food, even at the
risk of less personal care and attention.   It is well to
emphasise such cases, for there is no doubt an impression among some sections of the upper classes that women
go out to the factory from a craving for society, associated
work, talk, and so on.   There are such cases, no doubt ;
the present evidence contains a record of several women
who " like the factory," or feel " it's like home to work
at ——'s."   But such cases are rare.   As far as the
evidence from Yorkshire goes, the married women are pre-
dominantly, even fiercely, domesticated in their tastes and
feelings.   Again and again it is recorded that they think
no married woman would work unless she must ; and the
impression is evidently strong that if men's wages were
higher married women would not need to work for wages.
When they do so work, in a large majority of cases it is
to keep out of debt, to help build the home, to supplement
the man's insufficient earnings.   In cases of widowhood,

desertion, or husband's invalidity, as we have seen, the wife's earnings are the sole income of the family. In Mrs. D.'s (No. 15) simple words, " she would rather stop at home, but the children must be fed."

In short, poverty and low wages in nine cases out of ten are the causes that drive married women into the labour market. And poverty is seen here, as in other recent enquiries, to be due in a very large proportion of cases to irregularity of employment. This is not the place to enter on a subject which has been treated with such distinguished ability by Mr. Beveridge in his book on " Unemployment," and by Mrs. Sidney Webb and her colleagues in the Minority Report of the Poor Law Commission, Part II. It is only necessary here to point out that the irregular employment of men is not only a grave evil *per se*, but is a direct inducement of married women's work. Thus, to take a few cases only : of Mrs. E. (No. 1) we read that her husband, a miner, gets only 3 days' work a week ; of Mrs. E. (No. 4) that her husband, a pitman, averages only 4 days' work and 14/- wages per week. Mrs. E. (No. 5) has a husband who " brings it all home now," but he gets only 3 days' work at the mines and earns 12/- to 14/-. Mrs. E.'s (No. 10) husband could earn £1 a week full time, but the pits are being worked out or have bad seams, and there are long periods of short time.[1]

" Night combing " also appears as a highly irregular trade, which may be partly due to the unhealthiness of night-work. Mr. D. (No. 13) is a night-comber, very sickly, and suffering from an ulcerated stomach. His wife cannot depend on any regular income from him. She says " if he earned 25/- he would give her £1. But he can't give it if he hasn't got it." Mrs. D. (No. 17) remarks

[1] This account of Mrs. E.'s (No. 10) working experiences, collected in 1909, had a special interest in March, 1912, as an illustration of the troubles in the coal trade.

that "you can't say you have a pound a week regular with a night man," for they are the first to be stopped if work is slack. This statement is confirmed by information given independently by a trade union secretary, who says that with the slightest falling off in the trade the night men are stopped. They are engaged from night to night ; so that it is quite possible to find a comber at times earning 31/– a week, whose weekly average for the year will not exceed 9/–.

OPINIONS OF EMPLOYERS AND FOREMEN.

Some employers seem inclined to discourage the employment of married women workers, on grounds of morality and domesticity, a few because they think married women are more irregular and waste time more. Most seem however to regard the matter with indifference from the economic point of view. There is indirect evidence that married women workers are often highly valued in the fact that they are allowed, in some places, when they have a baby, to arrange for a substitute, and to return to their post later on. In one large mill the foreman in the " slubbing " room said the married women came in only three or four days a week, but he made no difference as long as the work got done. In another department of the same mill the foreman did not ask the women whether they were married or single, but in the " winding " room the foreman discouraged married women, and preferred not to employ them unless he were very much pressed, in which case he would perhaps send for some married women, by preference such as had worked for him before marriage. In two cases, foremen thought married women worked with a greater sense of responsibility, but one of these added that " they broke time oftener." The employer of another mill said he did not interfere or inquire if the women were married or single, so long as they kept time and could do their work, but this gentleman and his sister, living with him, both believed that if the husband earned enough, the woman with children would stay at home. Another employer thinks that in respect of quality or regularity of work there is no difference between single and married women. He also thinks there is a decrease[1] in the number of married women as compared with single, but does not attribute this to any conscious policy on the part of the employers. On the other hand, in a large and important mill run on co-partnership principles, women have to leave on marriage, but each woman who gets married receives a portion of £5 or £10 according to length of service. Reasons given for this regulation were (1) the neglect of children ; (2) the idea that the presence of pregnant women at the looms tends to the deterioration of young girls. The manager of another mill thinks that the employment of married women is not only prejudicial to home comfort, but has a tendency to prevent a rise in the standard of conditions.

It will be observed that these adverse opinions do not deal with the question of employment induced by poverty and necessity. This is recognised by a lady inspector in one of the most important woollen towns, who, while expressing the opinion that the employment of married women is detrimental to home life, added that economic pressure is so great that under present conditions married women often *must* go out. She is in favour of making a legislative experiment on the lines of prohibiting such employment and granting maintenance. This experiment would be limited to the group of mothers who had lost the breadwinner.

In conclusion, it may not be out of place to say a few words on the subject of the woman who really does like

[1] Another employer, however, thought an increase was perceptible, and attributed it to the decreased earnings of men.

factory work better than staying at home. For reasons given above, it appears to the present writer that this type neither is nor is likely to be numerously represented. But it undoubtedly exists, and is not without sociological interest. The investigator met one woman who worked as a wool-comber, having been first ill-treated and then deserted by her husband ; she had had six children of whom four had lived. She was miserable at home (the said home being in a terrible slum) and " as happy in t'mill as a queen in her drawing-room." A few cases somewhat similar may be discovered among those collected below. They are evidence, as it seems to me, of a growing sense in some women that work is a thing to take a pride and a pleasure in. There seems to be little doubt that women are developing far more industrial skill and ability than formerly. Our investigator was shown a new machine which, it had been asserted, no woman could ever work ; but one woman did learn to work it and taught several others. And undoubtedly in some cases women who take this pride in work, and have achieved their measure of skill and efficiency, will wish to continue at it after marriage, and will prefer to pay someone else to perform nursery work for their children. Has society any right to penalise these women, unless neglect or ill-treatment of the children be discovered ? In the well-to-do-classes of society it is a matter of course to employ paid help and service for young children, whether the mother has a profession to occupy her or not. Any attentively obser-vant person who has even a moderately wide circle of acquaintance can soon satisfy himself that there exists a certain proportion of women who may be quite capable of producing fine and healthy children, but have no natural gift for looking after them. It is unreasonable that in one class women should be bitterly blamed for finding a substitute for nursery work while, in another, such action is regarded as quite normal. The points at issue that urgently concern society are first, a proper period of rest for the mother before and after child-birth, during which society should surely provide for her needs if she has no husband or relations to do so for her. Secondly, that the children should be properly tended ; failure in that respect should be by all means brought home to erring parents without delay. But apart from neglect, there seems no reason to condemn the women who would rather earn for their children than stay at home and do their housework. In the industrial class such women do not appear to be many ; if men were well-paid, numbers of married women would be only too happy to stay at home. The tragedy of the domesticated woman who is driven abroad to earn has been amply demonstrated above. But all women are not of the same type. The mother who prefers to work may have quite as much mother love, and although clinging less to home, may very likely have a wider knowledge of life, a keener sense of citizenship, than the domesticated woman, and thus possibly make up to her children in one way what she lacks in another. " It takes all sorts to make a world."

PART II.—REPRESENTATIVE CASES. [1]

A.—WEAVERS.

THE largest section of our enquiry is that of the women weavers, who number 26. The first, whom we will call Mrs. A1, works only when her husband's work is slack. She stayed at home with her children until they could walk, and all were breast-fed. In spite of this precaution, out of six children she has lost four. Her wages are not often more than 8/-, and her husband's vary from 15/- to £1 a week.

[1] The reader is reminded that these cases were studied at a time previous to the recent trade boom.

Mrs. A2 also has not been a regular worker, since marriage. She stayed at home with the children when they were babies, and all are living. One is now, at 17, earning 18/– a week, and the other three are at school. Mrs. A2 has worked as often as she got the chance in the last two years, and is inclined to think she had better have gone out more, instead of trying to keep five persons on an income of 17/– a week, which she had to do at one time. " Then they clemmed." She now acts as what is called a " sick-weaver," which locally means, not a weaver who is herself in bad health, but one who is acting as substitute for a sick friend. Mrs. A2 averaged 14/– a week in the last five weeks before the visit. Her husband, a power loom tuner, is on short time. His standing wage is 30/–, but he has had much slack time through illness and slack trade.

Mrs. A5 is a woman of 54, having worked regularly both before and after marriage, with only short breaks. Her husband suffers from chronic bronchitis, and she is compelled to work in the mill. " Does not want to— could find enough to do at home." She has three children living, 22, 17 and 9 years old—one boy died. The first two children were put out to nurse and she paid 4/– a week for " minding " and 1/– for milk. She used to take the baby out at 5.30 in the morning and fetch it home at 6 p.m., and thinks " it is a dreadful thing for a mother to have to do." She stayed at home for two years with each of the last two children. Mrs. A5 earned 10/– and 12/– in the last two weeks respectively; her husband has averaged under 6/– in four weeks, owing to slack trade and illness.

Mrs. A6 has worked since 13 years old, with a short interval at marriage, and some months off at the birth of each child. Her husband drank, developed consumption, and died. She has two children, lives with her parents, and earns about 15/– a week. She works a " fast loom," and thinks it has a great advantage for women; there is no climbing up on the loom as with the old slow loom she used to work. The elder child (son) earns 10/– at the mill. Owing to her parents' help she has not known real want, untoward as her marriage circumstances were.

Mrs. A7 (aged 50) has worked as regularly as she can, because her husband does not earn enough to keep her at home. But she thinks " wed women ought to stay at home," and would gladly do so if her man brought in £1 a week. Her earnings are slack and irregular. One grown-up married daughter.

Mrs. A8 began as a weaver at 15, married at 19, and stayed at home with her babies, not one of whom she has ever reared. Has had 11 children and three miscarriages, " an' nowt to show for it." The babies were partly breast-fed, partly bottle. One child lived to 3½, another to 3¼ years, the others 8 or 10 months. She ascribes the loss of them to insufficient food,[1] and even thinks she *might* have done better to put them out to nurse and go to work herself. She is described as a very thin but wiry woman. The husband is weakly and asthmatical. The house spotlessly clean, nicely furnished, plants, etc. Mrs. A8 is a quick worker and could weave a " worset " in 10 days or a fortnight, which would bring in 30/–. She could at times earn £1 a week for eight weeks together. But again she may be " playing " for a fortnight. This woman is an extraordinarily hard-working, independent-minded woman. When staying at home with the babies she earned many a shilling, perhaps as much as 3/– or 4/– a week, with her sewing machine. She has, on occasion, stopped up all night to get her own washing, baking and cleaning done. She and her husband are on good terms, and the bitterness of life to them has

---

[1] It is also hinted that the husband's weakly constitution may have had something to do with the mortality of their children.

been the loss of their little ones. Both disapprove of outside work for married women if the home can possibly be otherwise provided for. Both are tender to suffering and will share their meal with a hungry man or woman.

Mrs. A11 is the wife of a miner who was disabled by an accident. She is therefore compelled to work for her six living children. She has lost three children, who died under a year old in each case, from teething and constipation. One child is tubercular, and ought to be taken to the hospital as an out-patient, but the mother has no time to take it. The father looks after it at home. The other children are healthy and very beautiful. Mrs. A11 can earn 15/- to 18/- but work has been slack, she has not averaged 9/- a week lately. She thinks the mill work does not hurt her health, but compels her to neglect home and children. She always worked close up to her confinements and returned to work within a month or six weeks. Her children were, however, all breast-fed, and she is a very healthy woman, which she ascribes to having had plenty of good food when young.

Mrs. A12, a woman of 41, worked as a weaver for 18 years in one place, but has now left work for five years. Has had seven children, including twins. One twin and another child died in babyhood. She was working up to a month or two before confinement with the first five children, but was at home a year before the twins were born, and nursed the twin that died. She went to work because her husband's earnings were insufficient to keep the family ; now her elder children are earning she stays at home. Both she and her husband are strongly against married women going out to work. " If men had more wages women wouldn't go out to work."

Mrs. A16 goes to work because her husband's earnings are not sufficient, and they have to support her mother and his father. No children. She would prefer to stay at home, but if she did her mother would have to work.

She does all her own work except washing, makes her own clothes and sometimes sits up to midnight sewing. Mrs. A16 keeps an account of her earnings which averaged 17/6 in 1908 and 14/2 in the first 13 weeks of 1909. The difference is due to a change in the machinery. She cannot make as much off the new fast loom[1] as she did off the old slow one, though the firm she works for pays the best wages in the district. Also there was more short time in 1909. 1908 was a very good year.

Mrs. A18 (aged 60) has been twice married, and has worked "right on" both before and after marriage, to keep herself and children. The first husband drank, and died when she was 29. She was a widow 25 years and then married again. The second husband never had steady work, and is now almost speechless, and unable to walk, through an accident. She has two married daughters living, and has lost two sons. This poor woman had worked from the age of seven upwards (first child-minding, then as doffer, spinner, and at 21 as weaver), and has never known what it was to be free from poverty. At the time of the investigator's visit the couple were being evicted for arrears of rent. She could not earn more than 9/- or 10/- a week now, and the husband had not averaged 6/- weekly since their marriage.

Mrs. A19 began work as a half-timer at 11, sweeping and doffing, then became a spinner and is now a weaver. She has two living children and lost one. She likes going out to work, and her mother lives with her and looks after the children. The husband earns 18/- " when at work." The wife can earn 11/- a piece, which takes about four days' work, but the work is irregular, and she is at home now, and anxious to start work again.

Mrs. A20 married at 19, but soon discovered the man was bad. He drank, gambled, and knocked her about.

[1] But compare Mrs. A.6, supra.

She would not have children by such a man and left him. Has had very bad health at times, and is consumptive, but can support herself by weaving, and earns on an average 14/– a week. In spite of so much trouble Mrs. A20 is not unhappy. She has a friend similarly circumstanced and the two bear one another company. Both think the wife should stop at home if the husband is "a decent sort" and that there should be a minimum wage for men on which a family could live. Mrs. A20 thinks most women would rather stop at home if they could, and that men should be made to keep their wives and families.

Mrs. A22 was a domestic servant before marriage, then stayed at home two years, then learnt weaving, and has worked ever since. She does not like to give it up. She has only one daughter, who is now working as a mender and earns 15/–. "They all go out together and all come home together." She agrees in principle that married women should stay at home, and says that if she had had more children she would have done so. The family earn over £3, father and mother each 23/–, daughter 15/–.

Mrs. A23 has four children living and three who died at birth or in infancy. She worked regularly before marriage ; not regularly, but a good deal, afterwards. Her husband's earnings are not sufficient for their needs, viz., 23/– or 24/– a week. She "does not work for pride" or for dress, or for savings, but to keep the children in some comfort. "Before she will stop at home she must have £2 a week from her man." The eldest girl, aged 15, takes care of the house while the mother goes out. Mrs. A23 can earn 26/– when she gets a good week, but the work had been uncertain, her earnings irregular, and she had not had more than 15/– for weeks.

Mrs. A24 has no children. She was a weaver before marriage, stayed at home 10 years afterwards, and had returned to work for six years, on account of husband's illness. She thinks no woman would go out to work if she could afford to stay at home. She earns about 15/-.

Mrs. A25 works because her husband cannot earn enough to keep them. She does not believe in married women working for wages, but thinks it worse to get into debt. She has three children, all girls ; all were breast-fed. Has not lost any children. She has been overworked always and too frequently underfed. The husband works in a dangerous trade. He used to earn 25/- but the wages are being steadily lowered, and at time of visit were down to 13/- or 14/-. Mrs. A 25 sometimes does a day's washing, sometimes goes to the mills as " feeder " or " sick weaver " (*i.e.* substitute for a weaver taken ill).

Mrs. A26 is a widow woman of 69. She began work at the age of four ! selling tea-cakes from house to house ; at eight began rag-picking, and afterwards became a weaver. Mrs. A26 has worked regularly whenever she could get the work to do, until recently, when her health had broken down. She married at 18 ; her husband was then earning 24/- weekly and she 6/6. But with the invention of the self-acting mule he lost his trade, and subsequently became a blanket weaver at about the same wage. When the power looms were set up in her town, Mrs. A26 became a weaver and earned good wages, taking home as much as 34/- or 40/-. About 1880 there was a strike and the trade went to Bradford. Her husband, always sickly, ceased work in 1886, and she had to work for both and meet the expense of a protracted illness. Her savings disappeared, and when he died in 1891 she owed £12 for rent. She has paid off every penny of debt, but been unable to save anything. She went back recently to rag-picking at 10/- a week, in the hope of keeping off the Poor Law until she can claim her pension. The struggle for existence in this town is intensified by the smoke nuisance. Children cannot play for half an hour in the yard without getting grimy, and even self-respecting persons who wash their children and themselves at least once a day, appear very dirty after their day's work. Mrs. A 26 is clean in her habits with all these drawbacks, and the toil involved must be very great. In spite of all her troubles and hard work, Mrs. A 26 has brought up a large family. She has had 15 children, of whom seven are living, and 22 grandchildren. In the early days of her married life, when suckling a baby, she used to go home to breakfast, ten minutes walk each way and ten to suckle the baby and have breakfast. Her mother would get things ready for her. When the children could walk, she would have them at the mill, and put them in a basket out of the way, till she was ready to go home. This is no longer permitted. She usually remained at the loom until near her time (except with the youngest, when she was at home some months before and after), and she returned at the end of a month or three weeks.

It is touching to learn that this old lady, having been ill, was fearful she would not live long enough to draw her old age pension. Perhaps many a great soldier's pension has been less hardly earned.

B.—Sheffield Trades.

Mrs. B1 is a young widow of 29 with three children, whom she brings up on 11/- a week. She has lost one child. She did not work except for a short time between marriage and widowhood. She is able to get home in the middle of the day to get the children their dinner, and they are all of school age. Her work is drilling bayonets by machine, on which women have only recently been employed. Mrs. B1 says the women do not seem to think they are taking the place of men, but only of boys, but the men in the works grumble about the women taking their work. All the women's work is machine work.

C.—Spinners.

Mrs. C2 is a widow, aged 29. She had to go to work before her husband's death, as he was not earning enough —*viz.* 18/- as labourer. He died in the infirmary before the baby was born. She has two children, earns 9/- a week, and lives with her mother. Mrs. C2's mother is aged 56. Her husband deserted her 29 years ago. She worked as a child as sweeper, doffer and spinner, and from 16 to 35 as weaver, subsequently as charwoman, in which occupation she has a regular connection. Her husband " never gave her a farthing " and she " was glad to be quit of him." This courageous lady did not regard work as a hardship, but liked going to the mill, " 'twas like going home to work at ——'s." She has five children living, four of whom have homes of their own, and has lost four. She used to work right up to her confinement, " had no time to sit about and think of trouble," never had a doctor, but paid a midwife 5/6 to 6/-.

Mrs. C4 is only 22, and has lost her one baby from pneumonia, at nine months. It was breast-fed. The husband is not strong, works as night comber and gets ill. Mrs. C. tried working in a combing-mill but became so ill she nearly died. On the other hand her sister works at the same mill, likes it, and is a strong, healthy girl. Mrs. C4 will do charing or any work she can get. She was a spinner before marriage, and worked up to within six weeks of confinement. Husband earns 22/-, and she 10/-, when in full work, but both have had broken time, and sometimes do not make 15/- together.

Mrs. C7 has to work because her husband's earnings are not sufficient. He is an outdoor man. earns 24/9 in a full week, but seldom gets a full week, and Mrs. C7 earns 10/6 as a spinner. One son, 17, earning; one of 11, at school; one baby died. Mrs.

C7 would rather stop at home, she "can make the stuff go further."

Mrs. C9 dislikes working at the mill, but has had to do it, "first to get a home together," then because her husband was out of work. She started as half-timer at 11, and worked right on save for intervals at confinements (intervals not defined). She has had two children, both born at seven months, one died; the present baby, who is very frail, is now five months. She nursed it for four weeks, then started mill work again, and the milk disagreed with the baby, who is now bottle-fed. She earns 10/- and does not have to pay for child-minding as a neighbour does it out of kindness. The husband is a fine young man, and very handy, was engaged in washing his own shirt when the investigator called. He had been tramping all round the town, trying to get work, from five in the morning. The wife said, "He is a good husband," and he said with a laugh, "Fact is, Miss, we're too healthy, we want too much to eat." The neighbours have been very good to them.

Mrs. C10 only works when her husband has a drinking bout, which unfortunately appears to be a regular observance. She has three young children and expects another. House and children dirty and neglected. She earns only 9/- a week. The husband is a hawker and can earn £1 "when he's teetotal," otherwise gives her only 6d or 1/- a day. She is of a degraded type.

D.—Wool-combers.

Mrs. D3 works as a wool-comber, only because her husband is out of work. She thinks there should be a law "to prevent wed women from working and to give men better wages." She would stay at home if she got 24/- a week from her husband. They have three children, 3, 6 and 8. The eldest looks after the other two. She comes home to meals but never lights a fire till evening. The children, however, are allowed to run into a neighbour's, opposite. She does her own washing, baking and cleaning, and looks overworked, though fairly strong. She earns 13/-. Husband earns 24/- as " teazer " and gives her 21/-. This is when he is in work, he has been " tacking " 8 weeks. Mrs. D3 said, " We're not living, we barely exist." Even when her husband gets work again, there will be arrears of rent before she can stop at home.

Mrs. D5 works because her husband is delicate and suffers from bronchitis. She has three children, and has worked regularly save for breaks of about two months for her confinements. She had to wean them very early, her milk being poor when she returned to combing, but they are all strong children. They get rough in the streets, however, and she feels very anxious about them at her work. She takes little food, only biscuits and tea, while at the mill, and appeared much exhausted. She cannot average 10/- a week. " Many a night she doesn't see bed, trying to keep some clothes on her children's backs." The husband gets 26/- as night-comber, but cannot work regularly on account of his health. Eldest girl earns 4/6 as half-time spinner.

Mrs. D7 is a widow and has only her earnings to feed and clothe four children and herself. She has only 14/6 a week and cannot keep out of debt. Whenever footwear or other extra is needed, the rent drops behind. She rather likes her work (wool-combing), and has had good health. Her husband earned only 17/- a week, and she continued working after marriage to help build the home. She returned to work three or four weeks after the children's births, except in one case. She would gladly stay at home if she had a pound a week to live on. She gets run down with overwork, and sometimes sits up all night to make or mend the children's clothes.

Mrs. D8, 34, two children, has to work because her husband fell out of employment, and she bitterly resents the fact. " I'd gie t'air off o' my head to stop at hoame," she said vehemently. Every morning she leaves at 5.30 for the mill, having previously washed the baby and dressed both children, and leaves them in their father's care. She was ill-nourished before the baby's birth, and looks very thin and overworked. The first fortnight she went back to work the baby got " the rash." She got milk from some charitable fund for it, and five out of 16 bottles were sour, and it got diarrhœa. She says anxiety about it is killing her. Husband appears to be a steady man, does not drink or gamble, and is a member of his union, but rather stupid and " unable to hustle." He worked in one firm 16 years, but it failed 18 months after his marriage, and he has been unable to get work since. He had 36 weeks' club money (first 10/-, then 8/-, then 6/-), but this stopped at Christmas. Her wages are 10/6. They are trying to pay contributions to keep the husband in benefit. They have pawned whatever they can spare. This poor woman said her husband must mind the children, and couldn't go out to look for work, until she came home, as her " heart turned over wi't' thought o' child in the cradle alone."

Mrs. D11 likes work—" her husband couldn't keep her idle." She has two children earning, one full time, 12/6, another half time, 3/6 ; and four small children who are brought up by her mother. The husband earns 24/6 as labourer and Mrs. D11 earns 15/- as comber.

Mrs. D13 has a sickly husband, only just out of the infirmary. He has not earned more than three full weeks' money in 12 months. She works to keep the children from starving, but would much rather stop at home, " for there's no comfort for anybody." She would like " to stop married women working by law if men could get regular work." She has four girls 12 years old and under, and two tiny boys. She earns 12/– weekly, has 7/– from the Union, and the children have school meals and occasional treats. She has to pay 4/– for minding the two youngest. The rooms are quite unsuitable for a family, no sink, all waste water has to be carried out. Husband is a night comber when at work. If he got 25/– he would give her 21/–.

Mrs. D14 is a young woman of 23, with one baby. She works because her husband cannot earn enough. He makes £1, and she only 9/–. They have an invalid uncle dependent on them, and an aunt and Mrs. D14's mother live with them, the two latter earning respectively 8/– and 5/–. Mrs. D14 resents the low wages, and says neither her husband nor herself "get what they earn." She would much rather stop at home. If her husband earned 30/– he would give her 26/– and she could manage on that.

Mrs. D15 has had a strenuous life. She is now 38. She started as half-timer at 12, and worked regularly except at her confinements. When she was at home she took in washing. Her husband never worked regularly, and has left her for months at a time, but is said to be " a good worker except when he's in the drink." She would rather stop at home, " but the children must be fed." Her first four babies were born dead, and she has lost two others at eight and six weeks old. She has four children living. Gets five days' work a week, and earns 12/–.

Mrs. D16 did not work till her youngest child was nine years old. They lived in the country, her husband being a signalman, but afterwards he was shifted to town and she got work as a blanket winder. She now wishes she could have worked when the children were little—" they would have had more to eat "—and she prefers winding to house work. Her children are now grown up and earning ; all very healthy.

Mrs. D17 has one baby living, and lost three. She must work, but says, " If husbands had better wages the wives could stop at home." She works as a " back washer," the work does not hurt her, " it's having to come home and set to work again, doing two women's work, that's wearing her out." She earns 13/- standing wage when at work. Her husband is a night comber and gives her £1 a week when in work. But " you can't say you have a pound a week regular with a night man," for the night workers are the first to be stopped if work is slack.

E.—RAG-PICKERS.

Mrs. E1 is 35, and was married at 17. She works intermittently as a rag-picker, but at present is staying at home to nurse the baby (9 months), the said baby, however, being observed playing on a stone pavement and already able to stand alone. She has a girl of nine years old, and has lost four babies within a fortnight of their birth. She earns 12/- when at work. Her husband, a miner, who gets only about three days' work a week, earns 12/- to 14/-. Mrs. E1 is a remarkably fine, handsome woman, but dirty and slovenly and the children are " bundles of grime and rags."

Mrs. E3 is a sad case. She was married at 15, and her first child was born before she was 16. She has buried no less than nine children. She has one living, a girl at an industrial school, " the only thing I've got to live for," she said. The husband deserted her with another woman. The Guardians do not consider Mrs. E3 a fit person to bring up a girl, and do not allow visits.

Mrs. E4 worked from 13 years old till marriage (at 20), and fairly regularly since. Her husband's work is irregular, he cannot earn enough to keep a family. She has one daughter earning, four younger children, and has lost six in infancy or babyhood. She is delicate, and all her children have been bottle fed. She earns 11/-, with deductions for time off. Her husband earns about 14/- as a pitman (averaging only four days' work a week), her daughter 6/–. She bakes three stone of flour every week and does her own washing and cleaning. She thinks married women should stay at home. " They've plenty to do there," but " I can't afford to stay home yet."

Mrs E5 has worked both before and after marriage. At first (after marriage) it was, in the expressive north country phrase, "to build the home"; afterwards, because of her large family, her husband's earnings being insufficient. She has seven children, of whom only the eldest is earning. She lost three others in babyhood. She earns 12/–, but cannot work full time every week. Her husband earns 12 or 14/– for three days' work at the mines. He " brings it all home now." He used to drink, but one Christmas he had been fined 11/6 for being drunk, and they had to go without food. He became a teetotaller from that time.

Mrs. E10 worked as a weaver before marriage, and continued at the looms until her first child was coming. She gladly stays at home when her children are young, and her husband in work, but for many years he has had periods of under-employment, and she has been compelled to go out. She now works as a rag-picker. He is a miner and has worked in the pit for 20 years. She has three little boys, 9, 5, and 1 year old. With the eldest and youngest she stayed at home only about a month, with the second she was at home 1 year and 9 months, and she says " he is the healthiest of the lot." The baby was born during the long slack time (1908), and she was herself insufficiently fed, and had to work " while feeling fit to drop." She has nursed all her babies. In her first pregnancy she had an accidental blow at the mill, for which, apparently, no one was to blame, and this child and two others were stillborn. Two others died in infancy. In all these confinements she was away from work only one month. She is not quite certain of the order in which the births occurred, but thinks her eldest living child was her third, and the one of five years old was the fifth. The children are washed all over once a week, and their hands and faces at least once a day. The two elder look healthy, but run wild when not at school. The baby is very sickly and ill-nourished. Mrs. E10 has very poor health herself. She thinks the work alone, or the housework and child-bearing alone, would not be too much for her, but the combined strain is wearing her out. She does her own washing, baking, cleaning, cooking, mending and sometimes making of clothes. She washes on Monday night, on Tuesday finishes the wash, mangles and mends. On Wednesday and Thursday nights she turns out the room, and on Friday bakes the bread. On Saturday— pay day—she goes to market. Her husband will walk to a more important market on Saturday nights, to buy a bit of meat cheap from the Butchers' Auction. In this way they " can get enough meat for 1/- to make Sunday's dinner and have a bit over for Monday and Tuesday " (for a family of 5 !) The wife and children often have to leave the meat for the father and do with potatoes and gravy themselves, not that he is greedy, but " she wills it so "[1]. He is a man who does his best, and would gladly, if he could, be the breadwinner for his family. He brings home all his earnings, and they agree together on the amount of " spending brass " he can keep for himself, " an' that's nowt, most weeks." On Sunday she cooks dinner and mends clothes. Mrs. E10 is a capable worker, and has been a twister and a weaver. She is now paid 12/- standing wage as a rag-picker, but all short time is deducted. In the week of the investigator's visit (the week following Easter) she drew only 3/10, and her husband only 7/-. His full time earnings are £1 0s. 2d., but the pits are being worked out, or have bad seams, and there are long periods of short hours. He most often works three days a week, and draws 12/- or 14/-. Mrs.

[1] *i.e.*, The breadwinner *must* be nourished.

E10 much prefers to stay at home when he is earning
enough to keep them out of debt. They have not had
poor relief. He is in the Miners' Union, and would have
lapsed but for his wife, who paid his arrears out of her
earnings. She will not go into debt for dress or food.
When they have no money they go without, unless a
neighbour brings food, and that often happens, because
when she has anything to give she never refuses food to a
hungry woman or child. Of this woman the investigator
remarks: " Her courage is magnificent." It would be
almost an impertinence to add further comment to such a
record.

F.—Miscellaneous Cases.

Mrs. F1 has no children. She does not approve of
women who have children going out to work, and intends
to stay at home when she has any. In the meantime she
works a " harness loom," and enjoys it, and says the
women " sing at their work." She had kept a record of
earnings for 16 weeks, ranging from nothing in one week
to 23/9 in another; average 15/9¾.

Mrs. F3 has a small business of her own, viz., corset
making. She worked at first, after marriage, with her
mother, whose business it then was, in order to improve
her position, and then because her husband did not give
her enough of his earnings. He was a butcher and had
a good business, but took to idleness, drink and dissipation. She has more than once in her 16 years of married
life saved £200 or £300, but it all went, first in
an attempt to save her husband's business, and afterwards to pay his expenses to America. Mrs. F3 has had
a very sad life, and believes that her husband's deterioration is partly due to her continuing work after marriage.
Her view is that " men are not self-controlled enough to
do without the steadying influence of responsibility."
She also told the investigator the story of a connection

of hers, a married woman who had a dressmaking business. One day the husband said, " You've made four dresses this week, you can do with less from me this week." The wife promptly replied, " No, I can't, and what's more, I'll never make another dress for other women ! " Mrs. F3's comment was : " And she has kept her word, her husband and her happiness." Mrs. F3 is in fairly comfortable circumstances and can spend 35/- a week on her clothes and housekeeping, but she is very much overworked and works excessive hours, starting regularly at 6 a.m. and continuing sometimes to 11 p.m. She has one boy of 13, who has done well at school, and is now office boy to a solicitor at 5/- a week. She lost one baby soon after birth. She stitched 25 pairs of corsets in the morning of the day it was born, and began work again in a fortnight. The husband is reported to be doing well in America and wishes her to join him.

Warpers and Winders.

Mrs. G2 is only 25, and is working till her first child comes, to get a bit in hand. She will stay at home then. She is not in favour of married women's work being prohibited, but thinks the health authorities should have power to give maintenance grants to married women. Wages not stated. Her husband is a spinner, earning 18/- to 25/-.

Mrs G3 works because her husband is in a lunatic asylum. She is very delicate, would be thankful to stay at home if she could, and thinks married women only go to work when they must. Her standing wage is 15/-.

Mrs. G11 is 50. She stayed at home when her children were little. Now both are married, and she wishes to add to her comforts, and also feels too lonely at home, and prefers to work when she can.

MANCHESTER.

W. ELKIN.

WHEN questions connected with married women's work are under discussion, it is extraordinary how frequently people, who are not in close contact with these particular problems, will argue to some much cherished conclusion, and ignore the vital question—why married women work. They often assume that economic necessity need not be considered as a possible explanation, or if they do not make this tacit assumption, at least imply that the same explanation can be given in all cases. It needs but little consideration to realise how completely arguments may be vitiated by this inaccuracy. In such questions as the connection between the rate of infant mortality and married women's work, it is obviously of vital importance to know the exact reason why the mother leaves the work which is ready to hand in the home, and seeks instead for work in the labour market. People often speak as if there could be no other answer than that the women prefer work in the factories, that they find it more interesting and more sociable than the combined duties of nurse and housekeeper in the home. It is clear that this could not apply to the very large number of women who do industrial work at home, and it is certainly wholly untrue as far as Manchester is concerned, where in the overwhelming majority of cases economic pressure alone was the explanation, in spite of the fact that slightly more than half the cases were concerned with women in the cotton trade, where it is customary for women to continue their occupation after

marriage. There were in all 120 cases, though in 13 no
reason was given for going to work. Amongst the 107
cases relevant to this particular subject, there were only six
whose position as wage-earners could be explained only
by their desire to have regular employment ; that they
liked working in a factory, or that they get tired of
being at home were the reasons given.

As a contrast to these women, who evidently regarded
their work primarily as a pleasant means of passing the
time, were the women who either temporarily or permanently were the sole or chief wage-earner for the whole
family. There were nine cases of widows, and four of
deserted wives, and in addition a considerable number of
married women who for the time being were forced to fill
the place of the husband as breadwinner. This latter
division included seven women whose husbands were ill,
one whose husband drank, and 11 cases where the man
was out of work. That is to say, there were in all 32
cases where the woman worked as the chief wage-earner
of the family. In two cases this meant that she alone
supported herself and her husband, and in 13 cases
there were young children to support as well ; the others
were helped either by children who had passed the school
age or by other relations who contributed towards the
expenses of the household, but even in these cases the
wife's wage was indispensable.

Amongst the women whose husbands were able to
work, there were three who earned also so that they might
support their own relations, a child by an earlier marriage of the mother, and there was one woman, evidently
with a love of independence, who said she worked so that
she might have something for herself. In every other
case, 65 in all, the reason given for the fact that the wife
went out to work was that she wished to supplement her
husband's wage. Exactly what degree of necessity is
implied by this phrase it is impossible to tell, without con-

sidering the exact circumstances of each family. A few
of the women worked for a definite purpose, to pay the
doctor's bill, or the cost of the furniture in a new home,
which practically meant that the wife was preventing
the accumulation of a debt, which would otherwise
probably have been a perpetual drain on the resources
of the family. But in any case, where the margin for
anything beyond the absolutely necessary expenditure is
small, an addition of even a few shillings a week may
become of vital importance, though exactly to what
extent this is so can only be realised by examining the
wages earned by the wife and the rest of the family.

The following table gives the wages according to the
different trades investigated. The cases in which the
wife was the sole supporter of the family have not been
reckoned in working out the contribution of the husband
and other members of the household. so as to give some
idea of the position where the wife's earnings were only
supplementary. The column giving the average income
for the whole family, on the other hand, includes all cases.

The amounts given as the wages of the rest of the family
are probably slightly under-estimated, as in many cases
it was the money that the husband gave his wife and not
his actual wages about which information was obtained ;
either the wife did not know his actual wage or else he
kept back some settled sum as pocket-money. This
would not, however, make any very considerable difference.
Apart from this possible modification, the particulars
given in each case of the wages brought in by the husband
or the children show that they rarely amounted to more
than 30/-, and the average, as has been shown, was between 21/- and 22/-. Considering that this sum was
needed to pay the rent, feed and clothe not only the
husband and wife, but perhaps three or four children
not yet earning, it is abundantly clear that even if it
were not necessary for the bare existence of the home

that the wife should help to swell the family income, it
would at least make an extraordinary difference, certainly
to the comfort, and probably to the health of the whole
household. An extra 10/- to a family income of 22/-,
may just be sufficient to prevent absolute squalor, and
whatever disadvantages may arise when the wife has to
be out of the house the greater part of the day, which
means too that she probably returns tired out, it is always
necessary to balance against these evils the extra food
or housing room, the additional comfort generally, that
her wages represent.

The sum of 10/8 given as the average of the wages for
the women in all the trades does not of course give a
very representative idea of their earnings, considering the
wide divergencies in the nature of the different trades.
The handkerchief hemmers were all home-workers, and
amongst the shirtmakers there were only three women
working in a factory. Of the women employed in the
miscellaneous trades three were homeworkers; two
made quilts and one covered umbrellas. The factory
workers under this head, 12 in all, included women in
various branches of the ready-made clothing trade, a
machine feeder in some lithograph works, and one woman
who worked in a calico bag factory. There was also one
woman earning 1/6 a week preparing potatoes in a chip
shop. Apart from these few factory workers the investigations in Manchester were concerned only with two
extreme types of women's work. On the one hand were
the home workers, with their entire lack of organisation—
only two belonged to the Homeworkers' Union—isolated
from each other, and suffering from the results of the
complete confusion that appears to prevail in these
trades. On the other hand were the women working in
the cotton trade, where they form a compact organised
body, with the force of the men's unions behind them and
recognised union rates of wages. No general statement

Trade.	No. of cases.	Wife's wages.			Wages of rest of family.			Wages for whole family.		
		Max.	Min.	Average.	Max.	Min.	Average.	Max.	Min.	Average.
Shirtmaking ...	20	16/6	4/-	8/1	53/-	9/-	24/1	63/-	19/10	28/9
Handkerchief hemmers ...	8	10/-	2/-	5/3½	43/3	18/-	24/9½	53/3	20/-	28/4
Weavers	18	20/-	5/-	13/7	38/-	5/-	23/4½	57/-	12/-	34/3
Reelers and winders	12	16/-	5/6	11/4½	38/-	18/-	23/1	44/-	8/-	28/10
Other occupations in the cotton trade	33	19/6	6/-	11/9	29/6	8/9	13/5	58/-	9/-	26/4¼
Miscellaneous ...	12	15/-	1/6	10/3½	34/-	12/-	21/3½	40/-	12/-	27/8
All cases ...	Average	...	...	10/8			21/8½			28/11

or comparison of the causes affecting wages can be possible under the circumstances.

The cases of exceptionally low wages all occur, as would be expected, in the home trades. There were in all only eight women earning less then 5/- a week, and it is noticeable that the wages earned by the husband or other contributors in these cases are distinctly lower than the average either for the particular trade or for all trades. The following details give some idea of the position of these women and the families they were helping to support.

Shirtmakers :

Woman earning 4/-, owing to bad health; husband a platelayer earning 20/-.

Woman earning 2/-; husband on the railway earning 17/10

Woman earning 4/- ; husband a mechanic earning 23/-.

Handkerchief hemmers :

Woman earning 4/-; deserted wife living with a married daughter and sons.

Woman earning 2/8 ; widow living with a daughter who earns 24/- and 5/- paid by a lodger.

Woman earning 2/-; husband an ironmoulder, earning 18/-. The husband had only just gone back to work after an illness of 26 weeks. The wife had not worked before this.

Woman earning 4/6; husband a labourer, gives 18/-.

Miscellaneous Trades—Woman earning 1/6 preparing potatoes. A widow living with her son, who is consumptive, earns 18/- when he is well enough.

These details show that on the whole where the wife's contribution was abnormally small the family, even apart from this, was in a particularly weak position. Any attempt to draw a conclusion from so small a number of cases, is of course absolutely impossible, but the facts, so far as they go, lend no support to the view that the women who accept work at particularly low wages have less need of the money than the majority of women who work. It is often assumed that when women wish to make a little extra money they do not mind whether it is a shilling or so more or less, that they undersell others and accept these astoundingly low wages, which would be entirely insufficient if they depended for their support on their own efforts. But there is always the other side of the case, which must not be overlooked ; for when the money is not of such vital importance, it is possible that it will have the result of making the women less willing to accept work which gives a very small return compared with the time and trouble that has to be expended on it ; whereas in cases of extreme need, they may be prepared to take anything, however badly paid, rather than refuse and run the risk of a long delay before anything better can be found.

It is however undeniably true that excepting some of the weavers, very few of the women earned a tolerable living wage, although, as was pointed out above, some of them had to keep both themselves and their family. How they managed to do so on wages ranging in these particular cases from 5/- to 17/- it is difficult to imagine. In one family, for example, where there were two young children, the wife was employed in making pinafores and aprons. The work came in rushes, and her earnings in consequence were most irregular ; for the preceding three weeks they had been 10/6, 5/- and 2/6 respectively, and averaged on the whole about 5/-. The husband was a fitter, out of work, and when he was in employment his wife said there was much broken time and his wages were small. It is improbable that under the circumstances there could be any savings for them to fall back on to supplement the woman's earnings ; if there were they could not have been anything but small and quickly

exhausted.   Another case was that of a family of five
children all under 14 years of age ; the mother worked
only when her husband was out of a job, and was earning
11/2 in a cotton factory as a reeler.   The husband was a
painter who was suffering from the invariable lack of
work in his trade in the winter.   These two are extreme
cases, but even with the most fortunate of these families,
the struggle to make two ends meet must have been
desperately hard.   Amongst these women who temporarily
at any rate bore the sole responsibility of providing
food and housing for the family, the highest wage earned
was 16/10.   The woman in this case was a cop winder,
with only one child of six months old, so that the expenses
in this household would be particularly small, but even
in such a comparatively favourable case it is obvious
what enormous difficulties face the married woman of
the working classes when the husband falls out of work.

In several cases it was only when the husband was out
of work that the wife sought industrial employment,
and this irregularity must put them at a peculiar disadvantage.   It practically shuts them off from all the
more highly skilled and highly paid trades, where practice
and regularity are essential.   Even in the lower grades of
work speed comes generally only with the frequent
repetition of some special action, and if the women have
not done any of the work since the husband's last spell of
unemployment, at the beginning, at any rate, their hands
will be unaccustomed to the work and their earnings will
naturally not be as high as would otherwise be the case.
Under these circumstances a general low level of wages is
inevitable.   Even when the women work steadily at their
trade it is generally not the same occupation as that at
which they worked before marriage.   Amongst the
home-workers 60% of the women were engaged in
totally different work from that which they performed
when they were unmarried.   The cotton industry is,

as is well known, an exception in this respect. How far this is one of the contributing causes to the fact that in few women's trades are higher wages earned, it is difficult to tell, but it is obvious that where a woman's career as an industrial worker is temporarily broken off at marriage, when she enters the labour market again not only is her choice of work limited, and limited to the less skilled trades, but her skill and her value to her employer must be appreciably less than if she had worked steadily without this break, which frequently comes just at the age at which a young woman has thoroughly mastered her trade.

Other influences are present too in the special case of homework, as the sums earned often do not represent a full day's work, and taken by themselves give a false impression of the conditions of the trade. Either of design or through necessity, the women do not give their full whole time or their full energies to their paid occupation. One woman, whose husband was making 18/- a week, and whose daughter, a ring spinner, brought home 11/3, made no attempt to earn more than 7/- a week. This was her second marriage, and for two years of widowhood she had to support her children, and frankly said that she did not attempt to work as hard as she did then. Another said she could do sufficient work to finish a dozen shirts a day, but that she actually did only two or three dozen a week. More often, however, it is the necessity of giving some attention to the housework that interrupts the women as wage earners. One woman who was employed in a shirt-making factory said that she had given up working at home as it worried her to be continually laying down her work to attend to the baby or to see to something in the house ; but the women who do homework are for the most part subject to these and other calls. A certain number, too, probably gossip at the door with their neighbours, and as two of the women visited pointed out, they are apt to count this as part of the time spent in finishing the work they have brought home. In two cases ill health was given as the explanation of the small sums that were made in the course of the week, and there can be no doubt that the average of the earnings for home-workers is lowered by the fact that women who are not strong enough to work the long and regular hours of a factory, will do as much work at home as their strength permits.

But though these considerations form a partial explanation of the low earnings so often found amongst home-workers, they must not be pressed too far ; an examination of the rates actually paid, and the cost of providing the sewing cotton or other materials needed, does not suggest the possibility of very substantial earnings, even apart from ill health and interruptions deliberate or unavoidable, and those who ventured an opinion on the subject were all agreed that prices were falling or that more work was expected for the same money. At the existing rates, several of the women said they could not possibly support themselves without help, one declared that even if she had no children and worked her very hardest she could not make more than 8/- a week, and would have to provide her cotton out of that. Another said that working at full pressure she might be able to make 9/- a week. This assumed that there would be sufficient work to fill their whole day if they worked steadily and quickly, but the irregularity with which the work was obtained was an almost universal complaint. The case already quoted in another connection of the woman whose earnings for three weeks varied from 2/6 to 10/6 is evidently not exceptional, and some firms only send out their surplus work, which must inevitably lead to great fluctuations in the sums they pay to their outworkers each week. It is impossible, too, in many cases, for these home-workers to avoid spending both time and money in fetching the work from the middleman or the factory. The fares still have to be paid even if they are fortunate enough to be able to send one of the children in their place, though probably the school hours prevent this as a general rule. Several of the women lived so far from their employer's place of business that every visit necessitated a car fare of 2d. or 3d. It is one of the disadvantages under which married women are forced to work, that the district in which they live is probably chosen so that it may be accessible for the husband and near his work, as the wife's occupation, when the husband is in employment, is generally regarded as of secondary importance. The work often has to be fetched every day, or rather the women have to go every day to see if there is anything for them, obviously with no guarantee that their journey will not be in vain. One of the women said that she was often kept waiting several hours before the work was given out, as the master went round each day to collect orders, which he might or might not find quickly. One woman who made children's coats informed the investigator that she did the preparatory stages at home, the coats then went to the factory and fancy stitching was embroidered on the collars and cuffs ; later on they were sent back again to have the button holes made by machinery, and then returned for the third time to the home-worker, who sewed on the buttons and did the finishing processes. This meant three journeys were made each way ; no information was given as to the arrangements made for this sending backwards and forwards, but it is probable that the worker would be responsible for this. It is difficult to believe that some arrangement could not be made to avoid the waste of time and labour involved, and some more businesslike method introduced.

Everywhere in these trades there appeared to be this

utter lack of organisation and methodical management. In some cases the price to be paid for the work was not known until it was taken back, or until the wages book was made up at the end of the week ; wrong entries apparently were not unknown, and whether they were accidental or intentional it would be equally difficult for the women to protect themselves against these mistakes. Another complaint was that with some of the firms any woman who applied for work was taken on with no regard for the actual amount of labour needed, with the inevitable result that all the employees had to be satisfied with irregular doles of work. There can be no doubt that the workers suffer in these and similar ways from the chaotic state of the domestic industries, and that with better organisation they would be able to obtain more reliable and probably higher earnings, even if the rates paid were not altered.

Considerations of this nature cover, however, only one side of the problem of married women's work ; there still remains the important question of its effect on the children and the homes. Many of the women when they went out to work made arrangements to have the children looked after, generally by the grandmother or some other relation ; but the work of looking after the house always remains for them to do. There is no reason, however, for assuming that because they gave the greater part of the day to industrial work, that their homes were therefore neglected. In any group of working class houses, there are sure to be a certain number that are none too clean, but the number of such homes visited in Manchester does not seem to be abnormally high. Of the 114 houses that were seen, only 16 were reported as being not very clean or actually dirty ; the worst two belonged to women who were employed at home and not as factory workers, so that their employment need not have prevented them from giving time to household occupations, and one would be inclined to imagine that it was lack of capacity, rather than their position as industrial workers, that accounted for this state of affairs.

On the whole, where the homes were badly kept, the income of the families was distinctly low ; only in three cases did the wages earned by both husband and wife together amount to more than 25/-, and in most cases they were considerably below this sum. In one case the husband was in India in the army and sent only small and spasmodic contributions home to his wife, who was earning 8/- a week and helped to some extent by relations ; in three cases the husband was out of work or only doing very occasional small jobs, and the wages earned by the wife were 14/-, 12/6 and 9/- respectively. It is perhaps not astonishing under the circumstances that the homes were not immaculate. Insufficient resources alone would not of course explain the lack of care shown by such homes, as other women succeeded in similar positions in keeping their houses spotless, but that such very restricted means increase the difficulties of good housekeeping and order is obvious, and a woman, who could manage to keep the house nice if she had a fair income to spend, might not have sufficient capacity to do so when 20/- or less was the total sum which had to supply the needs of the whole family. Many women, as the cases investigated show, do manage to keep the house in a thoroughly satisfactory condition, even though the income is small and they are working most of the day ; but it must remain more or less an open question, when the women are not sufficiently methodical or energetic to do this, whether they would not fail equally if they stayed at home, and had in consequence a smaller income to administer and a proportionally harder task to perform.

But a far more important question than the effect married women's work may have on the care of the home is its effect on the upbringing and health of the children,

and especially whether it tends to increase the rate of
infant mortality. Inquiries were made as to what arrangements were customary over the confinements, how long
beforehand the women stopped working, and how soon
after they returned to their employment. There were
only four out of the whole number who worked right up to
the time of their confinements, the number of births in
these cases being 15 ; on the other hand there were only
five women who did not work at all during the period of
pregnancy, which meant 21 children born under those
conditions. It is difficult to give any general idea of the
time taken away from work, as the arrangements made
in the different cases varied so, but anything from two to
four months taken away from work, both before and after
the birth of the child, seems to be a normal time. As far
as the question of infant mortality is concerned the table
below gives the number of children born in all the cases
investigated, and the corresponding number of deaths.

	Total no. of births.	Cases of infant mortality.	Deaths after 1 year.
Shirtmakers ...	110	30	14
Handkerchief hemmers	33	7	9
Weavers	71	24	2
Reelers and winders	40	3	4
Other occupations in the cotton trade	87	17	8
Miscellaneous trades	63	4	4
All trades	404	85	41

Taking these figures as they stand the infant mortality
rate would be 110 per 1,000, but several of the women

of whom the inquiries were made, were not industrially employed during the child-bearing period. The details of the infant mortality in these and the remaining cases were as follows :—

Where the mother was not in employment at the time—

	No. of cases.	No. of births.	Cases of infant mortality.
Shirtmakers ...	9	25	2
Handkerchief hemmers	3	12	5
Weavers	6	13	5
Reelers and winders	2	6	1
Other occupations in the cotton trade	9	28	10
Miscellaneous trades	2	6	1
All trades	31	90	24

Where the mother was employed—

Shirtmakers ...	13	85	28
Handkerchief hemmers	6	21	2
Weavers	16	58	19
Reelers and winders	11	34	7
Other occupations in the cotton trade	29	59	7
Miscellaneous ...	15	57	3
All trades	90	314	66

Curiously enough, the rate of infant mortality is higher in the cases where the mother was at home during the child-bearing period, than in the cases where she was in employment, the rate being 267 per 1,000 in the former case, and 210 per 1,000 in the latter. If only the cases in which the mother was working in a factory are considered, the result is practically unaltered, the figure being 214 instead of 210. Though the relation between the two tables can hardly fail to be accidental, it does suggest that the very high rate of infant mortality amongst the cases investigated cannot be explained only by the fact that the majority of the women were in some kind of industrial employment at the time their children were born. The general condition of the town must be largely responsible, and again the question arises whether, when the income is small, the disadvantages of married women's employment are counteracted or not by the additional comfort derived from their wages.

LIVERPOOL.

S. NEWCOME FOX.

To give a correct estimate of the effect produced by the industrial employment of women is in itself sufficiently difficult. But the problem becomes still harder when attention is directed solely to such portion of the sex as are either wives or widows, by reason of the introduction of a number of elusive factors in the shape of husbands and children.

All kinds of difficulties, economic, social and hygienic then arise thick and fast, so that a conscientious seeker after truth finds himself sorely perplexed. As a sample of economic questions, we are confronted with the following: Does the presence of married women in a particular industry raise or lower wages? What influence has their work upon the collective family income? How far does the fact that the wife was a skilled worker earning good money before marriage, tend to make the husband an inefficient workman, to induce irregularity or want of energy on his part, and tempt him to lay upon her shoulders the burden of financing the household? Are the wife's efforts called for by no fault of the husband but by the local incidents of his trade, and by other circumstances beyond his control? Where both husband and wife are wage-earners, is there any evidence that their respective earnings are thereby diminished? Is the wife often found working merely for pocket money? These and many other aspects of the industrial position of the wife force themselves upon our attention, and further complications ensue when we attempt to define the economic place of the widow either with or without dependents.

Quite a different train of thought is started when we examine from a social and hygienic standpoint the effect produced by married women being engaged as wage-earners. Questions of graver import may here emerge: questions that concern, not the rise and fall of wages in a given industry, but the welfare of the whole community. Is the mother's work a menace to the children of the nation? Does it mean a lower birth rate, or a higher death rate? Does it impair the vitality of the younger generation? Does it produce a neglect of parental duty? Is it detrimental to the health of the mother herself? Does it convert the home into a workshop, conducted under insanitary conditions? Some attempt will be made in the following pages to answer the above interrogatories, but the writer cannot hold out a prospect of dealing with them in detail, as the married worker often displays a great gift of reticence, and many of them when visited were clearly under the impression that facts were being elicited in order to stop their competition in the labour world.

Though the enquiry at Liverpool covers a wide range of occupations, attention has been chiefly concentrated upon four groups: tailoresses; machinists on underclothing; those employed in " bobbin-works; " and women working in a variety of factories and warehouses at jam making, hair-teasing, bag-mending, sack-sorting and other pursuits. Only the tailoresses, and those making underclothing, are working at home, with the exception of a few somewhat arresting types in the miscellaneous group who will repay attention on a subsequent page.

HOME WORK I.—TAILORESSES.

(A) VEST MAKERS.—Dealing in the first place with tailoresses, whether their husbands be alive or not, let us consider what economic result, if any, has been produced by their presence in the local labour-market. The story opens happily, as our investigator was confronted on the very threshold by a batch of " vest-makers," a class of home work in which the rate of wages varies to a remarkable extent, prices rising to 2/6 and even 5/6 a vest, and falling away to 1/- or 5d. Our case papers, from which certain extracts are here given, contain six typical instances :

(1) A widow who gets 2/3 for each vest and makes £1 a week, when busy ; has two children at school and a brother who lives with her and shares expenses ; she did the same work before marriage.

(2) A widow, getting 3/6 to 5/6 for each vest and makes £1 5s. a week ; has six children, two boys and one girl earning and a daughter who does home work ; did the same work before marriage.

(3) A wife, whose husband is a sailor earning £4 a month and sends her 10/- a week for expenses ; she herself earns up to 35/- a week, but usually makes less ; has one son, an engineer, out of work; did the same work before marriage.

(4) A wife, whose husband is a tailor ; his wages are not stated ; she gets from 3/3 to 4/6 a vest, and makes from two to seven a week according to season ; has only one child and did the same work before marriage.

(5) A widow, who has earned as much as £2 a week : has seven children, one earning 10/- : two others support themselves, and she has lost six. In this case her statements lacked precision, but she seems to be in comfortable circumstances, was paying 7/6 rent, and lived in a superior house in a good neighbourhood : same work before marriage.

(6) A wife, whose husband is a casual dock labourer earning 12/- to 15/- : she makes from 8/- to 12/- weekly, and has six children, two of whom earn 8/- and 5/- apiece : did the same work before marriage.

Economic Aspect.

The first five of the above cases give no indication that the worker, whether wife or widow, is willing to accept a low rate of wages : the evidence is all to the contrary, and seems to show that where a woman has been in the same trade before marriage, is a skilled hand, and knows what her work is worth, she is more independent and assertive than her unmarried sister and refuses to take less than a good wage. Case No. 6 is on rather a different footing, as here, though the wife had special knowledge of the trade, she takes much less money than the other five. This may be accounted for by the fact that the aggregate budget for her own earnings and those of her husband and children amounts to 33/- or 40/- a week, that she is content with a somewhat low standard of comfort and takes up her work irregularly. Or it may be due to a meritorious desire to have more time to make clothes for the four younger children and look after their welfare.

Social and Hygienic Conditions.

The vest-makers met with at Liverpool are the aristocrats of the groups investigated. They are all superior women, and their houses were clean and often well-furnished. Occasionally a piano and ornaments of various kinds meet the eye : one of them is described as being " elaborately dressed in fashionable style." Another, a widow, had six children, all strong, had done machining for forty years and had never found it hurt her, but she very rightly thought " it was about time her children kept the household going, in order that she might have a rest." Only in one case was there an invalid child. There is no sign that vest-makers neglect their household duties or families and they often say " they could do more if there were no children to look after."

(B) Jackets, Knickers and Trouser-work.—The next group presents some sharp contrasts to the last. It includes women working on jackets, boys' knickers and trousers in various material. Certain types follow:

(1) A wife whose husband is a mill-labourer getting 18/- to 21/- a week: he is " unsteady : " she makes drill jackets and boiler suits and averages 6/- a week. Before marriage she worked at the same trade in a shop and subsequently continued it at home, uninterrupted by marriage. Her work is stiff and heavy and she has to provide her own cotton and the machine : she pays 5/6 rent for four rooms and has two children.

(2) A wife whose husband is a dock labourer taking 15/-. She is at " dungaree " work,[1] making trousers at 4/9 a dozen, and earns 10/– weekly ; same work before marriage in a shop. She kept on working " as her husband never earned much and she liked to be comfortable " : has two children earning money and three at school, and the aggregate for the week totals £1 19/-.

(3) A widow, working on corduroy trousers, which she " finishes " at 2d. a pair, earning thereby 8/– a week. Before marriage was a tailoress in a shop, but gave it up " as her children needed attention." Has three children living and has lost six. Takes in a lodger who pays 3/6 : rent 5/6 for five rooms and a kitchen.

(4) A wife whose husband is a railway labourer at 24/–, but his work is irregular. She makes boys' knickers at the rate of 2/5 to 7/– per dozen, earning 10/– to 12/– a week : was a tailoress before marriage. Has twins one year old and says " it is hardly possible to work at home without interruption."

(5) A wife at dungaree work for which she gets 8/– a week : had no experience as she was an asylum attendant before marriage. Husband earns good money

---

[1] " Dungaree," a stout washing material, believed to be a mixture of cotton and jute.

at a coach-builder's, but he drinks and will not give her much. No children at home.

(6) A wife, making children's overalls, pinafores and frocks, and worked at the same before marriage. Formerly earned good pay but now makes only 4/6 to 6/6 a week, as her baby "takes up so much of her time." Husband makes 18/– to 25/– as a brush-maker.

(7) A wife with a husband who is a casual labourer at 12/– to 13/– a week : she was a tailoress in a workshop before marriage and still works in the same place during the season at the rate of 2/4 a day. In the winter she makes frocks for neighbours : has three children.

(8) A widow who makes 8/– a week on dungaree work ; was a servant before marriage but took up with machining at home because her husband said " he would never marry any woman who couldn't work, as his own wages as a seaman were insufficient to bring up a family upon." She has one child dependent on her and gets allowance of 1/6 from a married son.

(9) A widow who gets only casual wages for sewing and dressmaking and was in service before marriage : she has worked hard all her married life, as her husband was delicate : has two children, one of whom, a girl, earns 12/–, and a nephew who lives in the house earns 5/–.

(10) A widow, a tailoress both before and after marriage : she used to get well paid when working in a shop but took up home work for the children's sake and now gets very little. She gives a startling account of some of the prices paid, e.g. she does special boys' coats for one firm at 1/– each, and for another firm at 9d. each ; she once made a pair of knee breeches with seven buttons and button-holes on each leg for 1/– : the porter who brought the work told her that the waistcoat of the suit, of corduroy velveteen, was worked by another woman for 1/–, and that a Jew did the coat for 3/–. The suit was for an Irish farmer who paid £2 10/– for it.

Economic Aspect.

Here the wages are in some cases very low indeed, and this is due partly to the fact that the class of work adopted is always poorly remunerated, partly to want of working experience before marriage, and partly to irregularity occasioned by home duties. In such a trade the better the mother the lower the earnings. Over and over again the refrain is heard " it is hardly possible to work at home without interruption." The wives are at work because their husbands are often casual labourers and sometimes drunkards. But, however small the earnings may be, there is no evidence to show that these women are taking a lower rate of remuneration than is usual and are thereby injuring their competitors. The widows are in worse case even than the wives, for they are often engaged at a low class of work without any previous training. The plight of such a woman—and there are many of them—is deplorable, for, if left with dependants, she must take whatever offers or starve. Of course there is always " the House," but it is marvellous how the poor help one another in order to keep the home up, however humble it may be. The vendor of sweated goods battens upon the necessity of this unhappy class. From an economic point of view it cannot be doubted that these wages of starvation tend to multiply the small masters whose workshops are the centre of all that is evil. Those who run them, whether Jews or Gentiles, can only compete with the bigger workshop or factory where machinery exists and sanitation is enforced, by working for inordinate hours and paying the lowest wage to all whom they employ. And our poor widow is perforce and unwittingly helping to bolster up a rotten and pernicious system.

Social and Hygienic Conditions.

Though the homes are not infrequently classed as dirty, the children are as a rule clean and even well dressed. Instances occur where the desire to provide for household needs makes the mother reckless of her own health and that of her future offspring, and a high rate of infantile mortality is prevalent. Take the case of a widow who only stopped work a short time at her confinements : she has a total of five children dead, one stillborn, one dying at a day old and three under a year. Yet this woman's house was clean and tidy and the three children that survived are " well kept and healthy." Or the mother may try to get back time, lost during the day in maternal duties, by night work and overstrain her eyes— a not infrequent experience amongst home workers. But alas, it is still more common for the married woman, who is forced to work, to delegate the charge of her children to some one else : she gets a girl " to look after them," and the results are often disastrous. A widow in a workshop who had recourse to this expedient found her children were neglected and took to working at home, but not before she had paid a heavy toll by losing two of them.

In this trade, overcrowded as it is and notorious for its low rate of wages, the woman with a family is heavily handicapped by being deprived of that freedom of movement which is essential to effective competition. She is anchored to her home, and has to take the work that is nearest at hand. And not only is she bereft of the power of readily shifting from one market to another—an incident common to all the work of married women—but her meagre resources will not admit of the train or 'bus hire that would carry her further afield.

(C) Oilskins.—Comprised under the head of tailoresses we meet married women working upon oilskins either in factories or at home. They seem to make 2/9 a day in the factories and get quite a good return from home work. For example, " sou'-westers " are paid for at 1/10½ to 4/6 a dozen, according to quality, and a wife who was busy at home said " she could make three dozen of the common kind, and one dozen of the best in a day : she earned 10/- odd last week, only working two days, because she was moving : has earned £1 and over in a week." In oilskin coats, payment ranges from 6/- to 1/3 each, and a mother helped by her daughter made from 16/- to 26/- a week according to season. But in this instance the husband was taking 35/- at a stationer's, so it is probable that the wife did not deem it necessary to work with regularity.

No widows were found at this trade. It is undoubtedly stiff and laborious and is carried on in a rough quarter of the town. The married worker makes no attempt to underbid the unmarried : she is robust in appearance, with healthy children, and her social and hygienic environment calls for no special comment.

II.—Shirt Makers and Women Working on Under-clothing.

Machinists.—Most of the cases investigated were wives taking a fair rate of wages. In some instances the delicate health of the husband compelled them to work. Here and there we find women with a high standard of comfort, the weekly budget from the combined efforts of the family amounting in one case to £3 11/-.

Any widow met with was earning very little, and had to rely for support upon her children. One widow was leading a cruel life of penury ; she made but a hard-earned 8/- or 9/- a week by machining underclothing, with a shilling or two extra by darning sailors' socks, and could only work the treadle of her machine with one foot, as her other leg had been permanently injured. She had 8 children, 6 of whom were dependent, and is described as " a worn, delicate-looking woman." " Her brother," she said, " paid the rent, or she couldn't manage." Indeed it is difficult to see how in any event she can feed herself and her family.

Economic, Social and Hygienic Aspect.

These machinists are taking the usual rate of remuneration, fluctuating heavily, as it always does in home work, according to the nature of the trade. There is strong evidence to show that the woman, who has had no experience of such work before marriage and starts it when a wife, is injuriously affected by operating the machine. Not infrequently she will tell you that "machinery does not suit her"; that "she feels it rather because she took to it late"; or "she finds the work upsets her and the babies"; or "she has had ten children and has lost five," and when pressed admits that the doctor attributed their deaths to the mother working. On the other hand you have the strong, capable woman, inured to the strain of machining before the husband came on the scene, getting good wages and feeling no evil effects whatever. Such a one will express an opinion that her daughters "can't do better than follow the same trade."

But, whether with or without experience, there is a strong temptation for the married machinist to overtax her powers, and instances abound in which their labour has been carried on with a reckless disregard of the consequences both to their own health and to that of their offspring.

FACTORY WORK.

I.—Women Employed in "Bobbin Works."

With one exception the types given by our investigator of this trade are wives: all were engaged in it before marriage, and most of them continued their work uninterrupted by that episode. Cases are not unusual where husband and wife are employed in the same factory. The regular wage earned by women is from 8/– to 9/6 a week, plus an occasional bonus of 1/6 to 2/6. Hardly any husband takes more than 18/– and many less.

Economic, Social and Hygienic Aspect.

Several instances occur where a married couple have either never had children or have only a small family, and accordingly we find more comfort in domestic arrangements than could have been expected. We note comments in the " case-papers " to the following effect : " Nice, clean little house, comfortably furnished " ; " comfortable clean home " ; " house well furnished and beautifully kept " ; " nice house, very clean " ; " comfortable, inexpensive, neat " ; " comfortable, clean, well furnished home." The children moreover, when met with, are " bonny and healthy " or " fat and healthy " or " well cared for." However excellent the housewife, it is difficult to understand how she can produce such results from the meagre weekly stipend at her disposal. Undoubtedly something must be attributed to the low rents that prevail in parts of the Liverpool district, and to the salubrity of the climate.

Married and unmarried take the same wages in the bobbin works, so no economic question arises in this respect. There is no exceptional infantile mortality and no sign of the mother's health being injured by her occupation, but the children undoubtedly miss her maternal care when she is absent at the factory, and this is the most objectionable feature in a trade where the wife with a family is obliged to be from home. As regards the husbands it cannot be overlooked that in no case are they securing an adequate wage and in several households are merely on casual work. It is therefore possible to infer that the regular wages paid to his wife may produce a slackness on his part that prejudices the husband in the labour market.

II.—MARRIED WOMEN EMPLOYED IN A VARIETY OF MISCELLANEOUS TRADES.

With few exceptions all the work is done in factories or warehouses ; the wages paid are lower than in the trades already reviewed, and the wage-earner is of a rougher nature. We shall see her in jam, pickle and sweet factories, and as a hair-teaser, maker of boxes and bags, rope-worker, sack-sorter, and bag-mender. Out of thirty-one selected types ten are widows—a larger proportion than usual—two withheld information regarding their husbands and one is a deserted wife. A few characteristic examples of those engaged in these industries are given as an illustration of how the poor live.

JAM FACTORIES.—The jam trade is most in request. Here the regular hands are of quite a different type from the job workers, and it is in the latter class that we too often find the wife or the widow.

(1) A widow, aged 42, earns an average of 5/– a week as a fruit picker : says the work is very irregular ; pays no rent as she lives with her sister. Has three children, two boys of 10 and 8, in good health, and a girl of 4 who is delicate. She was in service before marriage and only worked when her husband died ; sometimes goes out charing when work is slack ; has had 1/6 a week " from the Lord Mayor's fund for the unemployed," and 2/6 on another occasion.

(2) A widow, aged 62, a fruit picker, earns 7/– to 8/– a week, and finds the work " fairly regular " ; was in service before marriage and began working at death of husband ; pays 1/6 for one room, described as " very clean and comfortable," and has only one son who is married.

She gives details of her factory duties :—" Oranges come in about Christmas, and marmalade making goes on till the end of March ; rhubarb starts in May, followed by gooseberries and stone fruit. When the stone fruit is finished there is a week or two pickling onions, but there is nothing from the beginning of October to Christmas." In the off-time she too goes out charing.

Note.—This woman, unlike the preceding one, has no dependants, so is probably more regular at work and gets a better wage.

(3) A wife, aged 35, but looks worn and old, prepares vegetables in a jam and pickle factory, getting 8/- a week ; was a servant in a gentleman's family before marriage. Pays 3/- for a cellar dwelling with 3 rooms that are fairly clean and tidy. Has 3 children, one of whom earns money. Husband is a casual dock labourer who has hurt his back working ; says " it's doubtful if he will get compensation as the dock doctor won't agree with the Hospital doctor as to the nature of the injury." Earns 4/6 a day " when he gets work." He is an old army man, served 7 years with the colours, and 7 in the reserve, and has good discharge papers, but says " it don't help you to get a job afterwards." A nice couple who make the best of it, and are quite above the average in refinement and intelligence.

(4) A wife, who is a season hand in a jam factory, and, when work is brisk, averages 8/- to 10/- a week ; was a servant before marriage ; is working to supplement her husband's wages of 15/- on dock labour ; pays 4/- rent and has a fairly comfortable little house ; there are four children living who look " grubby but healthy " ; three children died quite young, due, the mother fears, to her working right up to her time ; says her husband " was a drinking man, but about a year ago went into some mission place out of curiosity and became completely changed." Wife hopes if he gets more money " it will be

better spent than formerly and then she will not need to work out."

SWEET FACTORIES give employment to several married women, but some firms will only take on "old hands," or when there is a great rush of work.

(1) A wife, who does caramel wrapping and did the same before marriage, gets 10/- a week and is regularly employed. Husband is an engineer, but as he is now out of work, she has returned to the factory; she pays 5/6 rent, has a comfortable home kept very clean, and is described as "quite a superior little woman, evidently accustomed to better things"; has four children alive and has lost two infants. Her baby aged 4 months goes to a day nursery. "Relations," she says, "have helped them or they could not have kept on as they have."

(2) A widow, aged 30, at caramel wrapping, did the same before marriage and had to return to it before husband's death as he was paralysed for some years. Is only working for one, two, or three days a week on piece work, but has to go each day to see if there is any job; made 1/9 last week, and 3/- the week before; gets 5/- parish relief; occupies one room at 2/6, moderately clean; has four children, the eldest 8, "all being fat and rosy-cheeked"; lost one child at eleven months and has had five miscarriages. Her baby of 19 months goes to the day nursery.

(3) A wife, who does fancy packing at busy season and gets 8/6 when at work; same trade before marriage. Husband is a crane-driver for the Dock Board and gets 25/- to 30/- a week irregularly. She pays 2/6 rent for two rooms, which are clean and tidy, but the furniture is scanty. Has one little boy aged 4 who looks well cared for and healthy. Lost one baby from bronchitis, whose death the mother attributed to exposure at early and late hours, when she had to take him to the day nursery.

ROPE WORKS.—Here the women have nearly all worked

at the same pursuit before marriage, and continued it
during their married life. They are strong in build,
rough in type, and inclined to disregard household
cleanliness. The husbands, with one exception, are all
labourers on low wages and many are unemployed. The
children are not very carefully looked after. The wages
of these rope-workers average from 7/6 to 10/6 a week;
they entrust their babies either to relations or neighbours.
Most of them are forced to work in order to provide for
household expenses, but sometimes we meet an exception
to this rule. For example a young wife, recently married,
employed as a spinner and getting an average of 10/6 a
week, said " her husband didn't want her to work, but
she preferred to do so." Here the man was a farm
labourer at 24/– a week and there were no children; they
were paying 5/6 rent and living in a " nicely furnished,
sweet little house."

In Cotton and other Warehouses and Stores.—(1)
is a widow, aged 37, working in a cotton warehouse; the
work is intermittent and she gets 9/– a week when on full
time. When there is a fire in the warehouse her duty is
to pick over the bales and separate the cotton into three
lots: useless, fairly good, good. If not wanted she sews
and washes at home; pays 2/6 for two cellar rooms,
pronounced " fairly clean," and has four children, one of
them earning, all healthy.

(2) A wife, employed in a marine store as a rag-sorter
at 9/– a week; her husband is a casual labourer, out of
work; rent 2/– for a half cellar dwelling. Two children
of 7 and 5 in a verminous condition; house in a filthy
state; the children, she says, " manage for themselves."

(3) A widow, aged 29, a sack-mender in a warehouse;
makes new sacks out of good parts of old ones and gets
8/– to 9/– a week; " has worked all her married life as
her husband was drunken and cruel and for some time in
prison"; pays 2/6 for 3 rooms that are tidy; has two

children living and has lost two from neglecting to knock off work : is suffering now and should have an operation, but " does not see her way to leave the children."

(4) A wife, also a sack-mender, in a marine store : gets a regular wage of 8/– a week ; husband, a casual dock labourer often only gets 10/–.   She says that a number of women, chiefly married ones, are in this trade : occupies 2 rooms, pretty clean ; rent 2/9 ; has 3 children all at school ; did not work when they were younger.

(4) A wife, mending bags in a warehouse at 7/– to 8/– a week ; husband casual labourer, who " earned 2/6 last week and 4/– the week before " ; is given to drink ; she is on piece work and gets 1/– for 100 bags ; has five children, the eldest 12 ; they " have to look after themselves " ; she pays 3/– for some cellar rooms that are light and moderately clean.

(6) A widow, of 35, " a very respectable, uncomplaining woman," who thinks herself " lucky to have got back at her old work " ; makes 9/– a week by packing paper bags in a warehouse ; pays 2/6 for two rooms, neatly arranged and very clean ; has two children who go to school and are looked after by their grandmother who lives in the house : the latter gets 2/6 a week from the Guardians and 3/– comes from the same source for the children.

(7) A deserted wife, aged 38, in a hair and feather works ; she teases hair for mattresses and earns from 6/– to 10/– a week ; pays 4/6 for five rooms which she shares with a widow, who has a small shop in the cellar ; has only one child alive, aged 11, " who looks after herself," but lost four babies.

(8) A wife in a box-making factory ; now gets from 6/– to 8/– a week, as prices have fallen ; husband a labourer out of work ; has one child living and has lost two ; shares a house with her parents, who look after the child.

HAWKERS.—This glimpse at the work of married women

in Liverpool concludes with the picture of two wives who
are earning a precarious living as street hawkers. They
both seem contented though their life must be terribly
hard. The first, aged 26, was in a bottling stores before
marriage and took to hawking when her husband was
doing very little as a dock-labourer. She is clearly a
woman of some resource as she has improvised the following trade system : she buys mugs and exchanges them in
the Jewish quarter of the town for old clothes ; these she
sells in " Paddy's market " in the evenings. By this
process she earns from 9d. to 1/– a day, but says " you
have to be very sharp to get the better of the Jews." If
her husband has no work in the morning, he comes home
to look after the children, and the wife goes out, returning
at noon to allow him to take his next chance of a job at
the docks. The rent paid is 2/– for two rooms, described
as clean, but with poor furniture. The children are four
in number, " very healthy and clean."

The second wife hawks fruit and did so before marriage ;
she only makes 3/– or 4/– a week and her husband is also
a casual dock labourer, whose wages are most uncertain :
the rent is 2/9 for three rooms, which are moderately
clean ; she has three children attended to by a relation,
in the mother's absence ; and she is described as a " jolly
faced, healthy-looking woman of the gipsy type." She
works, from her own account, " partly to add to her
husband's earnings, partly because she likes the out-door
life."

ECONOMIC, SOCIAL AND HYGIENIC ASPECT.

In the foregoing cases that have been set forth in some
detail, what are the salient points that arrest our attention ? We can say with confidence that no question of
unfair rivalry enters here. The best paid are taking
normal wages. In the jam factories they are on " job "
work, the lowest branch of the trade, and are further

handicapped from having no previous experience and no connection with any firm who would employ them under better conditions.   In the sweet factories and rope works they are in a rather better position as regards remuneration ; but, like the jam workers, are mated with husbands who are on casual labour and do little or nothing towards household expenses.   There is in these industries some trace of mortality amongst the children, by reason of the mother working too near her time.   The worst paid women, employed in various warehouses and stores, are the victims of necessity, working mostly for sheer existence.   A first glance excites wonder how they support life at all, but we find them not only living but displaying a patient endurance of the ups and downs of fortune that is truly marvellous.   And how they must pinch themselves for the sake of their little ones, for we often note the comment " children in good health," " house clean and comfortable," or " children grubby but healthy."   True it is that sometimes they have " to manage for themselves," and then we may be sure that we have struck the bed-rock of destitution and despair. But despair is not a characteristic feature.   More often the mother bears a brave front before her troubles, and tries to bear up under her evil star.   She finds a neighbour, or better still a relative, who will look after her family. Amongst this class of labour the home is entirely dependent on a good house-wife, who will make the best of everything.   Nor can there be any doubt that in many cases allowances must be received from relations, friends, or charitable societies.

NEWCASTLE.

Annie Abram.

THE Council's investigator had great difficulty in finding
married women wage-earners in Newcastle, as the regular
out-worker is the exception. In the chemical works on
Tyneside young girls are largely employed to " pack,"
and in the " ropery " works marriage is a disqualifica-
tion. Almost all the married women who work in
factories have followed a trade before marriage, and have
been forced to return to it on account of the death or unemployment of their husbands. The men seem to
resent their wives working, and to feel the position un-
dignified and out of order, and the women consider it
a hardship which must be borne in silence. They prefer
to keep their work as secret as possible, and often live in
out-of-the-way bye-streets, or in rooms up dark passages.
So effectually do they hide themselves that the general
idea amongst men trade-unionists is that there are no
married women wage-earners except charwomen. Our
investigator gives details concerning twelve women
workers whom she visited in January, 1910 ; of these
three are in the rabbit down, two in the guano, five
in the sail and canvas, and two in the pottery works.
The rabbit down works employ five hundred women,
of whom half are married or widowed, the pottery about
the same number, a third of them being wives or widows ;
twenty-eight to thirty women are engaged in the sail and
canvas industry, and they are all married; but only twelve
women altogether in the guano works. The total number of women in these four trades is therefore about one

thousand and forty, and about four hundred and forty of them, that is a little more than forty-two per cent., are married or widowed. None of them enter into competition with men, as when both men and women are employed, they do different work. None of the women have any organization. One of them is Scotch, but the rest are English, and they are all town-bred.

RABBIT DOWN WORKS.—No machinery is used in the rabbit down industry, and the cleaning and dressing of the skins is very dirty work. It is carried on by women of a very poor class, and those who have worked at it when they were single are always taken back after marriage if there be enough for them to do ; apparently only the women who have been inured to it in their girlhood think it all right. About half a dozen men are engaged as packers and carriers, but there are no others in the factory.

The first woman visited had been in the works as a girl, but had left them to become a domestic servant, and had stayed in service until she was married. She returned to them soon after her marriage because her husband was so often out of work, and she went regularly. She was thirty-six, and had had six children, but only two —a girl of seventeen and a boy of three—were alive ; three died in infancy, and one, a year and a half old, had recently succumbed to bronchitis. Her husband was a joiner by trade, but he had been out of work for four years, and the daughter, who is also in the rabbit down works, lived with a relative, so the family apparently subsisted, it can hardly be called living, on the mother's earnings. She was an " opener," and did sixty skins for 5d., she could manage them in an hour and a half if they were in good condition, but much time was wasted if they happened to be poor. At the best she could make 9s. a week, but her average was 6/6. The hours were from seven in the morning to six at night, but married women could come and go as they pleased, as there was not much to be done. She worked as near as possible to her confinements ; the master would not have allowed it if he had known, but " as they sat at work it was not noticed." Her fellow-workers made collections for her ; last time they gave her 7/6, and a lady sent her 2/6, and she paid the woman who attended her by instalments. Her husband looked after the boy while she was out, and she used to pay 4d. a day to a *crèche*, for the baby when it was alive. She had the use of a wash-house, and a light airy room, which opened on to a wide street in a fairly sanitary position. She did the housework in the evenings, and the room, though untidy, was clean. The rent was 2/3 a week, and she then owed 9/–, as she was obliged to stay away from work when the baby was ill, but she must have paid it fairly regularly up till then, as she had been in the same house nine years. She kept her boy very clean, and his clothes were well patched, but it was not surprising to hear that at the time of the visit she had no fire, and only a few slices of bread and a little tea. She said " they never got what they ought to have to eat," and she did not know what would become of them " if married women were not allowed to work ; at any rate, it kept a roof and a crust for them."

The second woman was better off, as her husband was a labourer in a ship-yard, with wages of £1 a week, but he was often out of work. She was a " puller," and had to pull all the grey and white hairs out of the skins ; the women were paid 1s. for pulling five dozen, and a clever worker could do them in four hours. She earned 6/– a week, but she could earn 10s. if she worked all day, and all the skins were good. She was twenty-six years of age, and had one child a year and a half old. She lost one of pneumonia when it was a year and eight months ; she was not working then. Her husband minded the baby in her absence, and her mother lived in the room next to theirs ; she only went to the factory when her husband was out of work. She paid 2/- a week for one room ; there was very little furniture in it, but both it and the child were fairly clean and tidy.

The third woman had only worked during the last twelve months since her marriage. She prepared rabbit skins, and made down beds, etc. from 7 a.m. to 6 p.m., with an hour and a half off for meals, and received 9/- a week, and 2d. an hour for overtime. She was twenty-nine, and had had six children, and five of them, aged respectively ten, seven, six, four and two and a half years, were alive. She paid a girl to mind them when she was at work. She had two rooms at a rent of 3/3; they were warm and comfortable, and fairly clean. The children were untidy, but clean and well-clad. She was a delicate woman, and complained that the hairs got on her chest and made her ill, but her husband was in work again, and she meant to come home as soon as she could.

GUANO WORKS.—The two women who go to the guano works both thought their trade healthy ; about a dozen women were kept to sew up the guano in bags, and the rest of the workers were men. It is a seasonal trade, and the busy time is from February to April, when they prepare it for home use; later in the year they pack it for export.

One of the women could only be employed at the busy season, though she would willingly have gone more frequently, as her husband was often out of work. She earned eight to nine shillings a week. She was fifty-four, and all her children were grown up, except two who were at school. She had two rooms in a house in a nice street, but the investigator was not asked into them, and was not able to discover any further details.

The other woman, a widow of sixty-six, returned to work when her husband died twenty-nine years ago, and had been in the same place thirty-seven years altogether. She stayed indoors and mended bags. Her hours were from six in the morning to six at night, and her wages were nine shillings a week, but they used to be ten. She had brought up a family of five, and then lived with a married daughter in two rooms, which cost 3/3 a week. She was rather deaf and rheumatic, but maintained herself, and paid sixpence a week insurance.

SAIL AND CANVAS WORKS.—The sail cloth industry seemed to be dying, perhaps because the number of sailing boats on the Tyne had so greatly diminished : the mill only employed old hands, and they were chiefly occupied in making coarse, heavy covers for waggons, and a kind of coarse harding or fine sacking, which is very strong and hard wearing. The looms looked very big and clumsy, and reaching over them must be extremely tiring. Of the five workers visited by our investigator the first three were weavers, and the other two winders ; four out of the five said that wages had gone down because the material they used was bad, and it made the work slow. A few men were needed for the machinery, but none of them were weavers or winders.

No. 1 was a widow aged fifty-two, who was a half-timer in a Lancashire mill when she was eleven ; she did not work during her twelve years of married life, but was forced to go back to it after her husband died, to support her six children. A few years ago she earned sixteen shillings a week, but now she cannot make more than five or six. One of her sons, a boy of sixteen, worked for the Gas Company, and she hoped he would eventually earn 18/- a week, but another, " who ought to have been a good help," enlisted. A married daughter lived in the same house as herself, and she had a boy of eleven at school ; he had dinner there when she was at the works. She had one room, for which she paid 2/3 ; it was poorly furnished but clean. She said that she felt the bad effects of fluff on her chest, but she had never been off through sickness, she " couldn't afford to stay off " ; she would gladly stay at home, as she felt worn out, but she saw no prospect of doing so, for if she had been unable to earn she would have had to go to the workhouse.

No. 2 was a Scotchwoman, aged forty-eight ; she had worked intermittently for twenty-eight years, but the investigator was not quite sure whether she was a weaver before she married. Her husband who has only one arm, was employed in the same works as herself as an inspector of cloth, but his wages, though regular, were low and she was obliged to supplement them by her earnings, which amounted at present to 5/- a week. A married son helped her a little, and a daughter of sixteen went to a biscuit factory two or three days a week and brought home 2/3. She also had a boy of ten and a half, and a girl of eight, and had lost four, two of whom were stillborn, but she was not working at the time of their births. Her rent was 4/3, and she had two poorly furnished rooms, and a small yard. They were untidy but clean, and her children were clean and well dressed.

No. 3 was in a better position than any of the other women whose circumstances have come to our knowledge ; her husband was seldom out of work, and his wages would be enough to keep the family if it were not for a cripple son, who has undergone twenty-one operations and is still undergoing them. She worked to obtain aid for him. She was one of the best weavers at the works, and could make £1 a week twenty years ago, but now was glad of ten or twelve shillings, and usually earned less than that. Besides the invalid son, she had a daughter of sixteen who did the housework, a boy of eight or nine at school, and another son who had married and gone away. The investigator thought she said that four had died : both she and No. 2 declared that they never worked when their children were coming, or when they were small. She added that going to the works did not affect her health ; inspectors were often there, and saw that things were all right. Her rooms were very clean, and nicely furnished.

Nos. 4 and 5, the two winders, lived in dirty, miserable-looking slum dwellings, and both seemed rather hopeless. No. 4 earned 5/9 a week, and her two daughters, aged sixteen and a half, and fifteen, 3/6 and 2/6 respectively at the pottery works. Her son was a sweeper for the Corporation but she did not say what his wages were ; her husband lost an arm fifteen years ago, and had not worked since then. She had a girl between ten and eleven at school. No. 5 was a younger woman, and had only one child, of a year and a half old ; her husband took care of it when she was away, and she stayed at home when he had work. She was paid five to six shillings a week.

THE POTTERY.—The work in the pottery is very tiring, as it entails constant running about, standing, fetching, and carrying, but it is not otherwise unhealthy. The employer spoke very highly of the married women, and said they were more reliable than any other workers ; the men in the trade drank a good deal, and lost much time, but married women were always there when they were wanted.

The two women whom our investigator saw received 8/- a week time wages, for ten and a half hours' work. A was a widow of thirty-three, with four children dependent upon her. In addition to her wages she had 7/6 poor relief. She paid 1/6 to have the baby minded when she was out, and the other children had their dinners at school. Her rent was 2/9, and her two rooms were scrupulously clean. B had a husband, but he was in the Infirmary undergoing an operation, and a bad leg had prevented him from working for some time. She was consumed with anxiety about him, and most distressed at being obliged to take poor relief, but she had three children, the eldest twelve, and the youngest only eight months. Her money amounted altogether to 13/- a

week, and she paid a rent of 3/-, and 1/6 for the care of
the children. Her room was very poorly furnished, the
floor uneven, and the fireplace broken, and she said that
there was " no convenience " in the house ; but the beds
were neat and clean, and the children looked well cared
for and clean.

It is clear that these women are wage-earners from
necessity and not from choice; their work is unattractive
or tiring, and not one of them seems to take the slightest
pleasure in it. Their wages are extremely small, less
than 7/- a week on an average. Their standard of comfort is, with two exceptions at the most, low ; their
rooms are few and poorly furnished, but it is satisfactory
to notice that only in two instances were they pronounced
dirty. The investigator saw six families of children ; four
of them were clean, and the other two fairly clean, and
she does not suggest that any of them were insufficiently
clothed. Mothers going out to work always manage to
arrange that some one shall look after the little children.
Nevertheless, the death-rate, and especially the infant
mortality, is high ; in one family four out of six died, in
two others four out of seven, but the investigator was not
quite sure of the figures in one of these instances. Two
others had lost one child out of two, and one out of six
respectively, bringing the total number of deaths up to
fourteen, but the remaining seven had lost none at all.
We cannot give the exact number of children born to the
twelve mothers, because one of them only said that all but
two were grown up, but without counting hers there were
fifty-one, and it is not likely that she had more than six
or seven, so that we may fairly reckon that fourteen out of
less than sixty, that is more than twenty-three per cent.
died. Unfortunately we have very little information as
to the causes of their deaths, and therefore cannot tell
whether they were, or were not, due to the hard lives led
by the mothers.

In addition to these more or less regular workers, there are many married women who increase the family income by going out washing or charing, one or two days a week. Charwomen earn 2/- or 2/6 a day, and are provided with food.

Rag-gatherers are amongst the lowest class of women workers, and have no settled conditions of life. Some of them travel miles, just as rag-men do, and carry their sacks to the warehouse. The remuneration they receive depends upon the quality and quantity of the rags.

None of the women visited by our investigator had any suggestions for improving their position beyond employment for their men-folk. Physical exhaustion and a hopeless outlook seemed to her their outstanding features, but they dreaded any interference which might prevent them from continuing their work, bad as it might be, and the women who had not worked out before marriage, and whose homes were in a state of destitution, envied those who could earn a little. It is this which makes their lot so pathetic; they are undoubtedly wretched under the existing conditions, but to forbid them to work might only make them still more wretched.

LEEK AND MACCLESFIELD.

MARGERY LANE.

THE married women workers of Leek and Macclesfield are, as a rule, engaged in various branches of the silk trade. The exceptions are very few. A careful examination of the reports gives rise to certain conclusions with which it may be well to begin. The facts revealed are not very startling or very new; but they are interesting as confirming what perhaps most people already believe.

The average wage of a man in full employment is £1, certainly no more. A mill-owner in Macclesfield has lately roused the ire of the town by declaring that a working-man can bring up a family comfortably on 15/- a week. Perhaps he has forgotten the rise in the cost of living, or only made allowance for a very small family. The general consensus of opinion among the subjects of this enquiry, who are surely the best qualified to judge, is, that when there are only one or two children in the family it is possible by the strictest economy to keep house on £1 or 18/- a week, but that nothing is left over. If the husband's wages fall beneath this sum, as they often do, or if the number of children increase without a corresponding rise in the income, the mothers go out to work. When one adds the cases where there are other dependents, or where the husband is dead, ill, out of work, in irregular or insufficient employment, or morally unsatisfactory, it is clear that most married women who work do so through necessity. When both husband and wife work the average family income is 28/- a week.

Of the few out of the 82 cases investigated who are not

so hardly pressed about a dozen want " a little extra."
They desire to lay by a little for a rainy day, or more
often for an occasional holiday, or for little comforts
which in these days can scarcely be regarded as luxuries.

A still smaller number confess to liking the work, and
only three or four of these believe they could manage
without their earnings. On the other hand, very few
actually dislike the work. The great majority of them
have worked at the same trade before marriage ; some of
them have never left it, and all, if compelled, seem to
take to it again with very little friction. It must be
added in refutation of natural fears that those who enjoy
factory work invariably have well-kept homes, and clean
and healthy children also, where there are any.

It follows as a corollary from what has been said that
the standard of living sinks as the number of dependents
increases. Those are best off who have no young children,
or only one or two ; or where there are several adults in
a family. The largest families have often the smallest
incomes. A man and wife with a numerous flock of
young children must expect to see plenty of trouble before
their good time comes. Under modern industrial. conditions the blessings of a quiverful of sons and daughters
sometimes seem rather dubious.

Childless folk are generally very proud of their homes.
In two or three cases the wives work because they are
lonely. A piano is the sign of luxury. Comfort is far
more often to be met with than good taste.

Although the men comparatively seldom earn enough
to keep a wife and family, they are still the mainstay of
the home. So long as they earn a regular wage, even if
it is less than a sovereign, the home is fairly prosperous.
It is when this becomes irregular or fails for any reason
that the real trouble comes. Unemployment or irregular
employment is bad in every way. Especially at the first
the house-wife finds it difficult to adjust herself to a lower

standard of living. If the evil continues long it seems to result frequently in physical or moral deterioration.

It is quite impossible, however, to explain all discrepancies by a reference to wages. The welfare of the family, it is clear, depends ultimately more on the moral qualities and good management of the parents than on wages alone. Take, for instance, two families among the silk winders of Macclesfield. In one case the people are superior and the wife very intelligent ; and though the father is ill and out of work, and the family income, with relief money, only amounts to 24/- a week for nine persons, yet the home is nice and the children, all of whom are living, are clean and healthy. In the other the parents have been hawkers, though they are now trying more settled occupations ; the home is poor and dirty, five out of the eight children are dead, and the eldest, aged fourteen, is in Standard I : it is the worst case investigated. These are not isolated instances. Without insisting on its universal applicability, one may hazard the remark that the worst cases, that is, where the homes are not only poor but dirty, are associated with a general fecklessness ; while intelligent and efficient workers generally have good homes, whatever their incumbrances.

Many of the women have worked all their lives. The evidence does not prove this in itself to have very decided effects on them or their children. On the whole the women suffer most. If the family income has been low, and the number of children large, they generally show the result of the strain. But if they have been able to take things easily, they, their children and their homes are sometimes as prosperous as any. The comparative immunity of the children may be due in part to the noble services of the grandmothers of Leek and Macclesfield. In nearly half the cases where the arrangements for the care of the children are known, the grandmother is in charge of them, and does her work well.

The children suffer far more from dirt than from poverty alone, or from the absence of the mother during the day. In dirty homes the mortality among the children is frequently high, whereas in clean though poor homes they flourish. A high rate of mortality in families seems also often due to constitutional weakness.

The impression left by a perusal of the reports is one of strong admiration. The uninitiated can only marvel how the women contrive to keep their children and houses so well on so small an income and with so little time left from outside work. If these are fair specimens of the type produced by factory life, it must be a nursery of the domestic virtues. Only eight or nine homes were not clean. This desirable state of things doubtless arises partly from the fact that Macclesfield has only 34,000 inhabitants, and Leek 16,000, and that therefore the advantages of town and country life are in a great measure combined. The men also deserve praise. There are very few cases of really bad husbands, about half of these being due to drink. Drunkenness seems to be rare, and fortunately, judging from the condition of the homes of the transgressors. Only one woman is quoted as drinking ; it is no wonder that she does, but the children have suffered. When the husband is out of work he often takes the mother's place, and very efficiently. There are few dependents save the children : the exceptions in most cases are the mothers of husband or wife.

In all but four cases the women are natives of the town in which they work. Of the four exceptions three come from Manchester, and the other from Staffordshire, this last having been a servant all her life.

All but three women in Leek, and three or four in Macclesfield, worked in the silk trade before their marriage,

and in the great majority of cases in the same or practically the same department. This of course is only
natural, as it is the work for which they are best qualified.
Nearly all the children go into the mills when they begin
to work, and the majority of the husbands are also engaged there ; so that it is quite a family and hereditary
occupation. Some of those who were not in the mills
were in domestic service. The greatest diversity of
occupation is to be found among the eight cases labelled
as " Miscellaneous : Macclesfield." Washing, shirt-making and charing seem to be the most popular callings
with the few who are not employed in the silk trade.
Washing is, however, harder work than that in the
factories.

The home-workers are comparatively few in number.
They are paid at the same rate as those in the factories,
but the work is difficult to get, and very irregular. Otherwise not a few mothers would prefer to stay at home
when their children are quite young. Indeed the charges
for children put out to nurse are so high, 3/- to 4/- a
week as an average, that in a few cases where the babies
followed each other closely the mothers have been
obliged to stay at home, and take to poorly-paid homework, charing, etc. The objection of low pay does not
apply to the weavers and warpers, who earn the highest
wages of any ; but the old-fashioned hand-loom in the
garret is fast being displaced by the power-loom at the
mill.

The rate of wages varies enormously, but in Leek it
seems to strike an average of about 13/- a week. In
Macclesfield there is even less uniformity. The weavers
and warpers enjoy an average of 14/-, or thereabouts,
but two or three experienced workers said they could
earn £1 or more in good times. This is higher than anything mentioned at Leek. On the other hand the winders'
average is about 10/6, and in the " various " trades the

general level of pay does not rise far above 12/- a week. Those in service etc. generally take about 4/- a week, but they often have extras in the shape of meals and clothes. The Macclesfield women need an opportunity of making money, as there is little scope for the men.

The majority of the husbands are attached to the factories in some capacity ; but not a large majority. They seldom do the same kind of work as the women, but are often dyers, mechanics, lodge-keepers, etc. It cannot be said that their wages are high, but they are higher than the women's ; and in one case where this was shrewdly suspected not to be so, both husband and wife indignantly refused to give any details whatsoever. In fact the information about the husbands is very incomplete. It appears however, that work at the mill is fairly regular, save for such general disasters as the shutting-down of a factory, and therefore preferable to such occupations as those of labourers, whose work is very irregular and ill-paid, and even to those of painters or boot-menders. On the other hand regular and not highly skilled labour outside the mill is often better paid than that inside.

Women's wages are lower than men's, but more regular. All the women seem to be able to get work, provided they do not insist on working at home. But many of the men are unemployed, particularly at Macclesfield, and this through no fault of their own. It is therefore more necessary than ever that the women should help. Their work is regular, so that they are bound to follow it all the year round in order to keep it.

In Leek, so far as can be judged from the incomplete data, men earn on an average from 20/- to 22/- a week, and perhaps more in factories. The worst-off, however, are the least communicative. The men of Macclesfield find few openings. " There's nothing in this town for men," said one woman, and another gave as a reason for

working " Husbands don't get so much here, you see."
The average wage seems to be from 18/- to £1. But
there is great variation, and several are out of work, or
in irregular employment. One very decent man, with
three children, earns 6/- a week through slack time.
It is no wonder that the home is now dirty, though
in better days, when the mother was at home, it was
well-kept. Among the same class of workers, the silk
winders, the highest family income, 41/-, is enjoyed by
two families, the husbands earning 30/- apiece. In
other respects they differ. The one consists of a childless
couple ; the other of parents and five children ; the
mother has worked all her life, and likes it, the grandmother has taken care of the children, and the home is
extremely comfortable.

This instance supported by other evidence seems to
prove that, under favourable circumstances, it is possible
for a woman to continue working at the mill after
marriage without any very visible harm to herself
or her family. Not improbably the work is less trying
than the care of several young children. Indeed some
of the women who state that they like the life are delicate.
But it must be added that favourable conditions are
rare. A woman needs to be healthy in mind and body,
to be sure of sufficient support from her husband to enable
her to take a proper rest at confinements, and to be certain that the children will be properly looked after in
her absence. When these conditions are absent the mother
or children, or both, are likely to suffer. Among the silk
winders of Macclesfield, for example, four families have
lost children, about half the number born to them ; and
in every case the mother worked all through her married
life, the homes are poor and sometimes dirty, and the
husbands have been unfortunate. Three other families
have a numerous offspring, but have lost none. Of
these one is the exceptional case quoted above,

where the husband earned 30/- a week, and the wife liked going out to work. The others had seen better days, and the mothers were at home when the children were little.

Many mothers stay at home till the young ones are past infancy. Those who do not, generally stay at home two or three months at confinements ; unless detained longer by their own or the baby's delicacy. Unfortunately where the mother is the mainstay of the family or where there are many mouths to feed she is obliged to work very near the time. In the end this generally has a bad effect, though the results are not so noticeable as one might expect. Nine women of those engaged in the silk trade at Leek are mentioned as having worked up to the last : most of them have large families ; five have lost a child ; three look delicate and seem to have had a hard life. A Macclesfield silk reeler has six children under eleven, including twins of five months ; she has worked all her life, the family income is 28/6, and they had a hard winter ; she and the babies are in bad health.

A weaver in the same town who has been the mainstay of her household all her life lost all her five children when under one year ; she is a very intelligent woman and took every care over the choice of foster-mothers. Of two women in the smallware trade at Leek, who have worked all their lives, one, a rather dense woman, who nursed none of her children, has lost four out of nine ; and the other four out of seven, apparently from some tubercular complaint ; both homes are poor and untidy. One cannot help suspecting that constitutional weakness, or ignorance, have a good deal to do with these misfortunes.

When the husband is bad the wife and children invariably suffer a great deal.

The mothers do their best to nurse their own children,

and perhaps that is one reason why, on the whole, the children are very healthy.

After the examples given above it is cheering to look at a brighter side of the picture. A couple in Macclesfield have eight children, all living, four being in Canada ; the family income never exceeded 25/- a week and though the mother never went out to work she turned her hand to anything she could at home. A weaver in the same town who has been in the mill all her life has brought up eleven out of thirteen children ; eight of them are boys, and have all been apprenticed. Both homes are very good. It is evident that if the parents of large families can stand the strain they reap their advantage in later years. For instance, one family, where six out of the seven children are adults, enjoys a minimum income of £3 a week, though the father has been ill for several years.

Widows manage better than might be expected. Probably they have help from relatives and neighbours ; and besides the chief bread-winner is also the most expensive person to keep.

Factory-life appears to be healthy. Some of the women complain of the standing ; but most of them soon become used to it. The " gassers," of whom there are few, suffer the most, on account of the heat ; though the firms do their best to cool the rooms. One young mother with two children, one a baby a few weeks old, declares she will be obliged to give up that work as it is bad for the infant.

One of the worst and most constant results of an inadequate family income is that the elder children are put to work as soon as possible. They begin as " half-timers " at the age of twelve, whether they are physically fit or not, to the detriment of their health and education.

Only one or two of the husbands object to their wives

working ; and among these the most decided opinions are attributed to one long dead. This in itself seems to prove that married women's work is necessary under present conditions, and that it is possible to carry it out without causing much domestic unrest.

READING.

Celia Reiss.

The wages of married women and widows could not well be lower than they are at Reading.

As is usually the case the reasons why married women become wage earners are such as the following:—" To supplement husband's wages "—" Because of husband's ill-health "—To support self and children since deserted by husband."

In Reading Biscuit Making employs a fair proportion of women.

There is the case of the woman, aged 28, who returned to it two months ago, when her husband (bricklayer's labourer at 5½d. an hour) was out of work.

Her job is to feed the ovens, but she says she cannot stand it much longer; indeed her husband is just beginning work again, and if her mother-in-law can get a job of charing she hopes to be able to leave it off. Meantime her one and only child (a year old baby) is in the charge of her mother-in-law, and besides these two she has to help support her brother-in-law and sister-in-law, neither of whom is yet old enough to add to the family income. She earns 8/6 a week for 54½ hours' work (excluding meal times).

Another woman says her pay varies from 6/– to 10/– a week. Full time is from 7 a.m. to 6 p.m. but she manages to look after her own three children (varying in ages from 5 to 9), as they are all at school, and she can go home to mid-day dinner. She began the work two years ago,

when her husband (a cook ; away from home) was unemployed, and she has kept it on, as he only earns (or lets
her have) 15/– a week. We have a case of one woman
and her daughter earning 8/– and 5/– respectively to
support themselves and the rest of the family, *i.e.*, two
children and the woman's husband. The husband had
an accident and cannot get work, though he hopes some-
time to do light jobs.

One woman, aged 30, has an invalid husband who only
earns 8/– or 10/–, as a golf caddy, and has to take her share
in supporting the three children, the eldest of whom is 10.
She has even had to return to the factory a fortnight
after the birth of a child. She earns from 7/– to 9/– a
week. A neighbour takes care of her children, and her
home is clean, though scantily furnished, for she " had
to sell up everything to prevent her father going into the
Union."

PAPER BAG MAKING seems to be a little more profitable,
one woman managing to earn 14/– to 15/– a week, at an
average of 3½d. or 3¾d. an hour. She only needs to do
the work when her husband, a plasterer, is out of work.

RAG SORTING is a very dusty job, but one woman has
survived 33 years of it ! She works seven hours daily,
earning, roughly, 10/– a week, to support herself and her
incapacitated husband, with the help of her five grown
children.

Another woman (working from eight to six) earns
10/– a week at a SAUCE AND PICKLE factory, as her
husband " only has a newspaper round," bringing in
8/– a week, and they have two children (ages five and
eight), to support. Her age is 28.

Working in the chemical part of a FLY-PAPER FACTORY,
was unhealthy, so after her marriage one woman took on
a different job in the same factory, only leaving it when
her only child (now a sickly girl of 11) was born. She
was obliged to continue the work, as her husband is

frequently ill with abscesses and never earns more than 18/– a week.

CHARING is an occupation chiefly chosen by those who have had no " trade " before marriage or who have been in service.

One woman whose husband was a " bad lot " had to support herself in this way, till now, at 71, the old age pension and help from married children relieve her of toil.

Another charwoman is a widow who has to keep a home not only for herself, but for a grand-daughter, the child of her own dead daughter, and a worse than useless father. This woman earns 6/– a week and adds to that 5/– from a sailor son.

One case we have of a thrifty family accumulating enough to buy their own house, for which they have already bought the land. The father earns 19/– at the biscuit factory, the wife 6/6 to 7/– for " daily work " or " taking in washing," and the son 5/– or 6/– as typist, while only one other child is dependent.

Two shillings a day is the amount frequently earned for charing. In one case a widow does cleaning in the summer and seed-sorting in the winter, her average pay for the latter being 3d. an hour. Her only two living children —five having died before they were nine years old— earn their own livelihood.

TAKING IN WASHING seems a favourite job, though unre-munerative, and again we have to quote the case of a wife now aged 51 deserted—fourteen years ago, before her youngest child was born. Now four of her children are earning their living and only one is partly dependent, so the meagre 4/– which she earns for " washing " is supplemented by her children. But she has had to work too hard to be in good health, having been for years the sole support of her children. She made use of her prenuptial trade of " children's nurse," and went out nursing " under the hospital," as well as doing washing and charing.

TAILORING seems also unremunerative, for one woman says she gets only 3/– a week for two to three hours work a day. It was her trade before marriage, and in those days she was paid at the rate of 4d. an hour. Now she is unable to fetch the work on account of four young children. She and her husband (a groom earning 21/– a week) managed to save up a little to meet the expense of her confinements, and enable her also to stop work for about six weeks. At present they pay a rent of 6/6 weekly for six rooms. This seems about the usual rate at Reading, for we have cases of 7/6 for seven rooms ; 4/– for four rooms ; 7/– for five rooms ; 4/– for three rooms, a washhouse and a garden ; 7/– for six rooms.

For DRESSMAKING another woman earns 8/– a week. That was her trade before marriage also, but she did not take it up till four years ago, when her husband's health failed. Now he brings in 15/– a week, and two grownup children subscribe 14/– between them for the upkeep of the home.

Some widows return to SERVICE, as also do women who have separated from their husbands. Indeed we have one case of a woman (38 years old) who has to support her children in this way. Her husband was a drunkard and treated her cruelly, and she was at length legally separated from him. The court ordered him to pay 8/–, but as he never does so various help is given and kind friends maintain two of their four children, while the mother pays 10/– a week for the board and lodging of the remaining two, aged six years and three years respectively.

There is the case of a childless woman who prefers being servant to two ladies to taking in workmen lodgers. For this she earns 7/6, as well as coal and light and house room for herself and her husband. Another woman, whose husband earns 19/– to 20/– a week, goes out as servant five mornings weekly, but only when her two children are at school. She works in order to keep the house comfortable and not to take in lodgers.

Then there is the woman who " keeps the post office and the confectionery shop," in which she is helped by her husband, who has recently lost his work at the biscuit factory. And again there is a strong-minded woman who *cultivates an acre or so of ground to grow vegetables.* Her not very capable husband works in the garden under her direction, and her one child has recently taken her place in going round with the cart " vegetable selling."

The National Federation of Women Workers has a branch in Reading, though not a strong one.

GLASGOW.

Isabel Basnett.

See Preface, p. vi.

THE small investigation into the work of married women and workers which has been carried out in the Mile End and Anderston districts of Glasgow has revealed some very interesting facts. It may be wise at the outset to state that Mile End is at the east end of Glasgow and Anderston near the river, and they both contain many of those gaunt, dreary tenement buildings which are such a feature of this Scottish town. The " houses " in these buildings consist of one or two rooms. In Mile End rent is higher for one room than in Anderston ; 2/3 or 2/6 has to be paid in Mile End against 2/1½ in Anderston, but for two rooms rents are lower in Mile End—3/5 against 3/7 and 4/– in the district by the river. In Mile End the men are mostly artisans and labourers earning very low wages ; in Anderston, there are more dock labourers and men who only do casual labour of some other kinds; but men's wages are, when they are working, higher than those of the men living in Mile End.

The work of the women consists in Mile End of work in paper bag factories (parcelling, etc.), in clothing factories as shirt and trouser finishers ; in cotton mills as winders ; a small number do charing. In Anderston their work consists of cloth-lapping, which work is also frequently done by men ; in working in bolt and rivet factories, in printing works, in rag stores and a fairly large number work at charing, office cleaning, etc. In the majority of

cases investigated dire necessity was the reason of the
woman having to work—if married, to eke out the scanty
or irregular wages of the husband, or if widowed or
deserted, to keep a home together and a roof over the
children's heads.

To take a few typical cases :—

Mrs. C., Mile End, lives with her husband, who only
works very irregularly and at his highest only earns
18/- a week. The home consists of two rooms, rent 3/5.
She has two boys, 16 and 17, both in wire work, who
earn respectively 6/- and 7/- weekly. Besides these
two boys, she has a child of four and a half. She is out
all day working at parcelling paper bags in a factory, and
the husband looks after the child when he is out of work.
Mrs. C. earns 7/- a week, more or less, according to the
amount of orders.

Mrs. K., Anderston, is a forewoman in a cloth-lapping
store, and is obliged to work because though her husband
earns 30/- to £2, he is a drinker and takes himself off
periodically, so unless Mrs. K. worked her home would
be gone. She earns as a steady wage 12/- a week only.
She pays 3/7 for the rent of two rooms.

Mrs. M., Anderston, is a charwoman and has practically
to keep her husband. A delicate woman of 50, living
in one room and paying 2/5 a week rent.

Mrs. C., Anderston, a young woman of 25 with
two tiny children, has to put the babies out with her
sister while she works all day in a rag store for 8/- a week,
keeping herself and children practically, as the husband
earns only a very small irregular wage.

And so on and so on—we might continue multiplying
instances of women working all day for an absolutely
inadequate wage to keep the home going. In no case
do we find a woman in these two districts earning more
than 12/-, and freqently down to 7/-. In many instances
we find necessity compelling the woman to work up

almost to the hour when her child is born—with all the consequent bad results, ill-health for the mother and the early death of the child.

Wages have fallen in some trades, particularly in the paper bag trade and in the clothing trade, because of the increase of machinery. There seems to be little or no competition with men ; but in the rivet and bolt trade it is the exception for married women to be employed.

With regard to the work of widows, charing is the trade for the older ones, and among the younger, work in restaurants, blouse factories and cotton mills take foremost places—and the wages are, of course, as low as those paid to the married women. It seems deplorable that a young woman of 33 (who has been deserted by her husband) with three children, all under 14, should be unable to earn more than 7/- a week. This Mrs. T. received in addition 2/6 a week from the parish, making 14/- in all, on which to feed, house, and clothe a family of four. Or again, Mrs. D., a widow of 35, has one child entirely dependent on her and can only earn 10/- a week. In this case there was no poor relief, as there was some difficulty about the woman's settlement.

Inquiries as to health among the women elicited only somewhat indefinite answers on the whole ; but it was clearly shown in some cases that the health of the mother had suffered by her working up to the last day before confinement, and death or ill-health had been the lot of the child. On the other hand, some women said their health had clearly improved. The frequently overcrowded state of the house must be borne in mind in considering any question of the health of the women and children in these districts of Glasgow. Where two adults and three or four children have to live, eat and sleep in two rooms it is impossible that their health can be first-rate.

LEICESTER.

Margaret G. Skinner.

A SHORT time ago a very thorough investigation was
made of two typical working-class wards in Leicester,
and one result of this interested and sympathetic inquiry
is a detailed description of a large number of working-
class families. The observations in general are of
immense human interest, but chiefly valuable perhaps
for the definite facts they give as to why the mothers of
these families—contrary to the accepted domestic ideal—
engaged in paid occupations. The usual assumption is
that the woman can do best by staying at home, and
that it is a serious disadvantage if she carries on a trade,
and this idea seems to be supported by expert opinion,
for in the medical report of 1908 on the health of Leicester
—where are the two districts in question—it is suggested
that a great number of infant deaths were due to the
employment of married women in factories; and in 1909
the medical officer to the Education Committee stated
without any ambiguity that there are in his opinion three
remedies for the improvement of the home conditions
that produce such numbers of sickly, neglected and
deficient children, and these are : (1) the formation of a
strong public opinion against the marriage of weakly
persons ; (2) the reduction as far as possible of the
employment of married women in factories, and (3) the
raising of the school-age of children till 14 years. It is
interesting in the face of this to come to facts—since it is
probably true that ideas do not move so quickly as facts

—to discover how and why it is that such large numbers of married women do actually work at trades.

For the numbers are large. According to the census of 1901 over a quarter of all married women in Leicester were engaged in occupations, and the percentage must obviously be greater in the poorer districts, where the majority of unmarried women are self-supporting and where most young women have some kind of trade at their fingers' ends. In point of fact, the inquiry of which we speak shows that out of 560 families visited in St. Margaret's Ward and Abbey Ward in Leicester, about 43 married women in every 100 were earning wages. And basing our calculations upon the facts we have, of these 43, $16\frac{2}{3}$ earn supplementary sums of less than $\frac{1}{2}$ of the family income, $6\frac{1}{3}$ earn $\frac{1}{3}$ of the whole income, 8 earn equal sums or larger sums than their husbands, and 11 entirely support their families. Disregarding those women who earn smaller supplementary sums, we find then that $25\frac{1}{3}$ families in a hundred depend very largely on the money earned by the woman of the house.

St. Margaret's Ward is a very thickly populated district containing some of the worst slums in Leicester and also a number of very superior working-class streets. Abbey Ward is a better neighbourhood, but composed almost entirely of working-men's houses. The houses throughout were counted, and $\frac{1}{10}$ visited in each street—sometimes information was refused, but of 401 houses, that is, approximately, $\frac{1}{10}$ of St. Margaret's Ward, we have definite information as to 329, and of 286 houses, or approximately $\frac{1}{10}$ of the houses of Abbey Ward, definite information as to 231—this giving the total mentioned above of 560 families. And it is probable that this method of inquiry has given as widely a representative group of women as it is possible to obtain.

Although the women interviewed may roughly be divided into those who never intended to give up work at marriage, and those who took up work again after some years of married life, it is impossible to determine what proportion are driven to earn money by real necessity, for the standard of living is so varied. We find one respectable couple in a comfortable and neat house with a joint income of from £2 to £3 a week who say they cannot afford to have children—if they were sure of £3 a week " the wife would give up working," said the husband ; she said she could manage on less, though they " never could keep themselves respectable on a man's wage " (she earned about 16/- a week punching toe-caps at 3d. a gross, and he could earn about 35/- when on full time in a shoe factory). We know also of a woman earning 15/- a week who kept a sick husband and sent 2 children so neat and well-dressed to school that the authorities considered them too well-off to be granted free meals ! But take the opinion of the women themselves. Very few of them, as one said " go out to work for fun ; but it is better to work all the week and have things a little comfortable at the week-end than never any comfort at all." This woman's life is a miracle of good management. Married to a brewer's man who earns 18/- a week, she herself leaves every morning at 9 for the factory, having first made ready on the gas stove the meal which she comes to cook at midday for her 2 children who are at school. She earns £1 a week, and only gave up work whilst her children were babies, for later she entrusted them to her mother. A capable young woman of about 30, she expressed her opinions with reluctance but said she thought that married women's work should not be stopped, and that she was sure that many women who went out to work made their homes more comfortable than those who did not.

And if it is possible to generalize at all, the first statement we should make after a careful reading of our facts is that it is usually the intelligent woman earning a good wage who is the best manager and has most care of her family. And if it is difficult sometimes to agree with her that her contribution is necessary, it is usually possible to admire her for the reason that pushes her to work. For instance, the second wife of a foreman in a shoe factory, though childless herself, never gave up work. She was glad to help her husband, she said, to keep her step-children, since the mother of the first wife lived with them to look after the house ; and, too, she was able to help a sister who had a crowd of small children, by paying her to do the weekly wash. Another woman works to pay the rent of a larger house than her husband's wage could afford so that her boys and girls may have separate rooms " to keep them respectable." These cases are quite typical, and probably show sufficiently how value-less is any attempt to determine how often the woman's wage is not definitely necessary. On the other hand, however, by counting the numbers of neglected homes and well-managed homes, we discover that the wage-earning woman is just as likely to be a good housekeeper as not.

To take a few numbers at haphazard. Of 9 women engaged in corset making, 6 have clean and comfortable homes ; 2 of these where the husbands earn good wages are exceptionally comfortable, 4 are poorer but well cared-for, 2 are untidy, and one, the house of a drunken good-natured woman and drunken husband, is neglected and dirty. Of 26 women engaged in the woollen trade, 15 have clean and comfortable homes ; of 33 engaged in the hosiery trade 19 have well-managed homes, and of 31 engaged in the shoe trade 21 have well-managed homes. It is interesting in this connection to notice a statement of the medical officer in the report on the health of Leicester for 1895, concerning the illness which accounts for more infant deaths than any other single complaint— for he states that out of 82 deaths from diarrhœa of children under 6 months of age, the mothers went out to work in 21 cases only ; and of 137 cases visited of diarrhœa in babies the mother went out to work in 37 only.   For all these facts show that there is no evidence to prove that the married woman who goes out to work is less careful of her own and her family's well-being than are other women.

Our information then does not permit of any general statement against the married woman-worker. Roughly 25 per cent. of the families depend very largely upon the woman's wage, but it is impossible to show what percentage of these women, and still less what percentage of the other married workers are driven to work by real necessity.   And it is equally impossible to show that the woman who, not driven by poverty, yet deliberately choses to follow a trade is apt to neglect her children or her home, or to be lacking in self-respect.   It is obviously a physical impossibility for a woman to be the one efficient servant to a large family and an efficient factory hand as well.   But very few working-women attempt to lead this double life.   In all other classes, children are handed over to trained care.   Why should not the working-woman too entrust her children to another ? She can surely still love and protect them as richer women do.   Of six married cigar-makers in Leicester, one woman alone did not think her husband's wage quite insufficient, although she earned a weekly sum equal to his, and although he admitted that it was she who had kept the family going for many weeks when he was out of work. A delicate woman, she explained that she never could have done rough housework.   She had paid 5/- a week for her eldest child to be taken care of ; but for 9 years a widow whom she had rescued from the workhouse had lived with them to take care of the children and the house in return for her keep.   The husband, a warehouse-man earning 25/- a week, explained how it was that women had displaced men in the cigar trade, not only because they were cheaper, but because they were lighter-handed, and a lightly-rolled cigar draws best. Such prosperous and well managed homes as this seem to show that conscience and intelligence are not confined to one class. One is forced to ask, too, why heavy laundry work and the scrubbing of floors should be considered a woman's work rather than rolling cigars in a factory, shall we say ? And the case of the woman who gave as one reason for going out to work, that she was able thereby to help a sister, the mother of a large family, by paying her to do the household washing, prompts a question as to why it is customary for every woman in a street to devote every Monday to the washing of clothes, when the best laundress of them might, by using modern labour-saving appliances, do this work for them all, with little extra effort than her own " wash " demanded ? Such co-operation as this could not in any way arrest the improvement of home conditions, and would certainly lighten the burden of physical duties that presses so needlessly on working-women ; and such co-operation is only possible if women, married or independent, are free to chose their own line of work.

In point of fact we find, as we have said, that the intelligent woman capable of earning a good wage usually manages her home well—she sets out to earn money that she may manage it better. In the light of our facts, then, we cannot find any reasons for wishing to interfere with her liberty. And since we disagree with the medical officer to the Education Committee of Leicester when he advises the restriction of the employment of married women, we may perhaps say also that if the other two remedies suggested by him became effective that undoubtedly greater numbers of women will become wage-earners— not only will a higher standard of education with the consequent higher standard of living inspire greater

numbers of women to demand paid work, but with the
restriction of marriage many more women would perforce become self-supporting. It is obvious that as it
becomes more customary for women to become wage-
earners, it will become more necessary for each of them to
learn a trade thoroughly ; and it is the well-trained and
well paid worker who is so reluctant to give up her work
when she has a family, " just when the money is so
necessary." If the generally accepted idea that the
increase of the employment of married women is due to
the increase of female labour in factories is a true fact,
to restrict the employment of married women and at the
same time urge the other two reforms in question, would
seem as futile as to try to stop a cart by thrusting a
walking-stick between the spokes of its heavy wheel
when the driver is still whipping up the horses.

This extraordinarily interesting collection of facts
includes also the opinions—so far as they were willing to
give them—of all the employers of the women of whose
lives we have such intimate details. The majority dislike
employing married workers, although they cannot give
any definite reasons for this, except that they find
married women too independent—married women in fact
are likely to demand a fair wage ! One employer did say
that he found the married woman more reliable and
steady than the unmarried girl. But in all justice to the
employer, his prejudice springs undoubtedly not so much
from a mercenary source, as from the usual conviction
that the woman can do best by staying at home. And it
must be remembered that this idea must hamper the
women themselves by making it difficult for them to take
a proper pride in their work—and in this way a class of
poor and unreliable workers is created, workers who will
take up work spasmodically to supplement the husband's
wage, and will readily drop work again so soon as the
need—real or fancied—for the additional sum has been

satisfied.   Would not women be forced to leave the trades
for which they are less fitted, if an equal wage for equal
work were the rule ?   And it is probable that then greater
numbers of them would devote their energy and brain to
the duties closely connected with the household—to
trades in fact that would be directly useful to them as
mothers and housekeepers, and at which they could work
after marriage without incurring the chief criticism now
levelled at the married wage-earner.   In this way, too,
the work that women alone can do, would be better done
than it is at present.

The census of 1901 showed that in Leicester 9910
unmarried and 3969 married women were engaged in the
hosiery, textile, tailoring and paper trades, and 5924
unmarried and 2867 married women were employed in the
shoe-trade.   Now the majority of these unmarried women
inevitably follow a trade, and the majority of them must
be quite ignorant of cooking and catering when they come
to marry.   Does it not seem better that they should at marriage leave this domestic work to others and continue their
own trades ?   And this is what we find so many desire, and
some actually do.   At all events, in the absence of any
proof that the family of the married woman worker is
apt to suffer for the reason that she spends some—or
even most of her time—in work not connected with her
home, it is impossible to welcome any repressive measure
that robs her of her independence.   And a careful reading
of this most illuminating collection of facts about the
women workers in Leicester but strengthens the belief
that it will be only by granting every individual the
right to chose her own line of work that thrifty and
energetic and intelligent schemes of life will become more
general.

RURAL DISTRICTS.

M. F. DAVIES.[1]

THE work of married women for wages has been investigated in three rural districts, of which one is situated in Worcestershire, one in Essex and one in Wiltshire.

1.—WORCESTERSHIRE.

FIELDWORK.—Within the memory of people still alive women worked habitually in the fields in many parts of England. Now it is only in few and far apart districts that women are to be found who, as part of their daily routine, perform certain duties about the fields and farms of their own neighbourhood.

In the North West of Worcester and the contiguous parts of Herefordshire lies a tract where no great change has taken place in the work of women for the last fifty years, and where the young wife of to-day living "under a farmer" takes her share in the work of the farm almost as much as a matter of course as did her grandmother. Four parishes were visited, situated in the North Western arm of Worcestershire, spreading over many square miles of land and containing, at the census of 1901, a population of 663 persons. Of these 140 were male householders, of whom 23 farmed over 20 acres, 39 were small holders and 58 agricultural labourers ; while the remaining 20

[1] The articles about rural workers had not received their final revision at the time of their author's death and might have been altered in a few particulars. The wages, for example, were to have appeared in a tabulation which has not been found among her papers.

included the squires, clergy, school teachers, game-keepers, etc. There were also some women householders. The countryside is fruitful and extremely picturesque. No glacial period can have sent its rollers to flatten out this landscape. High ridge and deep valley are broken up with indescribable irregularity into a thousand hills and valleys watered by rushing streams. Even the different fields have each their well marked natural features and varieties. There are old-fashioned orchards where apples, plums and damsons grow together upon trees set in no rigid lines, and drop, when ripe, into rich meadow grass. There are gardens, hayfields and arable lands; and there are also hop-yards with their thousands of poles upright as a regiment of soldiers. Through the pleasant country the habitations lie scattered, here a hamlet bordering the highway, there a pair of cottages, then a single homestead buried in a crevice of the hillside and approached by a lane knee-deep in mire which entraps the stranger, while the native follows some scarce visible track through the long grass of meadow or orchard. The houses, too, are picturesque. Old timbered cottages, in the walls of which rough-cast lath-and-plaster has been replaced by mellow red brick generally contain three or four rooms. Within, the rooms are often whitewashed; hams and strings of onions hang from the oak beams of the kitchen ceiling; the great open fire-places are filled with blazing logs, and behind them run deep baking ovens. The red brick floors are uncovered, the furniture plain and simple, and there is an absence of useless litter that, together with the warm colouring, helps to give an impression of genuine comfort. The comfort, however, is too often rather apparent then real. So damp are the walls that where they have been papered the paper is generally peeling off; the bricks that pave the living room are often broken, and generally so porous that a bucketful of water poured upon them vanishes at once. Needless to say, rheumatism is prevalent, and although the disease is usually attributed to cider drinking, the dampness of these dwellings appears to provide a sufficient cause. Many of the men employed by farmers live rent free or nearly rent free in a cottage with garden or ' pig-run ' *i.e.*, orchard, belonging to their employer ; but it is a condition of so living—and there is usually no alternative—that the wife shall perform certain services for the farmer, such as tying a certain acreage of hops and helping in the hayfield at the busiest times. The monopoly of cottages by the farmers is a hardship to the labourer, who is rendered liable to be turned out at a week's notice, and who but for this circumstance would be in a very independent position, since labour appears by no means overabundant, and unemployed farm hands few. Rents for tenants who do not live " under a farmer " range up to £8 a year.

Agriculture is the only industry of importance, and the main branches, here, are stock raising, hop growing, and fruit growing. Ancient freehold small holdings are numerous, but diminishing ; the owners tend to sell, and most of the holdings are mortgaged.

Men employed as regular farm hands earn, broadly speaking, 12/- to 14/- per week, and are allowed in summer three quarts of cider per day. Little harvest money is given. An able-bodied day labourer earns 2/6 to 3/- per day, with cider.

Nearly all the cottages keep pigs or poultry, and it is estimated that they can make £2 to £3 a year by the sale of fruit. There is no market for vegetables but the gardens supply a large part of the food consumed at home.

About thirty women, known to be workers, were visited, most of whom were wives of labourers. Probably a chief share in the work of the homestead falls upon the wife, who also usually bakes her own bread and walks to the nearest town, some five miles distant, for her weekly marketing. Many women work three or four ten-hour days a week (from eight till six, or till dark) for the farmer, and a few go out to work every day in the week. Public opinion approves of wage earning by married women ; and the woman who abstains from working in the fields is taunted—even if she has young children—with being lazy. Various inhabitants of the district assert that the houses and children of the women who go out to work are better kept than those of the women who stay at home ; and appearances on the whole confirmed the assertion. The work of women is, nevertheless, tending to decrease, and probably no pressure is put upon the mother of young children, even when living " under the farmer," to go to work.

A woman who works for a farmer as a condition of occupying his cottage is paid 10d., or in some cases 1/- for her day's work, and is usually allowed one pint of cider if she cares to fetch it, which as a rule she does not. A woman whose work is not contributory to her rent receives 1/- per day. Piece work rates—which vary somewhat—yield different totals of course, according to the skill and speed of different workers. Employers and workers alike declare that the women are not pressed. They can take their children with them to the fields, and one farmer said that if his women took an hour or two off to go and look after their babies no complaint would be made.

By their own account they frequently stop to rest. In an orchard, one day, where they were " apple picking " several women were found in a picturesque group warming themselves around a large bonfire that they had lighted, and appeared in no hurry to resume their work.

Except farm servants, whose duties are of course, of a different kind, no women are employed regularly the whole year round. Those who desire regular work can have it for five to nine months of the year ; and during those months the most energetic often work almost daily, filling the places of others less willing to do so.

The following processes are those in which women are principally employed:

GROUND DRESSING, i.e., picking up bits of stick or stone from the fields, begins towards March.

HOP TYING is the fastening of wires up which the young shoots of the hop are trained. The fastening of each wire requires the worker to go three times round each pole. It is delicate work—some of the women said " fiddly " and tiresome—and the smaller hands of women are considered better adapted for it than those of men. The work is generally paid for by the piece, at 5/- an acre. Some women can earn 1/4 a day at it, but an unaccustomed and unskilled worker coming fresh to the district and bound to the farmer may be unable to make 6d. a day.

HAY MAKING often entails lengthened hours of work. As a set-off, however, tea is given by some employers ; and in some cases a bonus is also given at the conclusion of the hay harvest, which brings the rate of pay up to 1/3 per day. Some women are asserted to have earned 1/6.

ROOT SINGLING is often performed by a man and his wife together.

HOP PICKING employs not only nearly all the women and children of the district—including women who do no other field work—but also large numbers of people from Dudley and the Black Country, as well as from Bewdley and Kidderminister. The two populations seldom hold much intercourse, natives and visitors working, as a rule, in different " yards." Whole families, parents, children and even babies go together into the hopfields where the very young can be of help. Each family has a " vat " and the rate of pay varies according to the size of the hops. In some seasons eight bushels must be picked for 1/-, in others, only, perhaps, five.

FRUIT PICKING generally means, for women, the picking up of fallen fruit. Occasionally, however, women mount ladders into the trees and gather damsons, and for doing so their pay will exceed 1/- per day. One woman said she made 1/6 on piece rates.

The picking up of fallen fruit is paid in some cases by the piece, in some, by time. One old lady declared herself able to make 2/- a day by some knack of gathering up the apples into her apron ; she seldom, however, got employed at the work. Some women, especially, of course, those who are rheumatic, find the continuous stooping tiring. Apple picking is passing to some extent into the hands of men, although men are less skilful and more highly paid. Farmers probably prefer to employ their regular farm hands when these happen not to be fully occupied.

MANGEL AND SWEDE PULLING occupies the women in November. A worker said she was paid 10/- the acre for getting up the roots. The Annual Report of the Hereford Diocesan Social Service Committee states the usual rate to be 1½d. per 100 yards.

POTATO SORTING AND SACK MENDING affords employment on some farms for wet days, under shelter in the farm buildings.

THRESHING by machine often makes work for a woman who sits at the top of the machine to cut the binding round the sheaves.

2.—WILTSHIRE.

GLOVERS—Since the disappearance in the course of the industrial revolution of the clothing industry from the villages of Wiltshire a new industry, that of glove making, has arisen and greatly increased.

In Westbury or its immediate neighbourhood there are three or more factories, one of them employing as many as one hundred and seventy-five indoor workers, male and female, in addition to large numbers of home-workers (women) in surrounding villages and also in Oxford-shire and Devonshire. Seven parishes within a radius of five or six miles were visited. The great majority of the women interviewed stitched gloves by hand ; but a few button holers and machine stitchers were found living near the factory. Button holers received 2½d. to 8½d. per dozen pairs and could finish about that quantity in an hour ; machinists were paid 2/9 or 3/- per dozen pairs—about a day's work. For hand stitching the rates range between 4/6 and 7/- for the dozen pairs, and 5/- is the most general. Workers provide thread, wax and needles at a total cost of probably 2d. to 3d. per dozen pairs. Skilled stitchers reckon from two to four hours for making one pair ; three hours per pair is probably a good average for women who can work without interruption. Work is fetched and returned fortnightly by the stitchers who usually walk to and fro.

Glove stitching is thus a purely parasitic industry. No woman has been met with who attempts to support her-self by it ; those who work at it are married women, or elderly women depending upon private incomes or upon outdoor relief, and girls, who for some reason are living at home instead of following the usual practice of going away to service. Children are said frequently to help their mothers by " tying off " and also by stitching. Local byelaws permit the employment at home in indus-trial work of school children between 7 and 8.15 a.m. and 4.30. and 8 p.m. on school days. In one family two pale girls of ten and twelve help their mother and are immensely proud of doing so. The elder was reported by her mother to work on school days three-quarters of an hour before breakfast and three hours after tea ; on Saturdays and holidays the three together are able to get through a great deal of gloving. But the entirely sedentary occupation and the strain on the eyesight cannot be good for these willing young toilers. In another house a mother said that her daughter of thirteen had been helping her in the gloving for two years.

Few women sit steadily at this work or seem desirous of doing so ; it appears to be monotonous and uninteresting and it tires the eyes ; it is generally kept at hand and taken up at odd moments. The smallness of gloves facilitates this custom ; indeed, since they must be kept perfectly clean, gloves could hardly be made by home-workers if they were not small. Some notion of the ordinary output was obtained by noting the earnings for four weeks of twenty married women whose names were taken at random from the books and whose weekly average was 1/11 each. Yet it is the prospect of gaining these tiny sums that induces the women to take up this work. They need to eke out a husband's low wage or some other inadequate income or they desire to have a shilling or two of their very own, as they feel their personal earnings to be.

The husbands of the gloving women are in some cases employed in glove or tan factories, some are artisans and many work on the land. Incomes therefore vary greatly, but those of labourers with large families are seldom sufficient for the needs of the household. Rents are generally low, beginning at 1/6 a week for a cottage and garden. On the other hand many cottages are ill-built, small and dark. The most highly rented houses visited are in a row recently built at Ditton's Marsh by the Westbury and Whorlesden Rural District Council. These houses contain five rooms and a wash-house, seem well built and are let, mostly to factory workers or artisans, at 4/9 per week ; they have small gardens. Except in Westbury Leigh gardens are the rule and profits as well as produce are often derived from them. The ground plan of most of these villages is a line of straggling street, but in one or two the houses are scattered, singly or in hamlets.

The cottage floors are mostly covered with linoleum or carpet, and the living rooms crowded with furniture ; there will be table and chairs, often a sofa or couch of some description—not infrequently in rags—sometimes a wooden settle or screen filling or blocking up a good deal of space, almost invariably one chest of drawers and sometimes two. Very often there will be a collection of more or less useless decorations—various draperies, ornaments of glass or china, paper screens, perhaps a stuffed squirrel, cat or bird, and numerous indescribable knick-knacks. On entering one receives an impression of cramped discomfort and disorder, accentuated of course, where there is no second sitting room. Psychologically considered these redundances may perhaps afford relief in a life centred so exclusively within her own four walls as is that of the Wiltshire glover, but their presence in the kitchen-living room must add materially to the labour of cleaning—and it must be said that, with few exceptions, the homes visited were scrupulously clean.

The maiked characteristic of home life here—as in too many other districts of England, both rural and urban —is the isolation of each household. Not to be on familiar terms with the neighbours is regarded indeed as a sign of respectability. The man goes out to work, the children go out to school. It is upon the woman, left at home, that the evil presses especially, inducing a depression of spirits and a morbid exaggeration of minor ailments that rob her of pleasure in living, and that doubtless react in the form either of passive languor or of active ill-temper upon the husband and children when they return.

Perhaps the tonic to self-respect afforded by earning something for herself may be sometimes counterbalanced in the case of the glover by the eye-strain which, in the absence of suitable glasses, causes constant headache. It was certainly impossible to overlook the contrast that existed broadly speaking, between the glovers who seldom left their homes and the charwomen or other earners who went out to other people's houses. The latter workers were found to be generally alert, good-tempered and full of vitality, energy and cheerfulness. The most buoyant, perhaps, of all, was a woman who on market days helped relatives at an inn in a country town.

Depression of spirits accompanied by constant complaints of ill-health was remarked less frequently in lonely houses amid woods and fields than in villages or towns, where the isolation of the women is artificial, and was not so striking in cases where big sons and daughters brought in new and active interests. Certainly the Wiltshire cottage woman who goes out to work is a healthier, happier person, a better mother, and, presumably, a better mate than her home-keeping sister.

3.—ESSEX.

TAILORESSES.

WORKERS employed in the old-established tailoring industry of the Colchester district were visited in three villages. All three—and indeed the whole neighbourhood—are healthy and enjoy a bracing climate. Rowledge stands along the estuary of the Colne in which, during the winter, a number of private yachts are laid up ; while during the summer, these crafts are largely manned from the population of Rowledge and West Mersea. In West Mersea, an island possessing wild and beautiful coast scenery, agriculture and fishing are also carried on. Boxted, the site of the Salvation Army's recent experiment in small holdings, is, as far as men are concerned, a purely agricultural village.

The men employed on yachts, who are often absent for many of the warmer months of the year, receive 26/- or 29/- a week, together with a part of their clothes, but without board.   It is customary to send home £1 a week. Cooks, stewards and captains are more highly paid, and a captain receives also a retaining fee for the next season. During the months when the yachts are laid up some of the men remain at home, go fishing, or do odd jobs.   But fishing is declared to be no longer profitable and to bring only some 5/- or 6/- a week.   The rabbits on the heath are said to provide an unlawful supplement to the fare of some of the sailors at such times.   Others among them stay but a short time at home and seek employment on a collier or some other steam vessel where their wages are commonly about 30/- a week.

Agricultural labourers are more constantly employed, but at lower rates, and earn only about 12/- to 15/- a week in addition to some allowances in kind.

The women of this district are employed as outworkers by about a dozen firms or contractors in Colchester, and clothes are sent from firms in Manchester, East London and Leicester to be manufactured in this part of Essex. Curiously enough employers in Colchester send similar goods to be made in East London.   A great variety of garments is made here : cloths and tweeds for British wear : men's heavy greatcoats and reefers for little children ; light coats for export to hot countries which may be of flannel or may be the " silks " and alpacas for the skilful handling of which the women of Wyvenhoe and Rowledge have a long-standing reputation : children's sailor suits and white coats for cooks. In Boxted the women are employed exclusively on cloth trousers for one high-class firm.

The prices for making a garment quoted by the women

who were visited varied from 3d. to 1/4¾d. After certain
deductions had been made the incomes ranged from less
than nothing to nearly £1 a week. An average worker
employed by an averagely paying firm, and working from
after breakfast until tea-time would appear to earn about
7/- a week. The differences between one employer and
another are great, not only as to pay, but as to treatment of those employed. The best of the firms is spoken
of with complete satisfaction by the women who work for
it, but other women who had made the experiment
declared that firm " too particular." Certain of the
worse-paying employers seem to press for yet further
reductions. Many women mentioned that work had
been sent them to be done at 3/- or 4/- per dozen articles,
that they had sent it back, and that it had been returned
to them with the offer of an extra shilling per dozen.
A few women, exceptionally poverty-stricken or weak-
spirited were employed solely upon this ill-paid work,
which barely covered its own expenses, including, as these
often do, the hire of a sewing machine at 1/6 a week,
payment for making buttonholes at 1/- a dozen, " trimmings," *i.e.*, the needful thread, sewing silk, etc., always
provided by the worker, and usually carriage of the
parcel.

Differences of payment for very similar garments exist
even in work for the same firm ; these differences depending apparently not upon the amount of labour but upon
the quality of the material employed. Many women
who themselves receive their work direct from the firm
habitually put out to others some specific part of it, the
making, for instance of any buttonholes, or, at Boxted,
the " finishing," which represents half the work and half
the pay. As these workers at second-hand are not
included in the register of outworkers kept by the sanitary
authorities they appeared to constitute a danger in case
of any epidemic.

Some women prefer particular sorts of work, and succeed in getting these ; some for example, will only do " un-lined " garments, and object to the heavier makes, of which one delicate woman said that they " dragged her arms about and made her so tired that she could not sleep."

The health of the tailoresses seemed very good, although a few suffered from strained eyes and headache ; it is true that the young girls looked anæmic, but there is evidence that their health becomes rather worse than better if they go away to service. A marked contrast exists between the fine, vigorous women of Rowledge and the women of the agricultural villages, who, although they appear on the whole to be physically stronger than the Wiltshire glover bear more resemblance to her than to the sailor folk.

In the matter of housing, the Essex villagers generally are no better off than the dwellers in most other rural districts. Rowledge, however, is exceptional. Its habita-tions appear to have been mostly erected at about the same time, or from the same model and expressly to meet the needs of such people as now occupy them. Solidly built, containing four to six good-sized rooms, large and airy windows, and convenient sculleries or wash-houses, they provide " homes " in a sense rarely attained by the dwellings of English manual workers ; and the pros-perity of Rowledge is probably due in no small measure to the superiority of its housing accommodation.

The women re-paper their rooms every three years, regardless of the damp that may efface the freshness or peel the paper from the walls. It is significant that the people here insure their furniture against fire. This furniture is usually plain and simple. In one house visited, although there were both piano and harmonium, there was neither sofa nor easy chair. The absence of upholstered furniture and superfluous hangings (in house-

holds where no chintz or cretonne covers would find their
way periodically to the cleaner's) makes scrupulous
cleanliness possible, and the perfect freshness of the Rowledge homes is striking. A young girl engaged to be
married had filled an old sea chest of her father's with
needlework destined to beautify her new home, and the
treasures kept concealed from her neighbours' eyes
consisted mainly in hemstitched white linen table cloths,
covers and slips ; and in covers and chair backs of white
crochet ; only one or two more gaudily hued cushion
covers worked in wool appearing among them. In this
modern abode a sofa was doubtless to find a place. The
bridegroom asked, " Why wait any longer ? you have
got your home ready," but she, " as friendly with her
young man as though they were brother and sister,"
preferred to wait until a house entirely to their minds
should be obtainable in the place—a condition that
might postpone their marriage for some years. Rents
in Rowledge run from £7 to £10 per annum according
to the size of the houses ; and the landlords (among
whom are some of the sailor folk) seem able to keep
their property in good repair and obtain a fair return
for their capital. The water supply is satisfactory,
but the sanitary arrangements leave something to be
desired. Privies with pails or dead wells stand in the
gardens and the contents are removed by contractors,
a system which gives rise to foul smells and sometimes
to illness.[1]

In other villages the rents range upwards from £4 a
year. With few exceptions the cottages have each a
small garden ; in Rowledge, however, these gardens
are seldom tended, the women being otherwise occupied,
and the garden no good, as they say, to a " sailoring
man " who has spent his life on the water since

[1] Annual Report for 1908 of J. W. Cook, M.D., Medical Officer
of Health to Lexden and Winstree Rural District Council.

childhood and knows nothing about the land. Nor indeed could any horticulturist who was absent during all the warm months of the year hope to make much of a garden. The men when at home are not, however, idle; they generally do the housework and cooking so as to leave the women, who are then chief earners, free from domestic cares. In the villages where "landsmen" preponderate, as in Boxted and West Mersea, the gardens are often large and well worked.

Great diversity is to be found in the home-working tailoresses. The presence or absence of husband and sons, differences in the allowances handed over by husbands, and variations in the housing accommodation of each village are responsible for striking contrasts in home conditions. Moreover, on the principle that "whoso hath, to him shall be given" the industry pursued by the women still further accentuates the division between the happy and the miserable, since, not uncommonly, the woman who is most prosperous, free and comfortable, takes the pick of the work.

4. GENERAL OBSERVATIONS.

Though rural districts are often unsatisfactory as to housing, sanitation and water supply, yet the evil conditions of dirt, over-crowding and squalor which seem almost inseparable from industrial life in towns are happily absent in the country. On the other hand, the rural worker, in factory, laundry or home receives less protection from Factory and Public Health Acts than the townswoman; the ways of rural sanitary authorities are notoriously easy-going, and medical officers, having no security of tenure, are often chary of making complaints likely to bring down upon themselves the displeasure of influential landlords and capitalists.

Most of the outworkers visited in this branch of the investigation knew nothing of the Sanitary Inspector. The sanitary officials, however, of the Colchester district, were of opinion that the majority of homes in which registered outworkers lived had received a visit—usually, however, on some business not connected with the industry—at some time during the previous ten years.

The scope of the enquiry did not include visits to women who were not working for wages ; but some of these were met with, and of the wage-workers some had not long taken up the work ; moreover in all three districts, during a more or less prolonged stay, a good deal of information was obtained from people possessing intimate local knowledge. Thus it became possible to compare to some extent the life of the wage-earning and of the non-wage-earning wife.

The Essex tailoresses and the Worcestershire field workers, together with the charwomen and laundresses of these districts, show to advantage in comparison with their neighbours who are not industrially employed. They are physically healthier, mentally more alert, and last but not least, immensely more self-respecting, on account of having an income entirely their own.

The Wiltshire glovers did not exhibit the same superiority, either in body or mind. The very slight addition to the family income brought in by their work affords, however, a great satisfaction to themselves and appears to benefit their households. Here, the contrast between the women who work at home and those who, as charwomen, laundresses or marketers, do work which brings them into contact with others is again notable, and wholly to the advantage of the latter.

It is interesting to compare the number of children born to women in the three districts and percentage still living, or dead at the date the inquiry was made.

	No. of Cases	Children Living	No. of Children Dead	Average Children pr. family	Proportion of dead to those born
West Worcester-shire	25	138[1]	22	5·5	13·75%
West Wilts. ..	41	176[2]	30	4·3	14·6%
Essex	50	248[3]	26	4·96	9·5%

From this table it will be seen that the relatively low fertility of Wiltshire is accompanied by the highest rate of mortality in the children,[4] that the Worcestershire women, with the highest fertility, have also a high mortality among their children, and that the Essex women, with a fertility midway between, have a child mortality of little more than half that of Wiltshire.

It must not of course be assumed that these differences arise solely from the differences in the industrial employment of the women. Probably a thousand factors, difficult to trace, have their share. Not least among these is the greater fatality of disease suggested by these figures as incident to families where an inadequate income and poor feeding leave the children without power of resistance to childish complaints. In either case, whether the determining factor lies in the industrial employment of the mother, or in the prevalent general conditions, it is by reaction upon her, the wife and mother, and through her, the chief gainer or sufferer, that the various forces mainly shape the fate of the rising generation.

It is probable that the decline of industries and the many other influences which have conduced to the rural

[1] Also 4 stillborn.   [1] Also 5 stillborn and several miscarriages.
[3] Also 12 stillborn and several miscarriages, eight of the still-births occurred in one unhealthy family.
[4] A similar percentage of mortality was found in agricultural labourers' families in Corsley, in this district, as calculated from a different set of families. See Maud F. Davies' " Life in an English Village," p. 259, where the figure in the last column should be read 19·2 instead of 21·4 as printed.

exodus during the past century have affected Wiltshire to a far greater extent than the other districts visited, leaving in the villages a preponderance of old people, and sapping the vigour of social life, a depressing state of things which cannot fail to tell upon the home-keeping mother. Here, too, is found in an excessive degree, that principle, which, spreading to urban districts, is everywhere creating a morbid seclusion in the lives of innumerable women—the principle of " keeping ourselves to ourselves " and of avoiding intercourse with neighbours. This custom, which is regarded as a mark of respectability, is perhaps prompted by an overcautious desire to avoid " words " or possible unpleasantness of any description, or by dread of a too hasty intimacy with persons afterwards found to be undesirable. If these grounds are to be held sufficient for eschewing any familiarity with near neighbours, it becomes all the more important for the health and happiness of the woman at home and of her family that she shall be obliged, either by circumstances or by spontaneous vitality, to take part in some sort of social life outside her home.

Far healthier are the social conditions of the West Worcestershire woman, whose field work, inevitably involving change of scene and surroundings, is also usually carried on in company. The Wiltshire woman, in many a cottage, will tell you that she has always a headache, and will detail a variety of ailments, often in themselves insignificant. Her life is wearisome, she has no power of getting beyond her own narrow circle into a world of wider interests, and her own physical discomforts occupy all her attention and consciousness. The West Worcestershire field-worker, though she may have lacked opportunity to develop either physically or mentally to her full capacity, though she may be, as many of her elders are, stunted and wizened, is yet incomparably healthier and more wiry. Except for rheumatism, it would almost

appear as though illness and depression were unknown to
these Worcestershire women. One regular worker in the
fields, who also helped her husband with the pigs and the
orchard, a woman of about forty and the mother of four
children, never had a doctor or a day's illness in her life,
and only once, for a poisoned finger, had been for treatment to a chemist. Fulfilling a ceaseless round of duties,
in the house, small holding, or garden, in the employer's
fields, in the necessary tramp to and from market, lacking
leisure to adorn their homes or persons, or to chat for ten
minutes with a stranger visitor, they lead an almost ant-
like existence which, though not allowing the fullest
human development, is wholesome and certainly not
unhappy. Their children, healthy and gay, seem full of
the joy of life for which the mothers have no leisure.

The Rowledge women are all that women should be.
Full of vigorous health and spirits, they are equally ready
for work and for play. To three main causes the happy
condition of Rowledge may be attributed : firstly, the
general prosperity and sufficiency of the necessaries of
life ; secondly, the independent incomes of their own
which the women are able to secure ; and thirdly, the
unusual state of being a community devoid of social
distinctions. The general prosperity arises from the
good wages of the men, which enable nearly all the
inhabitants to demand effectually the provision of their
real requirements, whether in housing, clothing or food,
instead of making shift with the cast-off houses and
clothing of the rich or with the inferior commodities that
alone can be purchased by the very poor. There is little
poverty, partly because of the prevailing social equality ;
where temporary trouble exists friends and neighbours
know all about it, and " one will bring a loaf and another
the butter." These ministrations will not be extended,
however.

The independent income of the women brings them a

degree of consideration both from others and from themselves that educes and develops their personality, and causes each woman to become an individual interesting to herself and to others, even as her husband or her son is. In the house the woman is mistress, the man, when at home, adapting himself to her and doing the housework that she may not be interrupted in her industry. With her own earnings she is able to buy what she wants, pretty clothes for her children or for herself, a bicycle, a piano, or whatsoever else may appeal to her as affording the recreation which she takes for granted as her due, and as part of the normal routine of her life.

The absence of distinctions of rank makes for a cheery social life. " We are all alike here," many women remarked ; and with the exception of the resident clergyman, the resident doctor, perhaps a few persons connected with the engineering works, and a few little-heeded newcomers, the statement appeared to be absolutely true. A community of which two thousand or so members can hail one another as friends, and which is enlivened by the recurrent comings and goings of sailor kinsfolk, has, it may easily be imagined, no stagnant social life. For many months of the year the women are left without their men, but the fact does not appear to depress their spirits. They all said that they do not miss their husbands, because absence is what they expect ! It is common to see the women gathered together in their gardens for a spirited talk ; and this neighbourly intercourse by no means leads to quarrels, the women appearing to be very happy and good-tempered together. Of an evening friends will often pay visits to one another's houses.

These self-sufficient women are apparently excellent wives and mothers. The fact that there are no cases of rickets in the district and the small number of sons and daughters born here who, despite the extra risks of a seafaring life for the boys, have since died, furnish ample proof that the parents are not neglectful ; and no one who had seen these children or caught a glimpse of family life here would entertain any doubts about the matter.

Yet one other point remains to be considered. Even if the psychical and economic advantages of the mother's industrial employment be granted, is it not possible that the expectant or nursing mother or her infant may suffer physically in consequence of her employment ?

A scrutiny of these 116 families shows that ordinary work has no ill effect. In ordinary circumstances scarcely a worker in Essex or Worcestershire had lost an infant when there had not been some cause of constitutional weakness or disease in the mother ; while in Wiltshire, the percentage of infant deaths or of still births was greater in the families of twenty women who had not worked for money during their earlier years of marriage than in those of twenty-one women who had done so throughout their years of child-bearing, the percentages being respectively 17·1 and 14·8. Unless she is specially over-pressed the expectant mother does not overwork, and in the majority of cases is able to keep on with all her occupations as usual until shortly before her confinement. After the birth the Worcestershire women do not go out to work until they have been churched, and when they do resume work they often take the babies and younger children with them.

The case is different when, the husband being ill or out of work, the expectant mother is overpressed and compelled, perhaps, to sit at work half the night, and to go short of food at the very time when her conditions should be easiest. There are indications that in such circumstances the infant mortality tends to be even greater than when the woman is unable to earn money. The earnings, under such severe stress, seem to be made at the expense of herself and her infant, while the elder children, if any, profit by the sacrifice. Such cases afford, of course, no evidence as to whether the continuance of her normal work, without strain or worry, is or is not, beneficial to mother and child.

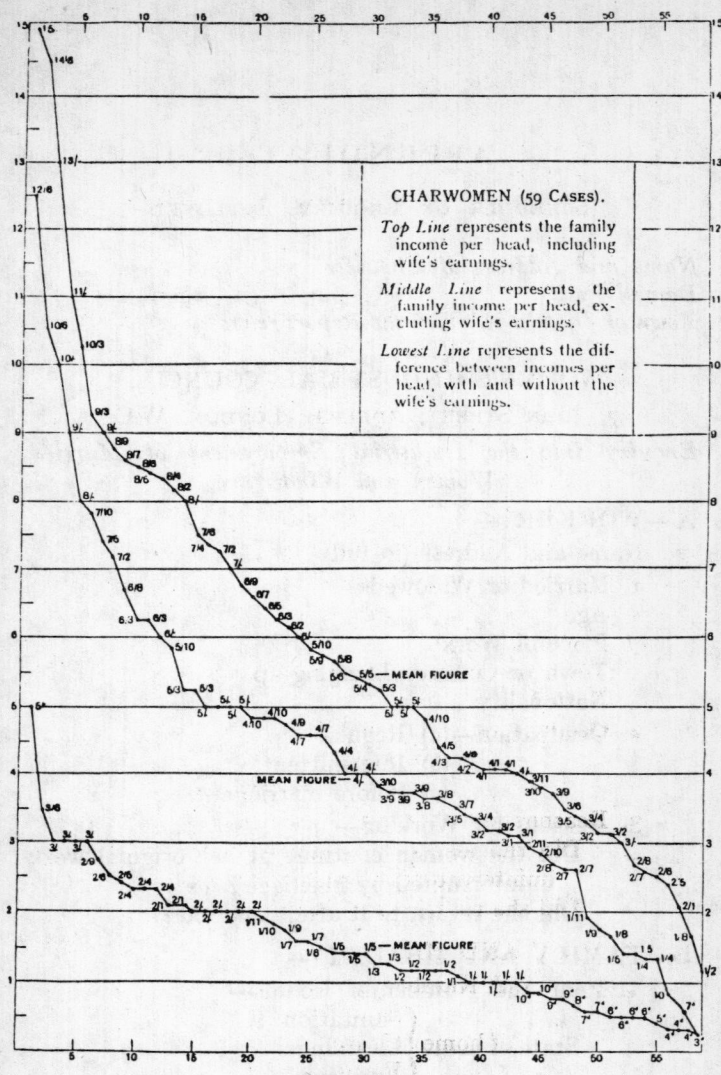

CHARWOMEN (59 Cases).

Top Line represents the family income per head, including wife's earnings.

Middle Line represents the family income per head, excluding wife's earnings.

Lowest Line represents the difference between incomes per head, with and without the wife's earnings.

CHARWOMEN.

Note.—The Scale at the base represents the number of cases, and that at the side shillings and pence.

APPENDIX I.

Name and Address of Enquirer
Date of Visit   1909
Town or District to which the Report refers

WOMEN'S INDUSTRIAL COUNCIL,

7, JOHN STREET, ADELPHI, LONDON, W.C.

Enquiry into the Industrial Employment of Married Women and Widows.

A.—WORKER :—

Name and Address (in full)

1. Married or Widowed
   Age
   Place of Work
   Town or Country Bringing-up
   Nationality

2. Occupation—(*a*) Regular
             (*b*) Intermittent
             (*c*) Before marriage

3. Reasons for Working—
   Did the woman continue at her original work uninterrupted by marriage ? *or*
   Did she return to it after a period ?

B.—FAMILY AND HEALTH :—

1. Rent and Number of Rooms—
   State of home { Sanitation
                  { Cleanliness
                  { Furniture
   State of Children

2. Number of Children alive—

   (*a*) Earning

   (Information should be given as to the nature of the occupation and the amount of the earnings of each child.)

   (*b*) Dependent

3. Number of Children dead—

   (*a*) Age at death

   (*b*) Cause of death

   (*c*) Had the mother been working during the year in which the child was born ?

4. Number of other dependents (if any)

5. Arrangements for care of home and children during absence at work

6. Effect of the work on the woman's health

   How long did she cease work at her confinements ?

   What provision (if any) to meet the expenses ?

C.—WAGES :—

1. Woman's earnings

   (Simple statements of average wages should not be accepted. Wherever possible, exact statements should be obtained of the earnings and hours worked over a series of consecutive weeks. Enquiry should also be made as to earnings in slack and busy seasons separately, and as to the length of these seasons. In the slack season of the woman's main occupation what other source of income or what subsidiary employment does she find ?)

   (*a*) Time wages

   (*b*) Piece rates

   (*c*) Average per week

   (*d*) Number of hours worked and average payment per hour

   (*e*) Have wages risen or fallen ?

2. Husband's occupation and average weekly earnings.

3. Total family income per week

From Husband   Lodgers
        Wife   Thrift, Friendly Socie-
        Children   ties, etc.
        Other dependents   Charity, Poor Law
        Allotments

4. Weekly budget

(If the total family income is in excess of the weekly budget, what is done with the surplus ?)

D.—REMARKS :—

E.—APPARENT ECONOMIC RESULTS :—

1. Does the fact that women work in the trade affect the men's wages ?

2. Are women actually working in competition with men and tending to oust them, or is it the other way about ?

3. Are married workers preferred to girls ?

4. Is the women's work being more and more done by machinery ?

F.—CHARACTERISTICS OF TRADE :—

1. Remarks—
   (*a*) Special characteristics of trade
   (*b*) Special characteristics of locality

2. Does the trade employ locally many
   (*a*) Men or boys
   (*b*) Married women and widows
   (*c*) Girls ?
   (Give approximate numbers.

3. Is the occupation healthy ?

4. Is the trade organised ?

G.—LEGISLATION AND GENERAL :—

1. Is legislation on the subject of married women's work desirable or not ?

2. Legislative Proposals
   (a) English   (b) Foreign

3. Schemes for the amelioration of Infantile Conditions
   (a) English   (b) Foreign

4. Schemes for Maternity Insurance

Reference to sources of information on any of these subjects will be welcome contributions towards the bibliography of the subject.

APPENDIX II.

HOUSEHOLD EXPENDITURE.

The investigator who studied these industries on the Council's behalf was able in a few cases to obtain details of the expenditure of the family income, and although these budgets are in most cases very imperfect, it seems worth while to give them here, as affording some little indication of how life is maintained by the poorer class of workers in these districts. The great difficulty in co-ordinating these budgets is the impossibility—from the evidence available—of making a correct estimate of the family income. In nearly all these cases the men's wages and the women's also are stated to be irregular in a very high degree. The income may be, for their standard of life, ample one week, then work may be slack, one or both breadwinners may be unemployed, or as they with half-conscious irony call it, " playing " for weeks together. From the facts given it is really impossible to estimate an average income. We therefore give a brief summary of the family circumstances in each case, and take the heading of expenditure as percentages not of income, but of total expenditure. The omissions are themselves significant, as showing what has to be provided out of the margin of income over outgoings.

Budget 1.

Weaver No. 8.

The husband, very weakly, earns only 10/– a week, the wife 17/6. Their earnings are, however, most irregular, and they are in debt owing to the illness of themselves and the illness and deaths of their 11 children, all of whom died in infancy or as quite little children.

One week's expenditure : 2 to keep.

	s. d.	s. d.	Percentages.
Rent		3 1	18·4
Coal		2 0	11·9
Insurance		1 0	6·0
Doctor		1 0	6·0
Hardwareman		1 0	6·0
Husband's spending ..		1 0	6·0
Flour	0 10½		
Sugar	0 5		
Tea	0 7½		
Yeast	0 1½		
Potatoes	0 3		
Butter and Lard	1 6		
Eggs	0 6		
Rice	1 0		
Meat	1 6		
Bacon	0 10½		
		7 8	45·8
		16 9	100·1

Remarks.—Nothing is included for wood, light, or clothes. The diet includes no milk, cheese, green vegetables or fruit.

BUDGET 2.

Weaver No. 23.

This is a very imperfect budget. The husband's earnings are stated at 23/6, the wife's are most irregular. She can earn 26/–, and probably earned 15/– in this week. She could give no account of what she had done with the balance. There are 4 children : 6 persons to keep in all.

			s. d.	s. d.	Percentages.
Rent and Rates	..	..		4 0	24·2
Coal	..	..		2 0	12·1
Insurance	..	..		1 0	6·1
2 stone Flour	..	..	2 9		
Potatoes	..	..	0 6		
Lard	..	..	1 1½		
Yeast	..	..	0 6		
Baker	..	..	1 0		
Meat	..	..	1 0		
6 lbs. Sugar	..	..	1 4½		
½ lb. Tea	..	..	0 8		
Milk	..	..	0 7		
				9 6	57·6
				16 6	100·0

Remarks.—No wood, light, or clothes are included. The provision of milk is obviously inadequate for 4 young children, and no cheese, green vegetables or fruit is included.

BUDGET 3.

Weaver No. 25.

The husband works at an unhealthy trade, and is also subjected to a system of lowering wages by deductions for loss which is really due to defective machinery. He brought home only 4/10½ in this week. Wife works irregularly, does charing, or goes as " silk weaver." There are 3 children. Rent and insurance had to stand over. Week's spending: 5 to keep.

			s.	d.	s.	d.	
Rent	..	..	..		3	3	} not paid.
Insurance ..	..	..			1	0	
1½ stone Flour	..	..	2	7			
4 lbs. Sugar	..	..	0	8			
Polony	..	..	0	1			
Potted Meat	..	..	0	1			
Yeast	..	..	0	3			
Fat ..	..	..	0	6			
			4	2			

N.B.—The neighbours gave some food and tea.

Remarks.—No coal, wood, light, milk, cheese, vegetables or fruit.

Budget 4.

Spinner No. 5.

This woman is quite young, 26, and has 3 children. She and husband support her mother, who minds the children when she is at work. She has no work at present. Husband earns 28/–, and her sister, who also lives with them, earns 10/–. It is not stated how much this girl contributes of her 10/–. Expenditure for 1 week: 7 to keep.

			s.	d.	s.	d.	Percentages.
Rent	..	..	..		4	2	22·7
Soap	..	..	..		0	6	2·7
Flour	..	..	..	2	9		
Yeast	..	..	..	0	3½		
2 lbs. Butter	..	..	..	2	4		
1 lb. Tea	..	..	..	1	4		
8 lbs. Sugar	..	..	..	1	4		
2 tins Milk	..	..	..	0	11		
Meat	..	..	..	1	6		
Rice	..	..	..	0	2½		
Cow's Milk	..	..	..	2	0		
Jam	..	..	..	1	0		
					13	8	74·5
					18	4	100·0

Remarks.—No coal, wood, light, cheese, vegetables, or fruit are included, and no payment for clothing.

BUDGET 5.

Spinner No. 6.

In this budget the income is below expenditure. The wife can earn 20/6 when at work, but is now not strong enough. The husband earns £1, gives her 17/–, and pays 1/– into a clothing club. There are 2 children.

Expenditure in 1 week : 4 to keep.

	s. d.	s. d.	Percentages.
Rent		2 6	12·9
Child-minding[1]		4 6	23·2
Clothing Club		1 0	5·2
Coal		2 0	10·3
Soap		0 2	0·9
Insurance and "Knocking up"		1 6	7·7
Furniture Payment ..		2 0	10·3
Meat, Jam, etc.	2 6		
Flour	1 9		
Yeast	0 2		
Milk	0 6		
2 lbs. Sugar	0 4		
¼ lb. Tea	0 4½		
Tin Milk	0 1½		
		5 9	29·6
		19 5	100·1

[1] She had only just left off work.

Remarks.—This budget shows what a large slice the payment for child-minding makes in a small income. The food expenditure appears very inadequate ; no cheese or vegetables, and milk very insufficient.

BUDGET 6.
" Ragger " No. 2.

The earnings of the family are highly irregular, and consist of what is brought in by the father, unmarried daughter, and a married daughter who has come back to live with her parents, the husband having turned out very badly. She has one baby. The income varies.

	Maximum.	
Father[1]	15/–	5/– or 7/6
Married daughter	12/–	9/6 or 10/– (only 7/– last week).
Unmarried daughter	17/–	13/6
	44/–	say 26/6

Expenditure in a week : 5 to keep.

	s. d.	s. d.	Percentages
Rent		3 2	20·4
Insurance		0 10	5·4
Soap and Soda		0 5	2·7
Paraffin		0 2	1·1
Sugar	1 1½		
Eggs	0 2		
Milk	0 10½		
Tea	1 0		
Meat	1 6		
Cheese	0 1		
Potatoes	0 7		
1 lb. Bacon	0 9		
Turnips	0 2		
½ lb. Butter	0 6½		
Lard	0 6		
Onions	0 2		
Flour	2 7½		
Fry Meat	0 4		
Yeast	0 3		
Porter	0 3		
		10 11	70·4
		15 6	100·0

[1] He had an accident and is incapable of hard work.

Remarks.—Vegetables and cheese are included in this budget, but only to the amount of 5d. altogether. The amounts for meat, butter, etc., seem very inadequate. No payment for clothing is included. Clothes would be a heavy item with 3 workers.

BUDGET 7.

"Ragger" No. 10.

This woman's standing wage is 12/- a week, but all short time is deducted. Husband's earnings at full time are £1 0s. 2d. a week, but the pits are being worked out, or have bad seams, and there are long periods of short time. They have 3 children.

The following is stated as the family weekly budget, "when income permits": 5 to keep.

	s. d.	s. d.	Percentages.
Rent		3 5	14·4
Child-minding		4 0	16·9
Insurance and Union ..		1 6	6·3
2 cwt. Coal		2 0	8·5
Groceries (including Butter and Eggs)	6 6		
Meat	1 0		
Bones	0 3		
Fry	0 3		
Onions and Carrots ..	0 1		
Potatoes	0 7		
1¾ stone Flour ..	3 0¼		
Milk	1 0		
		12 9	53·9
		23 8	100·0

Remarks.—Nothing for light, wood, or clothing is included. The diet includes no cheese, and only 1/- for meat.

Budget 8.

Miscellaneous Worker No. 2.

This worker is a widow aged 30.   She has 2 small children. She earns 11/– weekly, only 6/– at holidays.   Her relations give 2/6 towards rent, and share 2 rooms with her, but get their own food.

Expenditure in a week : 3 to keep.

	s.	d.	s.	d.	Percentages.
Coal, 1/– ; Cinders, 8d. ..			1	8	13·8
Rent			3	6	29·0
Child-minding			2	6	20·7
Insurance			0	4	2·7
Groceries	2	6			
½ stone Flour	1	0			
Milk	0	7			
			4	1	33·8
			12	1	100·0

Remarks.—Here the excess of income over expenditure is only 1s. 4½d., and has to account for wood, light, and clothing. The expenditure on food seems sadly inadequate for a woman doing hard work.

BUDGET 9.

Miscellaneous Worker No. 5.

This is a young married woman of 24, whose husband has gone to America in hopes of "making a fortune for her," but she has had no money from him for four months. She earns 11/- as a paper sorter, and employers occasionally give her some food. She has 2 children.

Expenditure in a week : 3 to keep.

			s. d.	s. d.	Percentages
Rent	..	..	..	3 6	35·3
Child-minding	..	..		3 0	30·3
Coal	..	..	..	0 6	5·0
Flour and Yeast	..	..	1 3		
Potatoes	..	..	..	0 2		
½ lb. Tea	..	..	..	0 5		
½ lb. Dripping	..	..	0 2		
Jam	..	..	..	0 1		
Milk	..	..	..	0 10		
			——	2 11	29·4
				9 11	100·0

Remarks.—Here the income exceeds expenditure by 1/-, and has to account for wood, light, soap, and clothing. The food expenditure appears very inadequate for a young working woman and 2 children, but is supplemented by the employer.

BUDGET 10.

Miscellaneous Worker No. 7.

This is a young woman aged 25, works in a packing ware-house, but has not yet resumed work since her baby's birth, 5 weeks previously. Her husband earns only 18/– a week; he is good to her, and gives her 17/– for the house. Both parents need better food, and the baby is not thriving.

Expenditure in one week: 3 to keep.

	s.	d.	s.	d.	Percentages.
Rent			4	9	29·4
Furniture Instalment ..			2	6	15·5
Insurance			0	8	4·1
Coal			1	1	6·7
Flour and Yeast	2	1			
Tea	0	5½			
1 lb. Butter	1	2			
2 lbs. Sugar	0	4			
Condensed Milk	0	2½			
Potatoes	0	4			
Stew Meat	0	9			
Meat for husband	1	10			
			7	2	44·3
			16	2	100·0

Remarks.—9½d. is left over, for light, wood, soap and cloth-ing. Note the inadequacy of the amount spent on fatty foods for a young nursing mother, and the absence of cheese, fruit, or vegetables other than potatoes.

Budget 11.

Woolcomber No. 1.

This woman has 3 children, aged 6 and 3 years, and 4 months old. She earns 12/-. Her husband is an ice-cream vendor, his earnings are very uncertain, and not stated. Her mother and her sister (a defective girl) live with them. The mother earns something, but not regularly.

Expenditure for one week: 7 to keep.

			s. d.	s. d.	Percentages.
Rent	..	..	..	5 0	25·1
Coal	..	..	..	2 10	14·2
Child-minding	..	..	3 0	15·1
Clothing Club	..	..	0 6	2·5
Flour	..	..	.. 2 3		
Sugar	..	..	.. 0 6		
Butter	..	..	.. 2 6		
Bacon	..	..	.. 0 3		
Yeast	..	..	.. 0 3		
Tea	..	..	.. 1 0		
Potatoes	..	..	.. 0 3		
Greens	..	..	.. 0 2		
Meat	..	..	.. 1 2		
Rice	..	..	.. 0 3		
				8 7	43·1
				19 11	100·0

Remarks.—This budget includes no milk, wood, soap, light, or clothing, except the subscription to the clothing club.

Budget 12.

Woolcomber No. 17.

This woman works at " backwashing," but is out of work this week. The husband is a night-comber, gives her £1 a week when in work, but it is very irregular. They have one baby, but she cannot nurse it.

Expenditure in one week : 3 to keep.

	s. d.	s. d.	Percentages.
Rent		3 6	25·6
Club		0 6	3·7
" Spending brass " ..		2 0	14·6
Flour	1 6		
Potatoes	0 7		
Meat	1 6		
Tea	0 8		
¾ lb. Butter	0 10½		
½ lb. Lard	0 3½		
3 lbs. Sugar	0 6		
Milk for baby	1 9		
		7 8	56·1
		13 8	100·0

Remarks.—No coal, wood, or light is included in this budget. A comparatively generous amount is spent on the baby's milk, but nothing on cheese, fruit, or vegetables other than potatoes. Nothing is said about clothing.

APPENDIX III.

Smaller London Trades in tabular form.

	Tie Makers.	Bookfolders.	Embroideresses.	Tailoresses.	Children's Clothes Makers.	Private Dressmakers.	Totals.
Marriage State—							
Married	5	5	7	18	9	10	54
Widowed	1	1	1	4	6	3	16
Deserted	—	—	—	1	—	1	2
	6	6	8	23	15	14	72
Reasons for Working—							
Like it	—	—	1	—	2	—	3
To support family	2	1	½	6	6	5	20½
Family income insufficient	3	2	1	14	4	3	27
Husband out of work, or seasonal work	1	3	3½	2	3	3	15½
Husband or other member of family invalid	—	—	2	1	—	1	4
Not stated	—	—	—	—	—	2	2
	6	6	8	23	15	14	72
Families having Persons per room—							
Less than 1 per room	—	—	2	—	1	—	3
1 and under 2	1	4	3	7	5	1	21
2 ,, 3	2	—	1	3	2	5	13
3 ,, 4	1	1	—	8	2	—	12
4 ,, 5	—	—	—	—	—	4	4
5 ,, 6	—	—	—	—	—	—	—
6 ,, 7	—	—	—	—	—	1	1
House	1	—	1	1	—	3	6
Not stated	1	1	1	4	5	0	12
	6	6	8	23	15	14	72

			Tie Makers.	Bookfolders.	Embroideresses.	Tailoresses.	Children's Clothes Makers.	Private Dressmakers.	Totals.
Families paying Rent—									
House ..	..	..	1	—	1	1	—	3	6
Not stated	..	..	1	1	1	3	6	—	12
2/– and under	2/6	..	—	—	—	—	1	—	1
2/6	,, 3/–	..	—	—	—	2	—	—	2
3/–	,, 3/6	..	—	—	—	1	1	1	3
3/6	,, 4/–	..	—	—	—	1	—	2	3
4/–	,, 4/6	..	—	—	—	3	—	—	3
4/6	,, 5/–	..	—	—	—	—	—	—	—
5/–	,, 5/6	..	1	—	—	—	1	—	2
5/6	,, 6/–	..	1	—	—	—	—	—	1
6/–	,, 6/6	..	—	—	—	1	—	1	2
6/6	,, 7/–	..	—	—	1	1	—	2	4
7/–	,, 7/6	..	1	1	1	—	1	3	7
7/6	,, 8/–	..	1	4	2	1	2	—	10
8/–	,, 8/6	..	—	—	—	1	—	1	2
8/6	,, 9/–	..	—	—	—	1	1	1	3
9/–	,, 9/6	..	—	—	1	3	—	—	4
9/6	,, 10/–	..	—	—	—	—	—	—	—
10/–	,, 10/6	..	—	—	—	—	—	—	—
10/6	,, 11/–	..	—	—	—	—	—	—	—
11/0	,, 11/6	..	—	—	1	1	—	—	2
11/6	,, 12/–	..	—	—	—	1	—	—	1
12/–	,, 12/6	..	—	—	—	1	2	—	3
12/6	,, 13/–	..	—	—	—	—	—	—	—
13/–	,, 13/6	..	—	—	—	—	—	—	—
13/6	,, 14/–	..	—	—	—	1	—	—	1
			6	**6**	**8**	**23**	**15**	**14**	**72**

			Tie Makers.	Bookfolders.	Embroideresses.	Tailoresses.	Children's Clothes Makers.	Private Dressmakers.	Totals.
Families paying Rent per Room—									
House	..	..	1	—	1	1	—	3	6
Not stated	..	..	1	1	1	7	7	—	17
1/- and under	1/3	..	—	—	—	1	—	—	1
1/3	,, 1/6	..	—	—	—	—	—	—	—
1/6	,, 1/9	..	—	—	—	1	—	1	2
1/9	,, 2/-	..	1	1	—	—	—	1	3
2/-	,, 2/3	..	—	—	2	—	2	1	5
2/3	,, 2/6	..	—	—	—	2	—	1	3
2/6	,, 2/9	..	1	1	2	3	1	—	8
2/9	,, 3/-	..	1	—	—	—	1	—	2
3/-	,, 3/3	..	—	—	1	1	2	2	6
3/3	,, 3/6	..	—	—	—	1	—	—	1
3/6	,, 3/9	..	1	1	1	1	1	3	8
3/9	,, 4/-	..	—	2	—	1	1	1	5
4/-	,, 4/3	..	—	—	—	2	—	1	3
4/3	,, 4/6	..	—	—	—	—	—	—	—
4/6	,, 4/9	..	—	—	—	—	—	—	—
4/9	,, 5/-	..	—	—	—	—	—	—	—
5/-	,, 5/3	..	—	—	—	—	—	—	—
5/3	,, 5/6	..	—	—	—	—	—	—	—
5/6	,, 5/9	..	—	—	—	—	—	—	—
5/9	,, 6/-	..	—	—	—	—	—	—	—
6/-	,, 6/3	..	—	—	—	2	—	—	2
			6	6	8	23	15	14	72

	Tie Makers.	Bookfolders.	Embroideresses.	Tailoresses.	Children's Clothes Makers.	Private Dressmakers.	Totals.
Families paying Rent per Person in Family—							
House	1	—	1	1	—	3	6
Not stated	1	1	1	3	6	—	12
9d. and under 1/– ..	1	1	—	3	1	4	10
1/– „ 1/3 ..	—	1	1	1	1	2	6
1/3 „ 1/6 ..	2	3	—	3	—	—	8
1/6 „ 1/9 ..	1	—	1	5	1	2	10
1/9 „ 2/– ..	—	—	1	1	—	1	3
2/– „ 2/3 ..	—	—	—	—	1	1	2
2/3 „ 2/6 ..	—	—	—	1	2	—	3
2/6 „ 2/9 ..	—	—	1	2	2	—	5
2/9 „ 3/– ..	—	—	1	—	—	—	1
3/– „ 3/3 ..	—	—	—	1	1	1	3
3/3 „ 3/6 ..	—	—	1	—	—	—	1
3/6 „ 3/9 ..	—	—	—	1	—	—	1
3/9 „ 4/– ..	—	—	—	1	—	—	1
	6	6	8	23	15	14	72
Children—							
No. living	20	26	17	63	35	58	219
„ dead	2	6	13[1]	18	17	10[2]	66
Under	2	—	4	18	8	10	42
at {school ..	13	—	7	19	9	18	66
Under & at {age ..	—	15	3	4	7	11	40
Over	5	6	3	22	11	14	61
Not stated	—	5	—	—	—	5	10
	42	58	47	144	87	126	504
Earning..	5	6	3	21	8	9	52
Out of work	—	—	—	1	—	1	2
Still-births	1	—	—	—	1	—	2
Other dependents ..	1	—	2½	1	1	—	5½

[1] 2 families only.   [2] 5 in one family.

	Tie Makers.	Bookfolders.	Embroideresses.	Tailoresses.	Children's Clothes Makers.	Private Dressmakers.	Totals.
Families having Total No. of Children in Family—							
None	—	—	—	—	1	—	1
1 child..	—	1	3	6	4	1	15
2 children	—	—	—	—	1	2	3
3 ,, ...	3	—	2	6	1	3	15
4 ,, ...	2	1	1	5	5	1	15
5 ,, ...	1	1	—	2	—	2	6
6 ,, ...	—	2	—	2	1	1	6
7 ,, ...	—	—	—	1	—	2	3
8 ,, ...	—	—	1	1	1	—	3
9 ,, ...	—	—	1	—	1	1	3
10 ,, ...	—	1	—	—	—	—	1
11 ,, ...	—	—	—	—	—	1	1
	6	6	8	23	15	14	72
Families having No. of Children Living—							
None	—	—	—	—	1	—	1
1 child	—	1	4	8	5	1	19
2 children	—	—	—	3	3	2	8
3 ,, ...	4	—	3	3	3	3	16
4 ,, ...	2	3	1	5	2	2	15
5 ,, ...	—	1	—	4	—	3	8
6 ,, ...	—	—	—	—	—	2	2
7 ,, ...	—	—	—	—	1	—	1
8 ,, ...	—	1	—	—	—	—	1
9 ,, ...	—	—	—	—	—	1	1
	6	6	8	23	15	14	72

	Tie Makers.	Bookfolders.	Embroideresses.	Tailoresses.	Children's Clothes Makers.	Private Dressmakers.	Totals.
Dead—							
None	5	2	6	14	8	10	45
1 child	—	2	—	5	2	1	10
2 children	1	2	—	—	2	2	7
3 ,,	—	—	—	3	2	—	5
4 ,,	—	—	—	1	—	—	1
5 ,,	—	—	—	—	1	1	2
6 ,,	—	—	1	—	—	—	1
7 ,,	—	—	1	—	—	—	1
	6	6	8	23	15	14	72
Families having No. of Children under and at School Age—							
None	—	—	2	3	6	1	12
1 child	2	2	2	10	4	1	21
2 children	—	—	1	3	1	4	9
3 ,,	2	1	2	4	1	3	13
4 ,,	2	1	1	2	2	—	8
5 ,,	—	—	—	1	—	3	4
6 ,,	—	1	—	—	—	1	2
7 ,,	—	—	—	—	1	—	1
Not stated	—	1	—	—	—	1	2
	6	6	8	23	15	14	72
Arrangements for Care of Children—							
Not working when children young	—	—	1	2	4	—	7
Own work allows	2	½	2	3	6	10	23½
Husband's work allows	—	1	—	—	—	½	1½
Elder children or relative	—	—	—	2	—	1	3
Neighbours	—	½	—	4	—	½	5
Day Nursery	—	1	—	5	½	2	8½
The children manage	—	—	—	—	½	—	½
No special arrangements necessary	—	—	—	3	1	—	4
Not stated	4	3	5	4	3	—	19
	6	6	8	23	15	14	72

Table of the Number of Children Living and Dead.

CHARWOMEN, &C.			Case No.	Alive.	Dead.	Case No.	Alive.	Dead.
Case No.	Alive.	Dead.	55	1	0	117	5	6
			56	1	1	118	5	1
1	2	1	57	1	9	119	10	2
2	3	2	61	3	6	120	4	1
3	4	0	62	7	6	122	3	0
4	1	1	65	2	4	124	7	0
5	6	1	68	4	4	125	3	0
6	5	1	69	2	1	126	3	1
8	1	0	71	3	1	127	4	1
9	2	1	73	9	2	128	4	0
10	3	0	74	6	0	129	6	6
11	3	0	75	5	0	130	5	5
12	5	0	76	7	1	131	7	3
13	2	0	77	4	1	132	4	0
14	3	2	78	6	2	133	4	2
15	2	0	79	3	3	134	10	2
17	4	4	80	2	2	135	4	2
18	6	0	81	3	1	136	5	2
19	6	0	82	5	2	137	3	0
20	8	0	83	4	5	138	7	6
21	7	1	85	4	1	139	1	1
24	3	3	86	4	0	140	4	0
25	5	2	89	5	0	144	3	0
26	5	0	90	4	7	146	3	1
27	5	5	92	9	7	148	8	0
28	5	0	93	8	1	149	3	0
29	4	4	94	2	8	151	4	1
30	2	0	95	8	2	152	2	1
31	2	0	96	3	0	154	3	1
32	4	0	97	6	1	155	4	3
34	5	4	98	10	1	160	5	2
35	3	3	104	5	0	161	5	0
38	3	1	104a	7	0	162	5	9
39	7	1	169	4	0	163	3	4
40	7	1	171	1	1	164	6	6
44	4	4	105	1	5	165	8	4
45	8	1	106	8	2	166	6	2
47	5	3	107	5	0	167	4	2
48	3	5	108	3	1	174	4	3
49	6	4	109	3	1	175	5	0
50	4	2	112	3	1	176	4	0
51	3	0	113	3	1	177	4	3
52	2	2	115	3	1	178	2	0
41	168	59	84	187	92	127	324	234

Table of the Number of Children Living and Dead.

MISCELLANEOUS.

Case No.	Alive.	Dead.
1	2	4
2	9	6
3	1	0
4	3	3
5	none	
6	9	5
7	5	0
8	3	1
9	1	1
10	5	0
11	4	0
12	2	0
13	1	0
14	1	11
15	6	0
16	2	2
17	0	4
19	1	0
22	3	1
23	2	2
24	5	0
25	8	3
27	4	5
28	7	1
29	1	0
30	none	
31	2	0
36	5	3
38	3	0
39	7	5
40	3	0
42	5	0
43	7	4
44	3	1
45	5	1
46	3	7
49	5	1
50	none	
51	2	0
52	2	0
53	5	1
41	**142**	**72**

MISCELLANEOUS (continued).

Case No.	Alive.	Dead.
54	2	1
55	2	0
56	5	1
57	4	2
58	1	0
59	0	2
60	3	2
61	none	
62	1	0
63	5	5
51	**165**	**85**

BLOUSEMAKERS.

Case No.	Alive.	Dead.
1	6	0
2	3	0
3	4	0
4	2	0
5	5	1
6	3	0
8	0	1
9	none	
10	1	0
11	3	8
12	3	0
15	3	11
16	3	1
17	2	0
14	**38**	**22**

UNDERCLOTHING.

Case No.	Alive.	Dead.
1	2	0
2	4	2
3	1	0
6	**7**	**2**

Case No.	Alive.	Dead.
4	4	8
5	3	3
6	7	4
8	4	3
10	2	0
11	1	0
12	4	1
13	7	0
14	4	0
15	none	
16	3	0
17	3	2
18	1	6
16	**50**	**29**

BOXMAKERS.

Case No.	Alive.	Dead.
1	3	0
2	4	4
3	1	0
4	3	1
6	2	3
7	2	6
8	5	0
9	4	6
10	5	0
11	4	1
12	2	0
13	6	0
14	5	2
15	6	2
16	2	1
18	none	
21	5	4
22	2	0
23	4	3
24	3	1
25	2	4
26	3	3
22	**73**	**41**

Table of the Number of Children Living and Dead.

Case No.	Alive.	Dead.
27	4	0
28	3	2
29	1	0
30	1	0
32	1	0
33	1	0
34	5	3
35	3	1
36	6	2
37	6	0
38	7	2
39	4	2
40	2	0
41	6	3
42	3	10
37	126	66

CASUAL DRESSMAKING

Case No.	Alive.	Dead.
1	5	2
3	2	0
6	6	5
7	9	0
8	1	0
10	4	1
12	2	0
14	5	2
8	34	10

EMBROIDERY, &c.

Case No.	Alive.	Dead.
1	3	6
2	3	0
3	1	0
5	1	0
7	1	7
8	1	0
6	10	13

ARTIFICIAL FLOWERS.

Case No.	Alive.	Dead
1	6	7
2	9	9
3	2	2
4	2	0
5	4	0
6	2	1
7	11	2
9	3	0
10	4	6
11	1	3
12	5	2
14	1	0
15	7	0
16	4	2
14	61	34

WOOD-CHOPPING.

Case No.	Alive.	Dead.
1	2	2
2	6	0
3	4	3
4	3	2
5	7	2
5	22	9

WAISTCOATS.

Case No.	Alive.	Dead.
1	5	8
2	3	6
4	11	2
7	1	0
8	4	5
9	1	1
6	25	22

UMBRELLAS.

Case No.	Alive.	Dead
2	none	
3	2	0
4	3	0
5	3	1
6	3	0
5	11	1

CHILDREN'S CLOTHES.

Case No.	Alive.	Dead.
1	7	2
4	3	1
5	1	3
6	1	0
8	3	3
9	2	1
10	2	2
11	4	0
12	1	0
13	1	0
10	25	12

PAPER BAGS.

Case No.	Alive.	Dead.
2	5	4
3	6	0
4	4	1
5	5	1
6	11	3
5	31	9

Table of the Number of Children Living and Dead.

TIE-MAKERS.

Case No.	Alive.	Dead.
1	4	0
2	3	0
3	4	0
4	3	2
4	14	2

Case No.	Alive.	Dead.
11	3	0
12	1	0
14	none	
15	7	0
16	1	0
9	20	3

STREET SELLERS.

Case No.	Alive.	Dead.
1	6	3
2	4	4
4	3	4
5	5	0
6	5	0
7	9	3
8	5	0
7	37	14

FUR SEWING, &c.

Case No.	Alive.	Dead.
1	3	0
2	9	2
3	2	0
13	3	3
4	17	5

MILLINERY.

Case No.	Alive.	Dead.
4	4	3
5	1	0
6	1	0
7	2	0
4	8	3

FEATHER CURLERS.

Case No.	Alive.	Dead.
8	1	0
10	0	5
2	1	5

JAM PACKERS.

Case No.	Alive.	Dead.
3	6	2
5	4	0
6	4	0
7	1	4
8	2	0
9	5	0
10	4	2
11	5	4
12	4	5
13	1	0
14	2	1
15	5	0
16	4	0
17	6	0
18	2	1
19	4	5
16	59	24

SHIRT & COLLAR MACHINISTS.

Case No.	Alive.	Dead.
1	4	1
2	4	7
4	1	3
6	5	0
7	2	0
11	6	0
12	1	0
13	7	2
15	1	1
17	2	0
18	4	0
19	6	2
21	2	1
22	4	1
23	2	1
15	51	19

COATS & TROUSERS.

Case No.	Alive.	Dead.
1	1	4
2	1	0
3	1	0
6	5	1
7	2	1
8	2	1
11	5	3
12	1	0
14	3	1
15	1	0
16	3	0
17	4	3
19	1	0
29	1	3
21	2	1
22	3	0
23	5	1
17	41	19

Table of the Number of Children Living and Dead.

BALLS.

Case No.	Alive.	Dead.
1	none	
3	2	0
5	4	1
9	2	0
10	1	0
11	4	0
12	none	
13	none	
14	3	0
16	1	3
17	none	
18	1	0
19	2	0
20	1	1
22	none	
23	none	
24	1	1
25	1	0
18	23	6

SHOES.

Case No.	Alive.	Dead.
1	1	0
2	5	0
3	5	1
5	5	1
8	4	6
9	9	0
10	5	6
7	34	14

BOOK-FOLDING.

Case No.	Alive.	Dead.
1	8	2
2	4	0
3	4	1
4	4	1
5	4	2
5	24	6

MANTLE MAKERS.

Case No.	Alive.	Dead.
1	5	0
2	5	0
4	6	1
6	4	0
7	2	0
8	6	0
9	5	4
11	2	10
8	31	15

SACK SEWERS.

Case No.	Alive.	Dead.
1	5	0
2	4	3
3	4	1
4	3	1
4	16	5

Table of the Reasons for Working in different Trades.

Trade	Widows.	Deserted or separated wives.	Husbands out of work.	Husbands ill.	To supplement husband's wage.	Other reasons.	Not stated.	Totals.
Charwomen, etc. ...	43	7	17	17	95	—	1	180
Wood-chopping ...	—	—	—	—	7	—	—	7
Embroidery, etc. ...	1	—	1	—	4	2[1]	—	8
Artificial flower-making	4	—	—	1	11	—	—	16
Waistcoat-making ...	1	—	1	2	5	—	—	9
Umbrella-making ...	—	—	—	—	6	—	—	6
Making children's clothes	5	1	2	—	7	—	—	15
Tie-making ...	1	—	—	—	5	—	—	6
Coat & Trousers-making	4	2	2	—	13	—	2	23
Ball-covering ...	6	—	—	—	18	1[2]	—	25
Shoe-making ...	—	2	1	1	6	—	—	10
Book-folding ...	1	—	—	—	5	—	—	6
Sack-sewing ...	2	—	1	1	—	—	—	4
Mantle-making ...	3	1	—	1	6	—	—	11
Making underclothes ...	4	—	—	—	15	—	—	19
Paper bag-making ...	1	—	—	—	6	—	—	7
Shopkeepers, street sellers	4	—	1	—	4	—	—	9
Fur-sewing ...	1	—	—	—	3	—	—	4
Millinery ...	1	—	—	1	8	1[3]	1	12
Jam packing, etc. ...	5	2	1	1	10	—	—	19
Shirt machinists ...	8	1	2	1	10	1[4]	—	23
Laundresses ...	9	1	5	3	43	—	1	62
Box-making ...	8	—	3	2	27	1[5]	1	42
Glove-making ...	4	—	1	—	3	—	—	8
Carpet-sewing ...	3	—	—	1	—	—	—	4
Eiderdown quilt-making	—	—	—	—	2	—	—	2
Blouse-making ...	3	—	—	—	12	2[6]	—	17
Miscellaneous ...	17	5	5	4	25	3[7]	3	62
	139	22	43	36	356	11	9	616

[1] To help mother; likes to work.
[2] To fill up time.
[3] Likes to do a little.
[4] To pass time.
[5] Husband drinks.
[6] Likes to work for comfort; going to cease on birth of first child.
[7] To fill up time; to keep invalid father; working with husband.

INDEX